Critiquing Whole Language and Classroom Inquiry

WLU Series

Whole Language Umbrella

The Whole Language Umbrella, an organization within the National Council of Teachers of English, is composed of language arts educators and others who view whole language as a dynamic philosophy of education. Through this series, WLU encourages discussion of critical issues within whole language, including promoting and disseminating research on whole language and facilitating collaboration among teachers, researchers, parents, administrators, and teacher educators.

Volumes in the Series

Beyond Reading and Writing: Inquiry, Curriculum, and Multiple Ways of Knowing (2000), Beth Berghoff, Kathryn A. Egawa, Jerome C. Harste, and Barry T. Hoonan

Parent to Parent: Our Children, Their Literacy (2001), Gerald R. Oglan and Averil Elcombe

Critiquing Whole Language and Classroom Inquiry (2001), Sibel Boran and Barbara Comber

Critiquing Whole Language and Classroom Inquiry

Edited by

SIBEL BORAN
University of Wisconsin Oshkosh

BARBARA COMBER
University of South Australia

National Council of Teachers of English
1111 W. Kenyon Road, Urbana, Illinois 61801-1096

Staff Editor: Bonny Graham
Interior Design: Jenny Jensen Greenleaf
Cover Design: Evelyn C. Shapiro

NCTE Stock Number: 23422-3050

It is the policy of NCTE in its journals and other publications to provide a forum for the open discussion of ideas concerning the content and the teaching of English and the language arts. Publicity accorded to any particular point of view does not imply endorsement by the Executive Committee, the Board of Directors, or the membership at large, except in announcements of policy, where such endorsement is clearly specified.

Library of Congress Cataloging-in-Publication Data

Critiquing whole language and classroom inquiry / edited by Sibel Boran, Barbara Comber.
p. cm. — (WLU series)
Includes bibliographical references and index.
ISBN 0-8141-2342-2 (pbk.)
1. Language experience approach in education. I. Boran, Sibel. II. Comber, Barbara. III. Series

LB1576 .C785 2001
372.6—dc21

2001030580

CONTENTS

INTRODUCTION

The Inquirers and Their Questions

SIBEL BORAN
University of Wisconsin Oshkosh

BARBARA COMBER
University of South Australia

Progressive movements in education, including whole language and inquiry, have reached a point where they must interrogate their own claims about and effects on the educational outcomes of diverse groups of students. It is no longer enough to assert a radical politics in comparison with proponents of transmission models of teaching. If these theories and associated forms of practice are to remain powerful and credible for educators, we must address their limitations and, where necessary, reinvent them in order to be able to demonstrate real learning improvements for socioeconomically and culturally diverse young people. This volume offers a critical reexamination of "inquiry" and "whole language" as tools for rethinking literacy, schooling, and humanistic citizenship in the complexities of today's multicultural world. We ask: What constitutes inquiry? What should young people inquire about in school? How can teachers assist young people to become critical inquirers? We examine the cultural politics of inquiry within global contexts of increasingly multicultural, English-speaking, postindustrial nations. In this volume, we explore the political implications of literacy theories and practices by asking: What kinds of inquiries promote or hinder the acquisition of literacies as tools for envisioning, critically exploring, and reconstructing knowledge and societies that are socially just?

We believe there is no apolitical inquiry nor neutral literacy. Messages about the world conveyed through literacy—by teachers, students, parents, administrators, texts, including today's technological media, and other social agents—are not natural but politically and culturally embedded phenomena. The ways in which students learn to access and examine messages about the world produce citizens with different forms of political awareness and critical resources. Inquiry practices are not innate, natural, or constructed in a social vacuum. They are acquired in ways that relate to dominant views of what counts as knowledge. Although inquiry is political, it does not necessarily lead to action, justice, or transformation. Young people need to learn that inquiry is not an end in itself but a process of connecting learning with social goals.

In *Critiquing Whole Language and Classroom Inquiry,* prominent whole language scholars, advocates of inquiry, and educators developing critical literacies reexamine the cultural politics of "inquiry" from three perspectives:

- whole language philosophy
- critical literacy
- multicultural global education theories

The contributors explore how particular theories may or may not contribute to politicized inquiry experiences in classrooms. Again, inquiry is not politically free. Rather, seemingly democratic models of classroom inquiry can incorporate hidden neotransmission models of learning. Inquiry approaches which purport to allow many voices to be heard but which ultimately protect some voices should be challenged. Natural developmental models of literacy and inquiry, while claiming to take students' interests into account, can sometimes camouflage conservative agendas. Questions need to be raised about what students should be immersed in; the extent to which natural development assumes a white middle-class natural developer; and what kinds of inquirers classrooms, libraries, and textbooks construct. We argue that inquiry approaches to learning need to incorporate a range of social and cultural practices which assist students to question the truths of texts, to ask different questions about texts, and indeed to seek out conflicting texts. Students need to learn that inquiry is not simply finding right answers to old and familiar questions, but that the questions themselves and the sources investigated must also be subject to interrogation. There is nothing intrinsically empowering about asking questions. The act of questioning may be just that if students cannot raise questions that count—questions about relations of power; about how knowledge is made and by whom; about historical, contemporary, social, and cultural practices. The object of critical inquiry is not to apportion blame for injustices, nor to identify victims of previous regimes, nor to romanticize earlier cultures, nor to find out the truth, but instead to assist young people to acquire the discursive and intellectual resources to conduct analyses about important questions and dynamic situations of relevance to everyday life.

Thus, the contributors to this book examine what it means to politicize inquiry. They consider how the belief systems underlying our literacy practices play a significant role in shaping the kinds of citizens we produce in educational institutions. Because students spend considerable time in our classrooms, educators possess at least some power to affect students' worldviews. Despite pressures on teachers to fulfill district-, school-, or state-mandated curriculum standards, the contributors show that there is space for politicizing our inquiry and literacy practices and call for further conversation and research.

Critiquing Whole Language and Classroom Inquiry questions the claims for universal or natural inquiry processes and calls for suspicion of literacy practices that sanitize curricula, exploring how we might politicize inquiry in English, English as a second language, and bilingual education classes in elementary and secondary schools. The book considers the potential of literacy curricula to provide educational access for culturally diverse populations and how multicultural global perspectives prepare young people to view and act in and on the world from politically ethical perspectives. And it argues that we need to move beyond politically correct questions in classroom inquiries.

In the opening chapter, Jerome Harste, an advocate of inquiry approaches for well over a decade, reexamines the territory and explains what constitutes inquiry as an orientation to education. He argues that such an approach means that reading and writing can be thought of less as identifiable skills than as meaning-making practices for getting things done in the world. By this account, inquiry is not a time slot on the curriculum but a process of developing a problem-solving, question-asking attitude and the associated investigatory practices across disciplines, modes, and media. Such an approach relies not on the lone curious individual but on a classroom collective pooling its research from across subject areas and in different modes. Further, Harste makes the case that while we may have learned to accept children's home literacies, we have not yet learnt to respect them. He goes on to outline the similarities and differences between an inquiry approach and Gardner's theory of multiple intelligences, and offers some advice about how to avoid inhibiting inquiry in the classroom. Ultimately, Harste's approach emphasises the need for children to learn *how* to learn and for them to assemble new and multimodal resources in order to solve the problems of tomorrow—in other words, to learn "how to be a good inquirer." Such a rethinking of the object of education, as Harste discusses, requires a radical rethinking of evaluation methods.

Kathy Short and Carolyn Burke explore similar themes by asking whether inquiry approaches are just "a different term for theme units" or whether what is going on in classrooms represents a paradigmatic shift in curriculum design and practice. Through a discussion of several stories of literacy practices, they consider whether changes in espoused beliefs are really leading to significant changes in the things that count, such as students' intellectual resources and teachers' relations with parents, or whether the changes remain superficial. Following a critical reflection of their own practices in designing and enacting curricula, they offer a model of curriculum as inquiry which involves students putting their knowledge and sign systems to work to pursue questions which are continually under revision. The authors see inquiry as an important component of educating for democracy and incorporating student diversity, and they make a strong case for teachers to take up inquiry positions in order to avoid self-congratulatory and limiting practices.

Susan Church explicitly tackles key political questions about the achievements and limits of whole language as a movement: how it has become in some places "a polarizing force," producing "camps" and "orthodoxies," and why there is a belief that whole language practices do not help children become skilled language users. By reexamining her own role in the development of whole language philosophy and practice in Nova Scotia, Church exposes a number of problems and assumptions that arose from the attempt to authorize whole language in district curriculum materials and in a book co-authored with teachers and administrators. The teacher audience for whom the book was written, however, was less than impressed and dismissed the work of the new teacher "experts." As Church points out, the move from top-down to a more democratically produced curriculum paradoxically resulted in the formation of camps and resistance to the book itself, which was still seen as imposed by the bureaucracy. She continues by detailing some of the hazards of misinterpretation of "whole language speak" and some of the unanticipated effects which can result. She argues that educators need to be more visibly part of a political agenda in times of funding cutbacks and neoconservative backlash in education and social policy and programs.

In the next chapter, Patrick Shannon explores the political interests in the work of progressive educators and the consequences of teachers' and students' inquiries. Having stressed the impossibility of being apolitical in pedagogy, he introduces a key problem which he describes as the politics of "niceness," wherein issues of power are seen as inappropriate or, as he puts it, as a "dirty business which teachers and children should avoid." What follows is a powerful interrogation of the assumed innocence of the child and a historical account which illuminates how gender, race, and class are implicated in idyllic versions of childhood. Shannon challenges progressive educators to address the consequences of difference in their desire to work for social justice and equality through literacy and schooling. In a wide-ranging discussion of the law, educational science, the market, and public schooling, Shannon argues that educators cannot ignore or gloss over questions of power and privilege and still claim to be working through inquiry toward justice.

In Chapter 5, Barbara Comber echoes some of the questions raised thus far. Beginning with an analysis of a discussion with her son about his history homework—to design a Nazi propaganda leaflet—she explores the kinds of histories, inquiries, and literacies being taught and learnt in school. She argues that students sometimes engage in simulations of assignments about language, power, and history that actually ignore what really counts. As she points out, students copy lies into their notebooks as though they were truths. Comber argues that inquiry approaches need to problematize how people come to know about particular versions of history. In other words, she does not take "the disciplines" for granted as knowledge to be appropriated, but rather approaches them as already inflected with interests, with knowledge-power relations constituted within their authoritative discourses. Further studies of classroom interaction suggest that different students are able to elicit different kinds of teacher help in response to their questions. Schools' material resources for inquiry such as libraries and access to the Internet also vary dramatically. Inquiry positions are not equal, and this chapter suggests a number of ways in which teachers and students might construct a curriculum of inquiry guided by principles of social justice.

In Chapter 6, Tim Lensmire discusses the weaknesses in the conception of student voice, within critical pedagogy and with writing workshop traditions. His project is concerned with how to link classroom writing with a critical democratic vision of schooling and society. Once again the assumed innocence of the child (in this case) writer and the child's experience is contested, as is the teacher's acritical positioning with regard to the child's textual productions. What happens when students produce racist or sexist texts in their search for personal voice? What happens when students collaborate to the exclusion of others? What happens when personal expression produces conflict between peers? Where does the teacher stand? Lensmire discusses the implications of his analysis for developing classroom inquiry communities.

Tim Shannon and Patrick Shannon also explore the social and educative functions of classroom inquiry communities, reiterating the impossibility of sheltering young people from complex questions about real world issues and out-of-school communities. Further, they restate the need for teachers and students to be skeptical rather than naive about the "answers" they find. Drawing on historical examples, they make a case for teachers recognizing and taking up an overtly social function as part of their work in teaching inquiry, and they show how in the past educators have made spaces for political and community inquiries in schools. Chapter 7 concludes with similar accounts of practice in contemporary schools and a call for relevant local action in communities.

In the next chapter, Jennifer O'Brien explains the work she did as an elementary school teacher to problematize books with young children. Taking the position that students' inquiries are sometimes limited by the texts provided, O'Brien reports on the ways in which she investigated children's analyses of books written for them. She describes how she helped students make critical readings of factual texts. Along with the students, O'Brien explores the hypothesis that factual texts written for children often fail to take them seriously "as researchers and knowers." O'Brien goes on to illustrate how to make both students' writing and factual texts designed for young readers the objects of students' critical analyses, and offers an account of key questions, talk, and tasks around text that destabilize textual authority. Inquiry in this classroom is not simply about finding answers to student-generated questions, but also about asking less reverent questions about the production of texts and disciplinary knowledge. Here the student reader/inquirer considers how information is selected and presented, why it is presented in such ways, how it might have been presented differently, and what else might have been included. This pedagogy engages with explicit ideology critique, and also makes space for young people at the start of their education to take a powerful position in relation to inquiry, sources of information, and knowledge production.

Also working in early childhood classrooms as a teacher-researcher is Connie White, who presents a moving and powerful account of the ways in which poverty in rural Nova Scotia affects classroom learning, particularly that of one young girl in her class. She focuses on the way a book shared in the classroom, Eve Bunting's *Fly Away Home*, opens up for discussion the topic of homelessness and poverty. As White notes, the initial discussion evoked by the book concerned plane trips and airports, even though few children had experience with either. But six-year-old Janice, from whom White draws many insights, sets up a problem for her teacher and her classmates by "telling tales" about her own many trips on planes. Both her teacher and her peers recognize that these trips are fictional; Janice's family is very poor and she has not traveled on a plane. White uses this critical incident to reconsider her classroom practice, rethinking what can be said in her classroom and what cannot, what can be named and what cannot, what positions different children can take up as participants, readers, writers, and inquirers. She asks what kinds of responses are possible for different children and deftly points out the ways in which social and economic class works in the everyday worlds of classrooms and literacy lessons. White takes up the challenge Janice poses for her in order to question how contemporary educational policy and practice maintain a cycle of blame with regard to poor children, their families, and teachers. As her teacher explores the conversations and stories Janice engages with, we gain a profound sense of how young children can explore some of the less "nice" (to use Shannon's term) topics of inquiry in school. Indeed, as White points out, children are living in poverty. How the subject of poverty might be productively and safely talked about in school is a question educators cannot afford to ignore.

White's chapter is followed by a contribution from Vivian Vasquez, also an early childhood teacher, working at the time the chapter is set in multicultural Toronto. Vasquez also demonstrates how young children can and do engage with complex issues about who exercises power, and identify and act on inequities in the classroom and school. She draws on her experiences as a young child whose family had immigrated to Canada from the Philippines. Recalling her classroom experiences as an elementary student, Vasquez points out how "foreign" the notion of "research" was to her. Her experience of being a student had been to answer questions, not to ask them. She indicates that what counts as proper learning or proper literacy is specific to the pedagogical occasion and that such occasions are shaped culturally. In this context, her beautifully written copied notes from the encyclopaedia elicited an angry response from her teacher, whose expectations of research were that the students would write the information "in their own words." Vasquez's narrative and analysis suggest that there is nothing universal or natural about children's inquiries. These practices are learnt in ways that relate to wider cultural and literate traditions. She goes on to show how as a teacher she attempted to allow young children to make genuine inquiries—through letter writing—about the ways things are in school.

In Chapter 11, Robyn Jenkin also considers students' research questions. Through her classroom research as a teacher-librarian in suburban South Australia, she discovered that some students' questions could be answered by books designed for children and others could not. Library books and schoolbooks designed for students to learn from have rhetorical structures and content that prescribe a style of questioning that teaches children what the "right" questions are. Jenkin's analysis further demonstrates that students' inquiries often follow gendered patterns as they select what is interesting to them from open-ended topics. As she monitors the process of several students, she notes that within the same classroom students are participating in entirely different inquiry processes about entirely different curricula. Jenkin explains how it is that some topics come to be "safe" areas for inquiry and others are excluded. She discusses the questions from students that challenged her as an educator in a Catholic primary school because they touched on matters that in that context were not considered open to contestation. This chapter reiterates and illustrates issues raised by Shannon, Vasquez, and Comber—questions which centre on what students are permitted to inquire about in particular school contexts.

The setting for the research discussed in Chapter 12 is a primary school in Exeter in the United Kingdom. David Wray, Maureen Lewis, and Carolyn Cox present an account of a project investigating how to assist children to read, research, and write nonfiction texts. Like O'Brien, Vasquez, and White, they report that young children just beginning to read and write can become powerfully engaged in the inquiry process when the work has relevance for their own lives. Through an account of a school gardening project, Wray and his colleagues elaborate on the pedagogical supports they designed to help young children engage in real, rather than token, literacies incorporating practical knowledge, complex ideas, and discipline-specific vocabulary. Richly illustrated with students' conversations (captured on videotape and presented here as dialogue), this chapter provides a sense of what "inquiry scripts" sound like in the early years and how teachers can scaffold these experiences to ensure that learning does take place.

Lee Gunderson's chapter unsettles any comfortable assumptions about whole language and inquiry approaches as operating for the universal good by raising some fundamental challenges about the impact these philosophies and practices have on culturally diverse communities. Drawing on research undertaken in British Columbia, Canada, he describes what happened in three contrastive school communities where cultural differences about the role and purpose of school education led to large-scale and wide-reaching reviews of whole language. Themes introduced by Vasquez are reiterated here as Gunderson discusses the mismatch between some parents' expectations for their children's schooling and the goals of progressive education. The objections of some recently arrived middle- and upper-middle-class families from Taiwan and Hong Kong in one school did not represent the whole parent community, nor even the Asian-parent community, but they generated significant conflicts about what education is, what it is for, and how it is best delivered. Referring to two other schools and particular classrooms, Gunderson demonstrates how progressive pedagogies conflicted with familial and cultural traditions, including ways of reading and ways of being a student. Teachers and students can become casualties in a process in which, despite the best intentions, school learning and English literacy produce cultural conflicts that disrupt the pedagogical relationship and make it counterproductive. Gunderson concludes with a call for more research and analysis of highly multicultural settings in order to explore further the effects of our practices on different groups of students and to envision how our theories of pedagogy and curriculum may need to change.

It is this challenge that Sibel Boran considers in the final chapter, as she explores how the educational community might genuinely engage with linguistic and cultural difference in redesigning classrooms of inquiry that investigate global matters. Working from her study of young people in an international school, Boran discusses how school-generated inquiries are often Euro- or U.S.-centric and discount or make invisible much experience and knowledge that young people from other places have to offer. She is an advocate of global education in which young people develop communities of inquiry marked by their diverse membership. Boran offers a range of practical starting points for teachers to consider in initiating conversations about difference and identity, and she outlines some risks in opening up these conversations. She goes on to explore how international literature might play a central part in generating such discussions, illustrating the effects of this approach by drawing on the comments of young people in high school. She reflects on the ways in which the impact of international wars and distant conflicts reverberates in the corridors and classrooms of U.S. schools far from the actual conflict.

The intention of *Critiquing Whole Language and Classroom Inquiry* is to open up conversation and to challenge progressive and critical educators to explore further how our pedagogies position different young people: to ask what kinds of inquiries we are fostering and what kinds of knowledge builders we are educating. It will have done its work if educators look again at what is going on in the name of inquiry, in the name of literacy, and ultimately in the name of education.

Chapter One

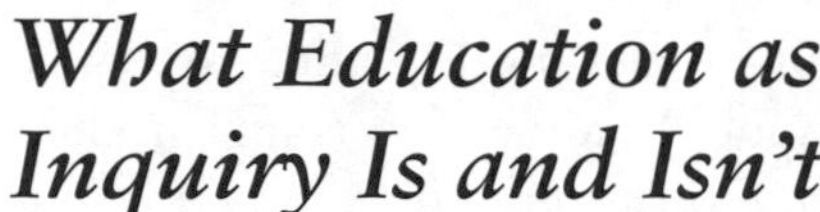

What Education as Inquiry Is and Isn't

Jerome C. Harste
Indiana University

Education as Inquiry Is a Philosophical Stance

I recently came back from a meeting with a group of middle school teachers who were interested in implementing a multiple-ways-of-knowing, inquiry-based curriculum. There was a good deal of talk about what inquiry was and wasn't, how one should and shouldn't go about implementing it, and what was and wasn't possible. Participating in that conversation, and reflecting on it later, helped me clarify what "education as inquiry" means to me.

Education as inquiry provides an opportunity for learners to explore collaboratively topics of personal and social interest using the perspectives offered by others as well as by various knowledge domains (psychology, anthropology, economics, ecology, feminism) and various sign systems (art, music, mathematics, language) for purposes of producing a more equitable, a more just, a more thoughtful world. In this way, curriculum becomes a metaphor for the lives we want to live and the people we want to be.

Since we don't have the answers to the problems future generations will face, I don't think we can afford to "train" children in the name of education. We need to give them tools with which they can outgrow us and yet help themselves. The problems we hand future generations—pollution, a depleted ozone layer, overpopulation, ethnocentrism, the haves of technologically rich countries versus the have-nots of economically developing countries—are not simple, nor will there be simple answers. It is going to take a good deal of research and understanding to unpack the problems and lay bare the issues that lie at the heart of finding real solutions.

For me, education is inquiry and inquiry is education. It is what schools should be about from eight in the morning to four in the afternoon. *Education as inquiry is not a clever new way of integrating curriculum.* It is a reorientation; a new way of conceptualizing schooling.

As I see it, all we guarantee the students we teach is that they will face problems of some magnitude and that no single individual is going to be able to fix the problems. If the messes we hand future generations are to be resolved, I suggest that it will take a lot of good minds that know how to learn and how to collaborate.

Many teachers think of inquiry in terms of six- or nine-week units of study. I see it as an attitude. In Jennifer Story's sixth-grade classroom, she and her students have been conducting "Twenty-Four-Hour Inquiries" and "Three-Day Inquiries" (Stephens, personal communication, 1993). On these days, the exploration of a single topic is all that gets done—no switching from mathematics, to language arts, to social studies, to music, to yet some other content area. Once these strategies have been introduced in a classroom, I would like to see "Twenty-Four-Hour" and "Three-Day" inquiries offered as options for students to elect to do any time the class is doing something that is not of compelling personal interest. This means that school schedules need serious work and serious rethinking.

I don't want inquiry to be relegated to an afternoon time slot, to be reductively thought of as something equivalent to a unit of study, a theme, or an integrated way to handle social studies, science, or other content areas. While education as inquiry is all these things, it is also more than any of these things.

Education as inquiry is a reconceptualization, a new way of thinking that challenges all extant definitions. Education as inquiry means rethinking reading, rethinking writing, rethinking classroom management. Reading as inquiry, for example, is very different from reading as comprehension. While reading as inquiry still focuses on making and sharing meaning, it goes further. The meaning we make has to be used as a metaphor to deepen understanding and make sense of some other part of our lives or world. This is "the inquiry," the search for ever broader connections. Writing as inquiry means writing as a tool for thinking rather than as a skill to be mastered. Writing as inquiry means using writing to establish one's voice, distance oneself from experience, observe the world more closely, share one's thinking with others, strategically search for patterns that connect, present what one has learned and reflectively take new action. Discipline as inquiry means that rather than implement behavior management procedures that allow you, the teacher, to control the situation, problems of discipline are matters of discussion, with alternatives generated by the group and with the parties involved invited to find solutions that work.

Education as Inquiry Calls for Radical Change

In the past, reading, writing, mathematics, science, and social studies have run roughshod over the curriculum. Say "schooling" to most people and they think of groups of children getting on a yellow school bus to be hauled to classrooms to engage in reading, writing, mathematics, and other content areas. In the old days, the students would be sitting in rows and taking tests. Today, even in whole language classrooms the structure hasn't changed much. Oh, they aren't sitting in rows or taking tests—now they're at tables, keeping portfolios—but they still have a writing time, a reading time, a math time, a theme time, and so on. Despite surface structural changes, the content areas are still the organizational device for curriculum.

The Core of an Inquiry Curriculum Is Personal and Social Knowing

Education as inquiry, while respecting the disciplines and what it is we think we know, is fundamentally about changing the way we think about instruction. Significantly, education as inquiry suggests that the personal and collective questions of learners ought to be the heart of curriculum. Rather than framing curriculum in terms of the content areas, learners' inquiry questions become the organizational device for curriculum. Integration occurs in the head of the learner, rather than in the daily schedule of the teacher.

Recently I ran into a middle school student wearing a T-shirt with the logo, "Been There . . . Done That," repeated on both the front and back. It struck me that metaphorically, at least, this is how we treat the subject matter areas in school. Rather than have students say, "Been there . . . Done that" ("I took ecology . . . I'm done with that"), I want them to see the content areas as available perspectives they might take during their inquiries. No matter what their question, at some point I would like them to look at the issues their inquiry raises in terms of science: What would an ecologist have to say about this problem, as well as this solution? The same is true for history: What would a historian want us to learn about this topic? What would an anthropologist want us to understand? an economist? a psychologist? and so forth.

Content Areas Reviewed

Each discipline or content area has a particular perspective—a focusing question, if you will. These ways of looking, often systematized and involving the use of certain types of research tools, have proved valuable. That is why they are still around. Rather than dead truths—something you learn and hopefully recall when *Jeopardy* comes on television—disciplines are tools for systematically exploring the modern world. We don't want kids to say they studied feminism and now they are done with it. Equity is an understanding we want them to keep foremost no matter what issue they are exploring.

More and more we have come to realize that everything is connected to everything else. Helping learners see the disciplines as devices they might use to unpack the complexity of issues surrounding the topics they study supports them both in thinking more deeply as well as in understanding the community and the connectedness of knowing.

Legitimizing Multiple Ways of Knowing

Sign systems represent ways humans have devised to make meaning: language, art, music, drama, movement, mathematics, etc.

Each of the sign systems is used by each of the knowledge domains as a tool and toy for inquiry. This is why much of mathematics is structured on language and why mathematicians use charts and graphs to convey their meaning. Music is very mathematical, a fact you can discover for yourself if you lay out the underlying patterns of your favorite song with a set of unit blocks. This is not to suggest that music, art, and language are the same. They aren't. Each captures dimensions of knowing that are unique. Meaning in language unfolds synchronically as words are temporally produced. Meaning in art unfolds as a whole; the juxtaposition of line, shape, form, and color holistically "means" simultaneously.

Currently, schools tend to value language and mathematics as ways of knowing. Art, music, movement, drama, and the like are relegated to the fringes, evidenced by the fact that whenever students in Australia, England, Canada, New Zealand, or the United States don't score well on a national or international examination, the typical response is to raise language and mathematics requirements for graduation. A multiple-ways-of-knowing, inquiry-based model of education is designed to change all that. It assumes that art, music, mathematics, drama, and other sign systems play a role similar to that played by language in learning. By denying access to these sign systems, we silence some students' ways of knowing. We don't do ourselves much good either. By making art, music, drama, and movement second-class citizens in curriculum, we limit our ways of knowing, too. Whole dimensions of what it means to know are silenced.

I assume different cultural groups have different ways of making meaning. Although we have learned to *accept* children in terms of their home literacies, we have yet to *respect* children and the home literacies they bring to school. If we truly respected our students' home literacies, we would routinely invite ourselves and the other students in our classrooms to inquire into these ways of knowing and try them on for size. At present we seem to accept multiple literacies but are determined to move them on toward school literacy.

The smallest unit of curriculum in an inquiry model of education is a focused study (see Figure 1.1), which entails a question of personal and social interest, at least one perspective, and

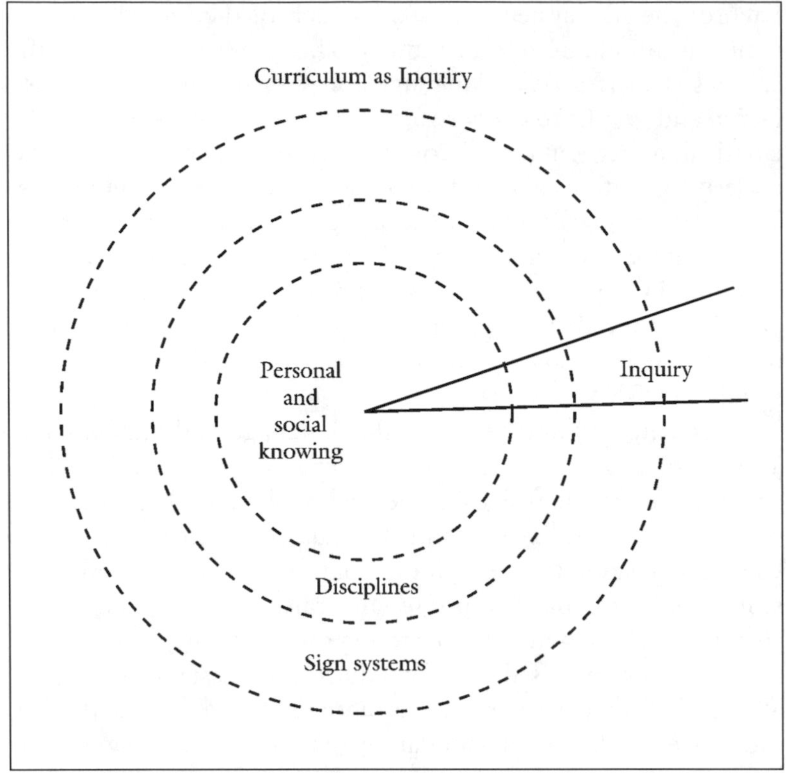

FIGURE 1.1. *Curriculum as inquiry (Short & Harste, 1996).*

total access to the various sign systems through which the topic might be explored. Marjorie Siegel says we should think of education as inquiry as a model which "invites learners to see themselves as knowledge makers who find and frame problems worth pursuing, negotiate interpretations, forge new connections, and represent meaning in new ways" (1995, 3).

Focus of an Inquiry-Based Curriculum

Figure 1.2 is a working model of the processes underlying an inquiry-based curriculum based on what we know about the role that language and other sign systems play in learning. Art, music, mathematics, drama, movement, and language each play a

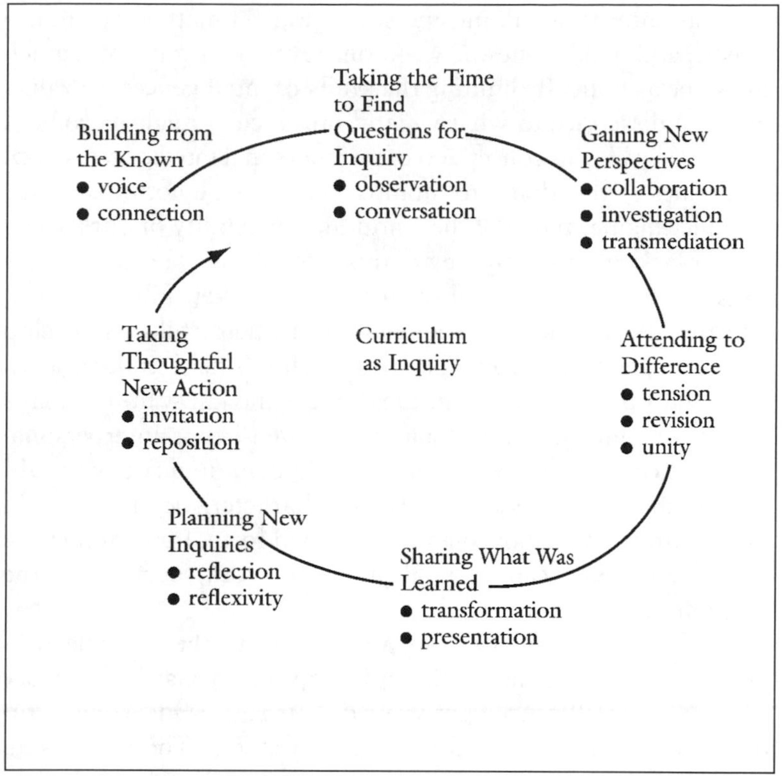

FIGURE 1.2. *The underlying processes of inquiry.*

role in the curricular development of voice, the making of connections, the more careful observation of our world, and so forth. A good inquiry-based curriculum focuses on learning how to learn. What students learn about learning today they apply tomorrow in the pursuit of a new inquiry. Part of this is metacognitive, knowing how to debug what went wrong as well as knowing how to position themselves with sign systems, disciplines, and other learners to capitalize on the learning potentials available in any situation. Mistakes are not problems, but the fodder for new inquiries.

Education as inquiry has some things in common with multiple intelligences, yet it is significantly more. Howard Gardner (1993) has proposed a theory of multiple intelligence in which he identifies seven major intelligences—spatial (which includes art), musical, interpersonal, intrapersonal, logical mathematical, linguistic, and bodily kinesthetic. At one level, his argument is much the same as mine. By limiting the kinds of intelligences we value, we do a disservice to what we and our society might become. I particularly like his conception of intrapersonal intelligence, which he defines as the ability to monitor one's own emotional needs. Gardner blames much of the emotional instability of our society on our lack of understanding of this intelligence. He sees teenage suicide, emotional outbreaks in which co-workers kill each other, and the like as evidence of our failure to help children develop this intelligence. He would like to see schools help students learn to monitor their internal emotional states and know how to make necessary adjustments for their mental well-being. Interpersonal intelligence is the ability to interact and communicate with others. Gardner sees it as an intelligence characteristic of persons in public office. In its most highly developed form, for example, we have a guru who can marshal others to work together for the good of the whole.

Although Gardner does not advocate using these intelligences as selection devices, many schools incorporating Gardner's theory of multiple intelligence have viewed their role as identifying students' strengths and nurturing these strengths. The result is an elitist approach to education. Kamehameha Schools in Hawaii, for example, use intelligence in one or more of Gardner's areas as the basis for admission. The Key School in Indianapolis not only identifies students by type of intelligence but also tracks them according to intellectual strengths.

In contrast to a theory of multiple intelligences, sign systems are democratic. Each of the sign systems is available to all of us. They represent the ways in which humans have learned to make and share meaning. While students may develop strengths in one particular sign system, the goal of the school is not to polish or hone this strength so much as to make sure that each student has ample opportunity to explore various ways of making and sharing meaning. *The goal of the language arts program becomes one of expanding communication potential* rather than systematically closing it down through the overemphasis of one sign system at the expense of others, or through the denial of access because some sign systems are thought to be more important than others.

On one level, an inquiry-based curriculum is problem centered. Yet I want to be careful in saying this. Students need time to find, as well as frame, their own inquiry questions. Outcomes aren't known as they are in discovery learning, but are instead open-ended, with students free to go off in directions and reach conclusions that were not anticipated. This does not mean that teachers do not need to plan. Rather, it means they need to engage in "planning to plan" (Watson, Burke, & Harste, 1989) by rotating themes through disciplines and sign systems for purposes of exploring the possibilities and potentials for learning. Inquiry is not so much a curriculum of objectives as a curriculum of possibilities.

The focus of an inquiry curriculum should be on how to be a good inquirer. Experiencing inquiry is a necessary but not sufficient condition. Students need to be able to gain new perspectives, articulate what inquiries do to sensitize them to issues, and reflexively interrogate their own and their society's values.

How long can students sustain inquiry? Forever, I would say. But we kill it by expecting reports, something to grade, and concrete products. Just as there are no prerequisites to inquiry except curiosity, so there are no specific terminal points other than more curiosity and the freedom to move in new directions if one so desires.

Often, inquiry begins not so much with a question as with an itch. Something doesn't feel right, but knowing what question to ask comes much later. For a change of pace, allow students to frame their inquiry questions through pictures rather than words. This invitation can give teachers as well as the students a new perspective on inquiry, as well as an intuitive feel for the complexity and possibility of the issues that need to be addressed.

I see it as dangerous to reduce an inquiry-based curriculum to either questions or problem solving. As Suzanne Langer (1980) has pointed out, by the time we have a question we also have a solution. Embedded in every question is an implicit, if not explicit, answer to the problem. Problem solving bothers me, too. Like questioning, problem solving implies a one-to-one correspondence: Here is my problem; here is my answer. Here is the students' inquiry question; here is their answer. Inquiry isn't the product of curriculum so much as an invitation to live a new curriculum. It is easy to reduce inquiry to fact finding. To do so, however, is to simplify a complex process. And as Carolyn Burke (cited in Harste, Woodward, & Burke, 1984) reminds us, while we can simplify a complex process, to do so does not change the underlying complexity of the process.

Inquiry is more about unpacking the complexity of issues than it is about coming up with simple solutions to complex problems. This does not mean that we cannot provide a supportive structure for our students as they learn about what inquiry is and isn't. I have developed inquiry journals that invite students to engage in observation, conversation, collaboration, reflection, and other key processes underlying inquiry (see Figure 1.2). As my understanding of the inquiry process grows, my questions and instructions change: Why is this topic important to you? What three questions do you have? For each question, you need to make an observation, read a book, conduct an interview, etc. Joby Copenhaver and Rise Paynter provided each of the students in their classroom with *A Wonderful Questions Booklet* (Copenhaver, 1991). Kathy Short and Gloria Kauffman hold a "Studio Time" each Friday during which students can use the various sign systems to conduct in-depth explorations of their inquiry questions (Kauffman, 1996). If an ample supply of computers and cameras is available, it is easy to envision a "Tool Time" during which students could be invited to explore the topics of their inquiries using these tools. In my experience, it is best to explore tools and sign systems as a functional part of inquiry rather than in isolation. The trick is to be clear about what processes you believe are an essential part of inquiry and then to create curricular engagements and structures that support these processes. If these structures do not work, revision—what I prefer to call "curriculum redevelopment"—is needed.

Inquiry is not about what kind of presentation students are going to make at the end of the inquiry. Often students will want to know this, and instead of inquiring, they begin planning their presentation. Fortunately, the process often takes care of itself, since in trying to present, students often end up having to inquire. Our options are either not to let students know what is coming up next or to trust the process. I have found that students find their way into inquiry through questions, exploration, presentation, conversation, and demonstration—that is, being around others who are similarly engaged. Over time, I have learned to trust both students and the learning process. I did not, however, manage this insight easily; neither will you.

Think about education as inquiry, and problem solving as the difference between philosophy and technique. In the old days of problem solving, we taught inquiry as something one did sometimes in mathematics or in science. It was a skill that once mastered could be applied whenever the need arose. I don't want inquiry treated this way. I want *everything* to be seen as inquiry, from the complexities of teaching to the complexities of learning and evaluation.

Evaluation Is Synonymous with Teaching

Education as inquiry calls for a total readjustment in our thinking about evaluation. In the past, evaluation has been anchored on outside criteria set by others; teachers and students either met expectations or they didn't. The view of evaluation was that of an outsider looking in. From an education as inquiry perspective, however, the view is different:

From an education as inquiry perspective on education, the only thing evaluation can do is help a learner or a community of learners interrogate their values. Over the years, teachers and pupils have been held more and more accountable while administrators, school board members, and other stakeholders have become less accountable. Under this outsider view of evaluation, the only persons truly vulnerable are teachers and learners. The evaluator and the standards, if not above reproach, are certainly not the focal point of evaluation.

From an education as inquiry perspective on evaluation, there can be no observers, only participants, in the evaluation process. Remember, the whole of education is inquiry. School

> board members need to ask themselves what they are doing to support the professional development of teachers and if this is the best use of the district's money. Teachers need to ask themselves if they are doing everything possible to provide instruction that is theoretically sound and based on what we know. Pupils need to ask themselves if what they are doing currently is the best they could do and perhaps, on the basis of this information, take thoughtful new action.
>
> *From an education as inquiry perspective, evaluation needs to track the changing inquiry questions of learners.* Experience, rather than age or developmental stage, determines learning. The information provided by standardized tests is useless to teachers in planning instruction largely because it provides information relative to the test designer's inquiry question rather than the inquiry questions of the learners. By tracking the inquiry questions of learners, information about the functions that language and other sign systems do and do not serve can be gathered. Only on the basis of this information can teachers plan meaningful instruction.

What is an inquiry-oriented educator to do in the name of evaluation? The answer, I believe, is one part "kid watching" (Goodman, 1978) and one part "invitation" (Short & Harste, 1996), by which I mean inviting students to track their own inquiry questions. Developing kid-watching skills is not easy. Recently I have been working with Diane Stephens on a kid-watching approach she calls Hypothesis-Test (Stephens, 1990). Teachers keep a four-column kid-watching journal. The first column is used to record observations, the second column to record various interpretations of each observation, the third column to record hypotheses generated from reading across interpretations, and the fourth column to record curricular decisions and future inquiries. Just mastering the difference between observation and interpretation is not easy. Reading through the list of interpretations that have been generated for each observation (Diane recommends five interpretations for each observation), complex patterns of interaction can be noted. For example, in one instance

I noted that when students asked their own inquiry questions during literature discussion, everyone seemed more engaged. Further observations of literature discussion groups could either lend credence to or fail to support this hypothesis. If my hypothesis were supported by future observations—which in this case it was—a curricular change in how I conduct literature discussion groups would be called for. In another instance, I noted that with the increased use of reflective drama as a technique in writing, more dialogue appeared in students' stories. Given this pattern, a whole new set of inquiries arose, from new things to read to new curricular directions to try. The focus is not so much on teaching as it is on learning. Curriculum is built from and with the students rather than something that is done to students.

Many teachers think of checklists as the way to evaluate an inquiry curriculum. The problem this poses is that it assumes we already know what to look for. For both students and teachers, curriculum then becomes a matter of running the hurdles rather than an ongoing process of inquiry grounded in research.

Students, parents, and other stakeholders need to be invited into the evaluation process. The intent is to inquire, not to turn evaluation into a horse race whereby teachers, students, and sometimes entire countries are pitted against each other in adversarial roles. Evaluation needs to put at risk what it is each of us thinks we know. Positions—not people—are put at risk. No person or position is privileged. It is by making all positions within the educational community vulnerable that we grow.

How do I get the kids I work with to the point of wanting to investigate? I'm convinced nothing teaches like demonstration. By being inquirers ourselves, we provide students with the best invitation to inquiry I can think of. And we need to be upfront with students about what we are doing. They need to understand the inquiry questions we have about them as learners, as well as how we plan to investigate our questions. Instead of talking behind our students' backs with a colleague, saying that we are concerned about Jordan, a first grader who is not demonstrating any knowledge of grapheme-phoneme correspondence in his writing, we need to say, "Jordan, I'm concerned. I'm wondering what I can do to support you to write like the other kids in the room. See, they write so that I can read their writing. What can I do to help you learn to write this way? I know next year's teacher is going to be expecting you to be writing like them."

Statements like this may seem brash, if not wrongheaded, but curiosity, not correctness, starts the inquiry cycle for teachers as well as students. Embedded in statements of this sort are your beliefs about how schooling operates, what constitutes growth and development in writing, as well as what you see as your role in the big picture of things. While there may be several things wrong with the position you hold, by first clarifying and then interrogating your stand, you, like your students, grow.

Most curricula are built from memory: This is what proficient reading looks like . . . This must be the way we get there. This is what being a mathematician means . . . Logically this is how someone must get there. In lieu of these adult-logical views of curriculum and curriculum development, think of evaluation as an opportunity for you, your students, and the wider educational community to build a new curriculum for our society through research.

Focusing on evaluation may, however, be an error. At this historical moment, there are so few instances of true inquiry-based education that to talk at length about evaluation seems premature. After all, it is hard to evaluate a dream if you have never first given yourself permission to have one.

Inquiry Curriculum Musts

I liken curriculum to drama. Because I see curriculum as a metaphor for the lives we want to live and the people we want to be, I envision curriculum as an attempt to "dramatize" a new way of being in the world. This is why curriculum is more about sociology than psychology, more about research than memory, more about experiences than exercises. The lived-through experience curriculum offers and the new interaction patterns it fosters make all the difference. How you teach and what you teach are both important. In fact, how you teach often determines what gets taught. *Issues of equity and justice need to be embedded in the presuppositions one makes about curriculum, frontloaded in cur-*

riculum as class topics and themes, as well as experienced and interrogated as part of the inquiry cycle.

Too often, even in whole language classrooms, we schedule one engagement after another. Rarely do we take the necessary time to reflect on what we have learned from these engagements or what our participation in these engagements means for how we will operate in the world anew. Even less often are learners asked to interrogate new understandings in terms of who benefits and who doesn't. *Learning does not end with presentation but rather with reflection, reflexivity, and action.* As a function of learning, learners need to position themselves differently in the world: business ought not to go on as usual.

An inquiry curriculum is not neutral. It begins with voice, inviting all learners to name their world. It ends in reflexivity and action, inviting all learners to interrogate the very constructs they are using to make sense of their world. Naming one's world is not a neutral process. Because we are born into a world that is already named, it behooves learners to examine critically the meanings they make, the systems of meaning in society that support those readings, as well as the available alternatives. Phrased differently, learners must take responsibility for ideas as well as for the personal and social actions that result from ideas. I'm not for a minute suggesting that learners can both name and interrogate their naming simultaneously. I am suggesting that the very process of inquiry allows us to distance ourselves from experience and to look at it critically. Just as surely as inquiry must begin in naming and framing, it must end in interrogation and action.

How you view inquiry makes a difference. *As I see it, an inquiry-based curriculum allows us to use what we have learned about creating holistic and supportive environments for learners and to build from this base.* At the same time, an inquiry curriculum raises the stakes, forcing us to address issues of critical literacy as they relate to democracy and schooling. Some see inquiry as a new paradigm in competition with whole language; I see it as an extension of the whole language model. The potential for critical theory and inquiry has always been there. It has simply taken us this long to begin to explore its potential.

In her keynote address at the 1995 National Council of Teachers of English Annual Convention, Carole Edelsky identified various ways that issues of equity and justice could be addressed in curriculum without violating what we know about the role that language plays in the learning process. In addition to a unit on "bears," she suggested we can and must study topics of greater social significance. Without question, curriculum as inquiry mandates that we position ourselves as advocates for the disenfranchised.

Whole language is about hearing new voices, starting new conversations, and putting in place structures whereby those conversations can continue. I want learners to understand inquiry-based instruction philosophically as a diversity model of education. *In lieu of the conformity and consensus model that now operates, diversity and difference should be seen as an educational asset, one that puts an edge on learning.* Although there is no singular outcome—no one vision of democracy toward which we must all work—curriculum as inquiry is only democratic to the extent that it supports thoughtful new personal and social action by today's learners and tomorrow's citizens.

Just as whole language benefited from the involvement of many teachers in the movement, exploring its potential as well as expanding how it might be done, so curriculum as inquiry will benefit from your inquiring voices. Education as inquiry will be what we curricularly and collaboratively make of it.

References

Copenhaver, J. (1991). Instances of inquiry. *Talking Points K–5, Premier Issue,* 6–12.

Edelsky, C. (1995, November 17). Justice, equity, and petards. Keynote address given at the Whole Day of Whole Language program, 85th Annual Convention of the National Council of Teachers of English, San Diego, CA.

Gardner, H. (1993). *Frames of mind: The theory of multiple intelligence.* New York: Basic Books.

Goodman, Y. (1978). Kid watching: An alternative to testing. *National Elementary Principal, 57*(4), 41–45.

Harste, J. C., Woodward, V. A., & Burke, C. L. (1984). *Language stories and literacy lessons*. Portsmouth, NH: Heinemann.

Kauffman, G. (1996). Creating a collaborative environment. In K. G. Short & J. C. Harste, with C. L. Burke (Eds.), *Creating classrooms for authors and inquirers* (2nd ed., pp. 229–49). Portsmouth, NH: Heinemann.

Langer, S. (1980). *Philosophy in a new key: A study in the symbolism of reason, rite and art* (3rd ed.). Cambridge, MA: Harvard University Press.

Short, K. G., & Harste, J. C., with Burke, C. L. (1996). *Creating classrooms for authors and inquirers* (2nd ed.). Portsmouth, NH: Heinemann.

Siegel, M. (1995). More than words: The generative power of transmediation for learning. *Canadian Journal of Education, 20*(4), 455–75.

Stephens, D. (Ed.). (1990). *What matters? A primer for teaching reading*. Portsmouth, NH: Heinemann.

Stephens, D. (1993). Personal communications. [See also EDCI 431 course syllabus (Mimeographed). Honolulu: University of Hawaii.]

Watson, D. J., Burke, C. L., & Harste, J. C. (1989). *Whole language: Inquiring voices*. Richmond Hill, Ontario: Scholastic TAB.

Chapter Two

Curriculum as Inquiry

Kathy G. Short
University of Arizona

Carolyn L. Burke
Indiana University

The perspective of curriculum as inquiry involves theoretical and practical shifts in how educators view teaching and learning within school contexts. As educators examine their beliefs and actions, they take control of their learning and work with their students in creating more democratic learning environments. Within these environments, students have the time to explore and find the questions that are most significant in their lives as inquirers.

> We get to figure out what we know and what we want to do. We are trusted to learn, to talk, and to share. We are expected to ask more questions and find out more.
>
> Amber, *age 10, Gloria Kauffman's classroom*

> I did work out of workbooks. I was hoping for a good education. I could tell I was not getting what I wanted. I was wild all the time. I was getting in trouble. I was worrying too much about my friends. Now I like to move around and work with others. I need others to understand me and my ideas. When I work with others, I learn. I need to learn. I share my ideas even if they are not good. I ask questions. The atmosphere in this class has changed my thinking. Others have started to want to learn. I knew if I would try, I would get somewhere.
>
> Jennifer, *age 10, Gloria Kauffman's classroom*

While educators have debated at length about the value of democratic classrooms and inquiry-based curriculum, students such as Jennifer and Amber who have lived in these classrooms speak powerfully about the new potentials in their lives. Some students initially resist a curriculum based on inquiry and democracy because it involves learning new ways of thinking and acting in the classroom. Over time, however, they come to value and demand such a curriculum because it builds from their own ways of knowing and living in the world. This curriculum, therefore, can never look the same from classroom to classroom, nor will it realize the same potential in all students.

Voices such as Amber's and Jennifer's, however, persuade us to continue our struggles to create democratic classrooms based in inquiry. We realize that such classrooms challenge educators to make major changes in current school structures and in beliefs about learning and curriculum. This struggle must therefore include a consideration not only of democracy and inquiry but also of the process of change and how this process affects curriculum when education is viewed as a democratic institution.

In this chapter, we begin with a consideration of the attributes of change within and across shifts in paradigm and the relationships between collaboration, change, and diversity. We then use these understandings about the change process to explore the implications of adopting the perspective of curriculum as inquiry. One of the questions we want to address is whether inquiry approaches to curriculum are simply a different term for theme units or actually reflect a different theoretical and practical approach to curriculum. Does curriculum as inquiry change what we do in schools, or simply put a new label on what we are already doing? Throughout this chapter, we share our personal experiences and stories of change as educators, realizing that many of the changes we have experienced parallel those of other educators.

Examining Our Beliefs and Actions

For us, *curriculum involves putting a system of beliefs into action* (Short & Burke, 1991). When we engage in inquiry about curriculum, we examine and reflect on our beliefs as well as our actions in the classroom. In thinking about the changes in curriculum that we and other educators have made, we realized that some of these involve changes in actions within the same paradigm of beliefs, whereas others involve changes in actions and beliefs that spread across paradigms. That is, sometimes we build on our current beliefs to further develop our teaching practices and the learning environments we are creating with students. Other times we rethink our beliefs and make difficult shifts in both our beliefs and our actions. Both kinds of change are essential to our lives as teachers, but they involve different challenges and ways of thinking about teaching.

A work of children's literature, *Dear Willie Rudd* (Gray, 1993), helped us understand why these distinctions in the questions we ask and the changes we make as educators matter. The book opens with a woman rocking on her front porch, lost in thoughts that are causing her to feel tension. Miss Elizabeth thinks back fifty years to when she was a young girl and Willie Rudd was the family's African American housekeeper. She realizes that Willie was not treated fairly but knows that she cannot make amends to Willie, who is no longer alive. Finally, she writes Willie a letter, telling her all the ways in which she would treat her differently and letting her know that she loves her. Miss Elizabeth attaches the letter to a kite and releases the letter and kite into the night sky. She then returns to her porch and continues rocking.

We have found that change for us begins with similar feelings of tension. Something isn't right but we are not quite sure what it is. Over time we begin to get a sense of what is bothering us and so we take action. What often happens, however, is that our first steps stay within the same paradigm of beliefs and, like Miss Elizabeth's, lead to a surface change in actions. Miss Elizabeth has rearranged her memories and relieved her feelings of guilt. The question left unanswered, however, is whether she is willing to make more substantive changes in her beliefs and actions. Will she alter how she thinks and acts with others? Will she continue to reflect on her beliefs and seek out others in order to continue her inquiry?

We are *not* criticizing Miss Elizabeth's first steps toward change. They resemble our own first steps. They may not go far enough, but they are a beginning and they count. The issue is whether her learning stops because she believes she has answered her questions and achieved a deeper change in her beliefs and prejudices. Are writing the letter and letting go of the kite her only actions? If she sees herself as now acting without prejudice and feels no need to take further steps, then we have concerns.

These same issues are present when educators mistake their initial changes in action within the same paradigm of beliefs for substantive changes across paradigms of beliefs. When they make this mistake, they are prevented from inquiring into and making the deeper and more substantive changes that are needed to transform themselves and society. They need to keep inquiring, not assume they have *the* answer.

These issues are always present in our inquiries as educators. To understand these issues within educational inquiry, we share several stories of change from our own experiences that highlight changes in action within and across different paradigms.

Examining Educational Inquiry through Change Stories

The first story involves change in our questions about spelling in the classroom. For many years, spelling has meant teaching isolated words, chosen for their graphophonemic patterns, through spelling lessons, workbooks, and the weekly spelling test. Discontent with that approach led us to reject textbook lists and to begin selecting spelling words from classroom theme units or from student writing.

This shift, however, did not involve a change in the questions we were asking. It was not until we moved away from asking questions about how spelling words get chosen to asking questions about the purpose of spelling within the authoring process that our inquiry was pushed to a different level of understanding. This shift allowed us to explore the role of spelling within the authoring process and to see *spelling as a realization of language* (see Figure 2.1). Spelling lists and isolated word study gave way to a focus on spelling strategies and the role of editing in the authoring process.

A second change story relates to the role of parents in the curriculum. Our oldest model of parent involvement is that of schools reporting to parents through sending home report cards

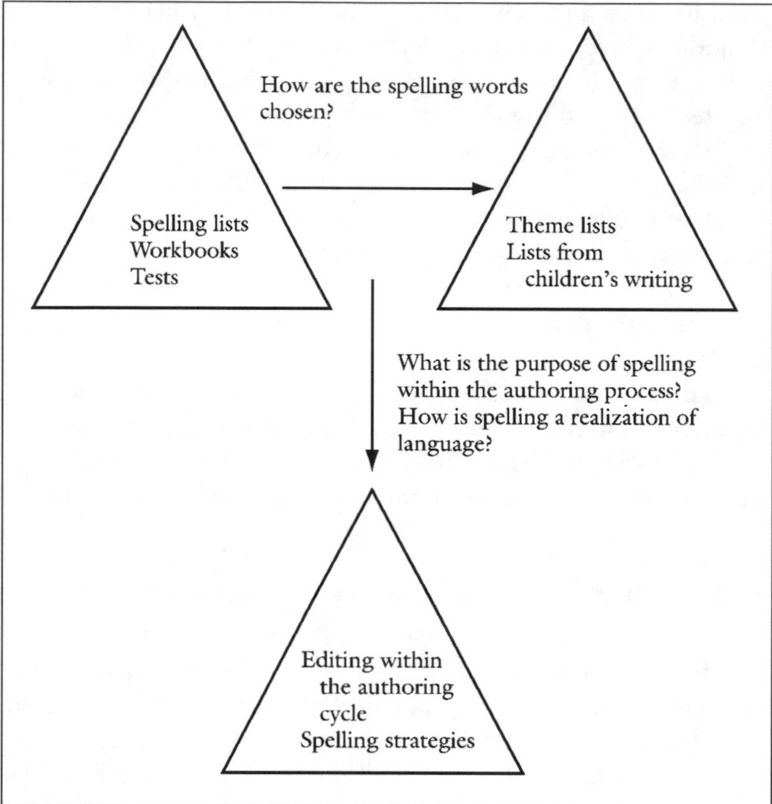

FIGURE 2.1. *Changes in understandings about spelling.*

and announcements and inviting parents to attend school plays or assist on field trips. These teacher-parent relationships are those of a professional reporting to an amateur, with teachers remaining in control of the standards.

A recent shift that is fairly substantive in its physical form but not in its function is the move toward narrative report cards and more parent participation in classroom learning events. This shift involves the same relationship of professional to amateur with the teacher in control and asks the same question of how teachers can report *to* parents. It's more friendly and welcoming, but operates within the same belief system.

For the paradigm to shift, we needed to initiate a *three-way conversation* between teachers, parents, and students (see Figure

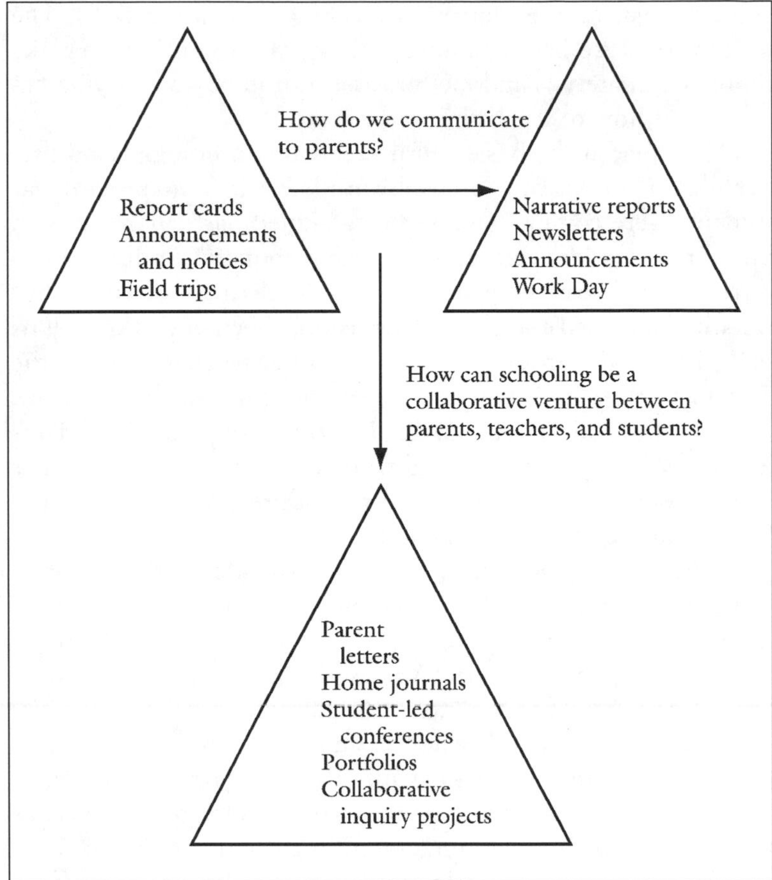

FIGURE 2.2. *Changes in the role of parents within schools.*

2.2). Instead of parents remaining outside of the main relationship between teachers and students within the curriculum, they have begun collaborating with teachers and students within the curriculum. This collaboration gives parents some ownership of classroom events and a share in the risks as they participate in classroom life.

The question of how to teach students to read and make sure they comprehend has dominated approaches to reading in schools. When we began teaching, we answered this question by using basal readers, ability groups, round-robin reading, workbooks, and emphasizing the sequential teaching of reading skills. The shift to literature-based reading programs led us initially to make changes in materials and methods but not in our underlying beliefs about how to teach children to read.

We replaced the basals with literature anthologies and lists of children's books categorized by grade level. To make sure that students were comprehending, we assigned particular topics in their literature logs and graded their responses. Ability groups were replaced by heterogeneous literature discussion groups, but we still controlled the content by asking open-ended questions that directed the groups' discussion. Other teachers control the discussion through a cooperative learning format in which responsibilities and roles are divided among group members. Thus we shifted away from one right answer, but not from teacher control: there were still preferred procedures to follow and preferred interpretations and themes.

When we changed our question to how literacy functions as an inquiry tool in lives of learners, our focus moved from how to teach students to read to *reading as part of the ongoing personal and social inquiry in children's lives*. We moved beyond reading "because it's good for you" to reading because it allows students to pursue questions and issues of significance in their lives (see Figure 2.3). Instead of making sure that students have comprehended, we focus on providing opportunities for readers to construct and explore their understandings with others through conversation, story, and dialogue. Through collaborative inquiry in literature circles, readers explore different perspectives and actually *think* together, not just cooperatively work together. Everyone, including the teacher, participates by listening carefully to others and working together toward understanding.

The changes in writing have paralleled the inquiries of educators in the previous areas. In writing, our primary concern used to be teaching students *how* to write, a focus that entailed grammar lessons, handwriting practice, and skills workbooks. Learning these separate skills, however, did not ensure that students could actually write to communicate, so we explored ways to get students involved in writing through using creative writing and story starters. Students were given a topic and a set of procedures or steps to follow to produce a particular piece of writing

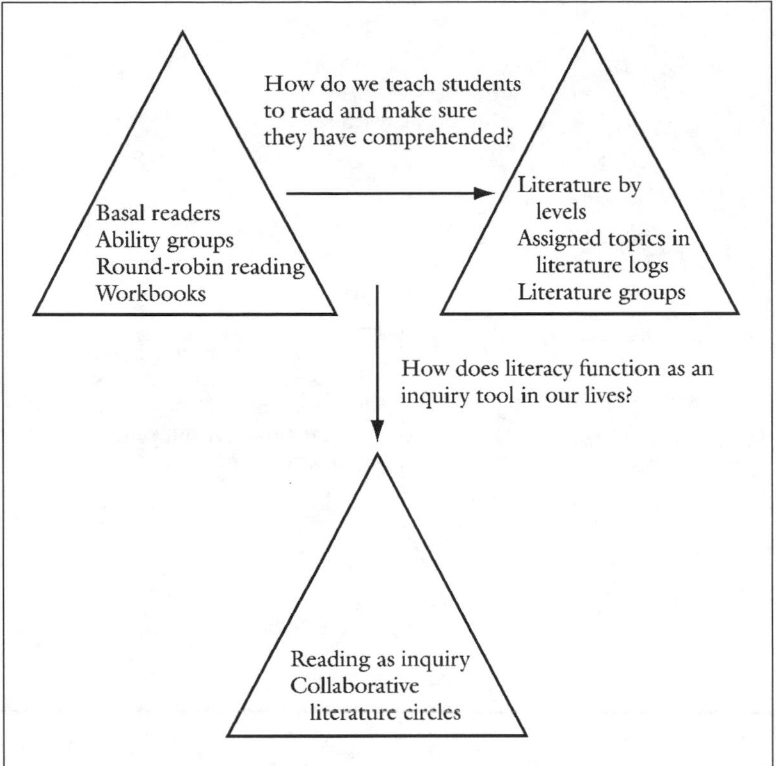

FIGURE 2.3. *Changes in our understandings about reading and literature.*

within a certain time span. But our question of how to teach students to write remained the same.

The work of Donald Graves (1983) and Lucy Calkins (1986) encouraged us to ask new questions about how we could support the authoring process so that *writing is a tool for thinking and communicating within school contexts*. These questions led us to explore writing workshop (Graves, 1983), writers' notebooks (Calkins, 1990), and the authoring cycle (Harste & Short, 1988) as curricular structures and engagements to support authors in constructing their own texts for authentic purposes (see Figure 2.4).

Recently we have been exploring other sign systems such as music, art, movement, and mathematics as tools for thinking and

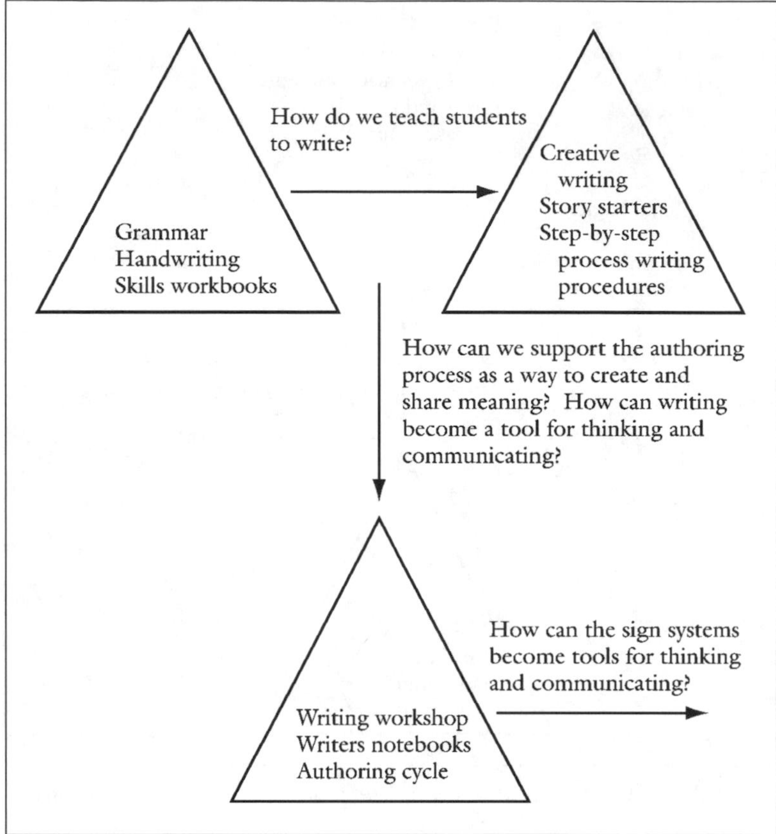

FIGURE 2.4. *Changes in understandings about writing.*

communicating in schools (Short & Harste, 1996). We have assumed that these explorations are within the same belief systems as those which underlie language and the authoring cycle, and have acted as though the same universal meaning-making processes underlie each of these systems. While we have made these assumptions in order to move ahead with our inquiry, we are aware that our work with sign systems may involve a move to another belief system at some point.

As we examined these change stories, we realized that when we shift paradigms, new relationships, constructs, and constituencies become possible that were not available within our previous paradigm. The availability of new potentials and relationships in particular became evident as we considered the relationship between reading, mathematics, social studies, and the other subjects that have composed a traditional curriculum as a discrete and independent set of knowledge. We have come to new understandings of these subjects as knowledge systems and sign systems that interweave to provide the parameters and structure of knowledge and to form the basis for inquiry. In trying to examine these relationships, we found it helpful to return to *three visual models of the reading process* which were developed many years ago. These models helped us rethink our beliefs about curriculum, knowledge, authoring, and the integration of content and process in the classroom. They have helped us explore curriculum as inquiry.

Exploring Curriculum as Inquiry

Carolyn sketched out the three best-known models of the reading process in order to highlight how each model emphasizes individual systems and components within the reading process (see Figure 2.5). The first model, *the phonics model*, is based on letters that lead to families of words that eventually build to word definitions. The second model, *the skills model*, is what our generation experienced as elementary students. The same systems operate in this model, but the emphasis changes. Instead of choosing words based on their family patterns, they are chosen because of their frequency. Readers are taught a range of word-attack skills instead of depending solely on graphophonemic correspondence, and their focus goes beyond word meaning to story comprehension.

The third model, *whole language*, views reading as a process that cuts across the cueing systems of meaning, syntactical structures, and surface structures (for example, graphophonemic correspondence). In this model, the pragmatic context becomes a necessity for illustrating the importance of the social context within which the learner is reading. This model illustrates the uninterruptable and embedded nature of the systems of language and their relationship to each other.

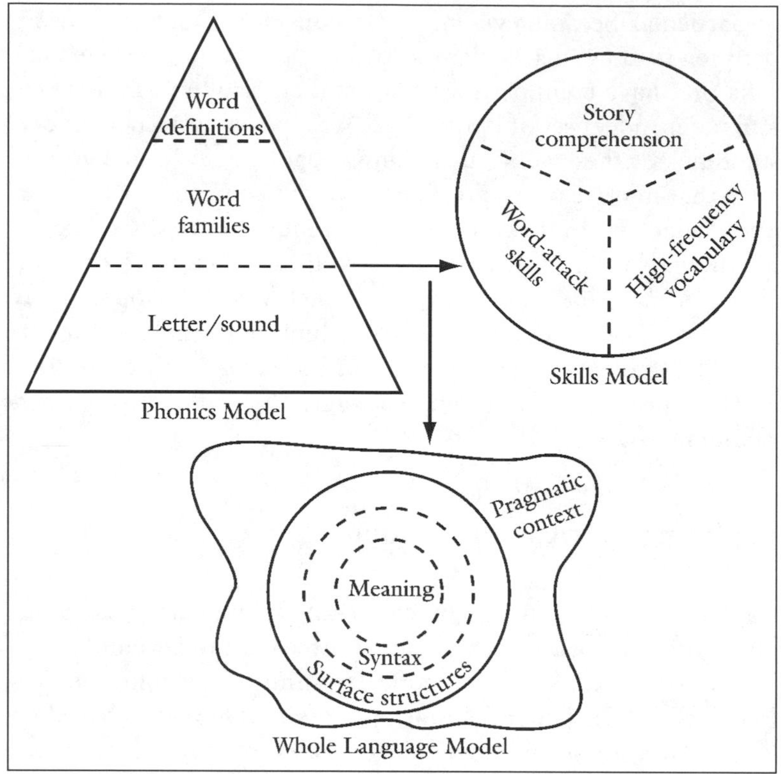

FIGURE 2.5. *Models of the reading process.*

These understandings and visual models of the reading process gave us a way to rethink our beliefs and models of curriculum as inquiry. The model that has dominated schools for many years is *curriculum as fact* (Figure 2.6). When we were students, we spent our time studying different content areas where a common core of predetermined knowledge was broken into parts.

The smallest unit of curriculum in this model is a fact, so isolated facts and procedures are the basic building blocks. We memorized dates, people, events, facts, and formulas. In mathematics problems and science experiments, we followed exact procedures that could not be varied and led to one right answer. Over time we learned sets of facts that were then combined into concepts. Because we learned each topic and each subject area in isolation from everything else, we never got to the point of form-

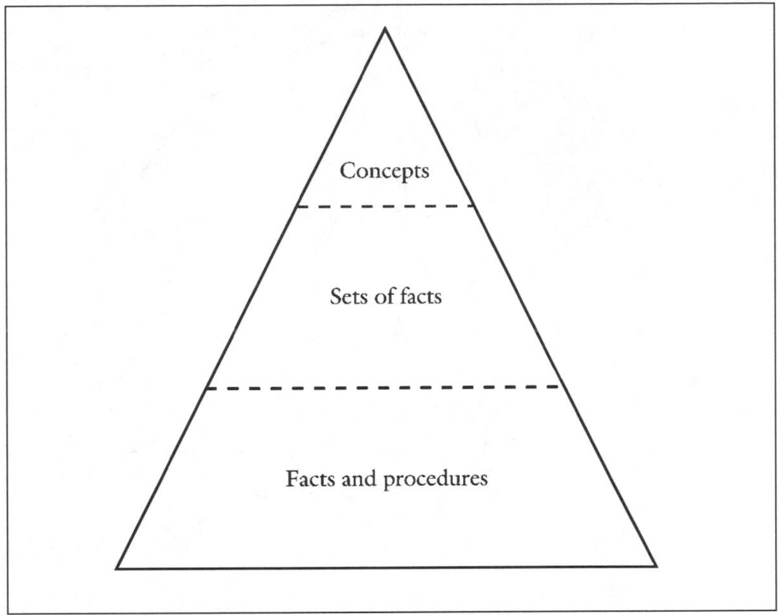

FIGURE 2.6. *Curriculum as fact (Short & Harste, 1996).*

ing broad generalizations that cut across the different subject areas.

Our focus was on "covering" the topic, and we did so by reading the textbook, filling out worksheets, giving teachers correct answers in class discussions, and taking tests to see if we had mastered the information. Research consisted of copying facts from the encyclopedia into a little booklet and handing it in to the teacher. We covered lots of facts and memorized many details that were forgotten the day after the test. We covered few topics in any depth and ended up with superficial knowledge and no desire to keep learning—we were *done* with that topic. School was something to endure, not a place of significant learning.

Our frustrations as students with textbook approaches to content areas led us as teachers to explore theme units. This approach of *curriculum as activity* then dominated our teaching for many years (see Figure 2.7). Sometimes we chose activities because of the facts that could be learned; other times we chose activities according to particular skills and procedures that we felt students needed. Still other times we chose activities because they

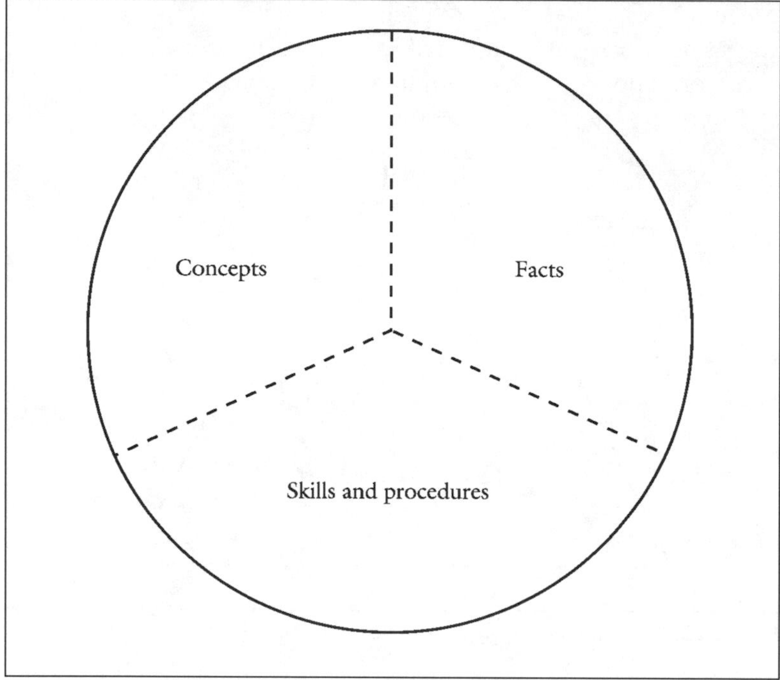

FIGURE 2.7. *Curriculum as activity (Short, 1993).*

supported the development of certain conceptual understandings.

In developing thematic units, we took a topic such as kites or the Civil War and listed activities relating to different subject areas such as mathematics, science, social studies, art, or reading. Underneath those subject areas, we listed activities that would lead to the acquisition of particular facts, skills, and procedures. Other activities were listed because they were fun, not because they were tied to any fact or concept. Later, we webbed topics such as kites by concepts and subtopics such as wind, Japanese folktales, kite making, paper folding, celebrations, and weather.

These units were more interesting and engaging for students and allowed us to replace the textbook with well-written fiction and nonfiction. When we looked more closely, however, we realized we were still covering topics and supplying facts, just in more interesting ways. The units still compartmentalized knowledge by subject area or concept. Our goal was an integrated curriculum, but what we had created was a correlated curriculum. While the activities were related to each other because they were all on the same topic (for example, kites), they did not build on each other or support students in pursuing their own questions.

In addition, the topics of the units often seemed trite and the connections between activities and the topic forced. We felt as though we were engaged in activities at the expense of critical and in-depth knowing of larger conceptual issues. Even though students had more choice, they were primarily engaged in gathering sets of facts on narrow topics and questions.

As teachers, we spent a lot of time inventing activities and creating the curriculum. Because the units were limited by our own knowledge of the topics, student research stayed safely within what we already knew; students were assumed to be discovering what was already known. We remained within a deficit model of learning in which we assumed the unit would teach students what they didn't know and take them from a more confused to less confused state (Dewey, 1938). Although the package was more attractive, we were still developing the curriculum and delivering it to kids.

The tensions we felt in our use of theme units remained vague until we realized that we had changed our actions as teachers but not our belief systems. Our movement away from the belief that we needed to "cover" topics began when we examined the ways in which we go about learning and inquiry in our own lives. Just as our assumptions about reading and writing changed once researchers looked at how people actually read and write outside of school, so our beliefs were challenged once we asked ourselves how *we* lived as inquirers in the world.

Exploring Our Understandings about Inquiry

One of our first insights was that inquiry is a process of both problem posing and problem solving (Freire, 1985). Inquiry involves becoming immersed in a particular topic, having time to explore that topic in order to generate questions that are significant to the learner, and systematically investigating those questions. Educators have acted on the assumption that research begins with a question. Students are asked to immediately identify what they know and what they want to know about a topic and then quickly choose a subtopic and gather facts. They are able to stay close to what they already know and believe. Although they may end up with interesting information, they are not pushed to consider questions of broader and deeper significance because there isn't time to explore and find those questions. Inquiry is not just a matter of finding a problem, but of having time to find a problem *significant* for that learner.

We knew from our own inquiry that finding the question often is the most difficult aspect of our research and occurs quite late in the process. We begin with an area of interest that we explore, and the specific question grows out of that exploration rather than preceding it. Sometimes we do begin with questions, but those questions change, and we discover new questions and issues through our explorations (see Figure 2.8).

Creating a visual model of curriculum as inquiry allows us to see that inquiry is an entire process that cuts across three knowledge sources—personal, system, and signs (Harste, 1993)—just as reading is an entire process that cuts across the cueing systems. It is not separated into different subject areas with separate activities, facts, procedures, and concepts to be added up to cover the topic.

At the heart of inquiry is *personal and social knowing,* the knowledge that learners bring from their personal experiences of living in the world and being part of specific cultural groups and social contexts. Inquiry can only begin with what learners already know, perceive, and feel. All voices need to be heard, including those with whom teachers might disagree. The inquiry process allows learners to reflect, critique, and take further action, but they need to begin with their current beliefs.

The second knowledge source is the *knowledge systems* such as history, biology, and economics. These knowledge systems were constructed by humans as a way to structure knowledge to make sense of the world, just as grammar emerged as the structural system of language so that humans could communicate. They developed because a group of scholars shared a set of questions and a domain of intellectual inquiry and over time created a set of questions about the world, ways of researching those questions, and a continuously evolving body of knowledge.

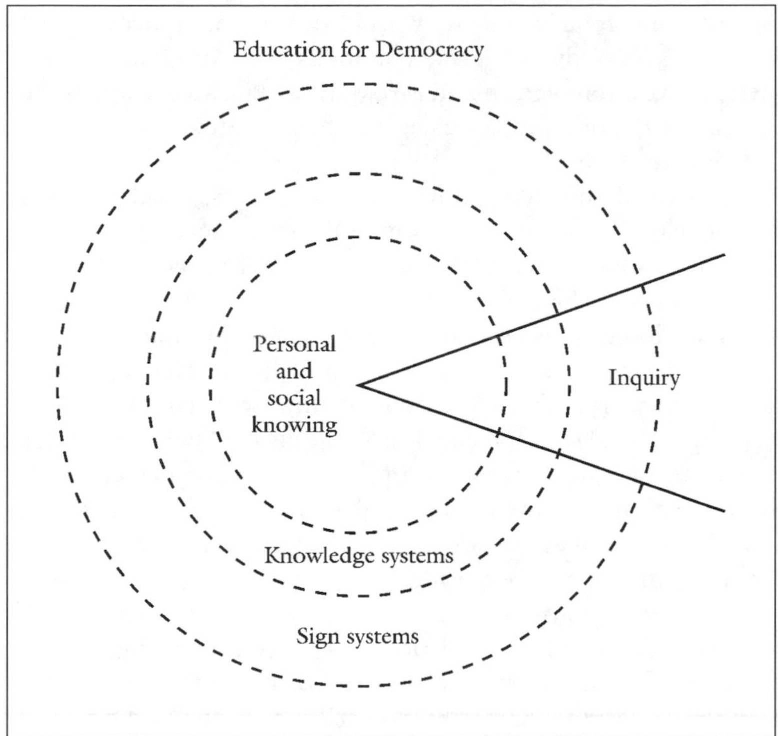

FIGURE 2.8. *Curriculum as inquiry (Short & Harste, 1996).*

We see two major differences between knowledge systems and the content areas as traditionally taught in schools and universities. The first concerns what is considered significant. The content areas in schools have taken the broader knowledge systems and reduced them to isolated skills, facts, and concepts. What is significant about knowledge systems, however, is not the specific pieces of information but the alternative perspectives each system provides about the world. Each knowledge system looks at the world through a different lens and asks a different set of questions about the same event. These systems also provide us with different methods of research and different tools to use in those investigations.

The second major difference is that content areas are taught as separate entities. Instead of teaching each area separately and developing science units and social studies units to cover particular facts and concepts, inquiry involves the simultaneous use of multiple knowledge systems. The focus is on bringing multiple perspectives from within and across many knowledge systems to an issue or topic, not on using the topic to teach a particular subject area.

The third knowledge source is *sign systems*, which are alternative ways of creating and communicating meaning with others, such as language, mathematics, music, art, movement, and drama (Eisner, 1982; Leland & Harste, 1994). All of these systems are basic ways of making and sharing meaning, but they allow humans to know and communicate different meanings about the world. Outside of school, multiple sign systems are commonly used simultaneously. In schools, however, one system at a time is taught, often separate from the thematic focus of the classroom. Inquiry involves having all sign systems available so that students can use the ones that best meet their own purposes at any point in time (Berghoff, 1993; Clyde, 1994). This realization has led us to question the writing workshop because of its exclusive emphasis on students constructing meaning through language. We are interested in a studio time during which students can select the sign systems most appropriate for their meanings and their inquiries.

Through inquiry, students come to new understandings that are temporary rather than final answers. Students do not cover the topic; instead, they begin a lifelong inquiry, and so their understandings and questions continue to grow and deepen in complexity over time. We believe that progress in inquiry is marked by new questions to ask, because answers last only until learners have time to ask new questions and until more compelling theories are generated. Learners don't inquire to eliminate alternatives, but to find more functional understandings, create diversity, and broaden their thinking. They don't go from more confused to less confused; they move on to new questions that are more complex and reflect deeper insights. These questions cannot be framed ahead of time by teachers and experts: students have to be involved from the beginning. Educators have learned how to build curriculum for and *from* students; the challenge they now face is how to negotiate curriculum *with* students.

Inquiry involves a major shift in thinking. Instead of using the theme as a rationale for teaching reading, writing, and content, the knowledge systems and sign systems become tools for exploring and researching students' questions. The major focus is on inquiry itself, not the traditional subject area distinctions that have dominated the curriculum through both textbook and theme unit approaches. This shift involves using many of the same materials and activities that were part of theme units but for different purposes and within a different theoretical frame. This shift is a difficult one to make, and we continuously find ourselves moving back into previous ways of thinking. Although it is beyond the scope of this chapter to provide specific descriptions of classrooms based in inquiry, some of our initial explorations in classrooms are described in Copenhaver, 1993; Short & Armstrong, 1993; Crawford et al., 1994; Short & Harste, 1996.

Education for Democracy

This model of curriculum as inquiry indicates that the pragmatic context of the school and classroom makes a difference in inquiry. The classroom contexts and social relationships that most powerfully support inquiry are those based in education for democracy (Edelsky, 1994). Inquiry is theoretically based on collaborative relationships, not the hierarchies of control common in most schools. While our long-term goal is to work toward changes in the overall structures of schools, in the short term we have worked at changing our own classrooms and our relationships with students. Because education for democracy is essential to inquiry, the phrase "collaborative inquiry" becomes redundant because inquiry is at heart a collaborative process.

Pat Shannon (1993) defines a democracy as a system in which people participate meaningfully in the decisions that affect their lives. It involves a participation and negotiation among equals in which participants are not just given a choice among options determined by others behind the scenes, but are part of the thinking behind the scenes.

We believe that education for democracy involves these essential properties: (1) assuming that people are naturally inquisitive; (2) realizing that the significance of learning lies both in *what* you do and *why* you do it; (3) understanding that accepting a new alternative does not mean devaluing the contributions of current and past beliefs; (4) realizing that each individual has a personal responsibility for critiquing and envisioning; (5) taking responsibility for problem posing; and (6) valuing and seeking diversity, not sameness.

We are particularly concerned with valuing and seeking diversity so that difference is seen not as a problem to be solved, but as offering new potentials for a group of learners. The role of the school in society has often been viewed as producing a model citizen. We find ourselves in disagreement not with the goal of producing contributing citizens, but with the belief that this "model" citizen is monocultural, with particular characteristics that are the same for everyone. This view of a model citizen led initially to a "melting pot approach" in which schools made no adjustments to accommodate student backgrounds but insisted that all individuals be "ready" for schools. The curriculum was predetermined and students did all of the adjusting or they were left behind (Banks, 1991).

In some schools, the current focus on diversity has led to changes, most notably the willingness to take into account the different life experiences that students bring with them to school. Starting from students' own life experiences, building on these experiences, and recognizing their cultural diversity has increasingly become part of the curriculum. While culture has been defined most frequently in terms of ethnicity or race, we believe that culture also includes gender, socioeconomic class, religion, language, type of community, and so on—the many ways in which we live and think in the world.

Diversity has been recognized not only in terms of the life experiences students bring to school, but also in how they learn. In some schools, teachers have adapted their ways of teaching and their expectations for how students will go about their learning. Students are encouraged to express themselves through art and drama, for example, and not just language. They are also able to function as bilingual learners, using the language that best fits their needs and thinking for particular learning events.

The valuing of diversity currently breaks down, however, when outcomes are considered. Schools recognize and use the differences that exist between students to shape the same model citizen. Students are led to believe that schools value who they are, but then they are forced toward a mainstream model of a citizen; the valuing of diversity is used merely as a way to begin the conversation, but then students are funneled down to the same standards. Diversity is fine *as long as* students can speak standard English, write a persuasive essay, and pass the standardized tests. Although democracy is rooted in diversity, schools aren't comfortable with that diversity because it builds on strengths, and schools can't always predict what the variations will be or determine the exact outcomes, leaving educators feeling nervous and uncomfortable.

Schools have recognized and accepted diversity but have not respected or acted on difference as essential to learning and democracy. We believe that it is difference, not sameness, that makes a democracy strong. Through building on the different ways of thinking and living in the world that students bring to the classroom, schools can open new possibilities for those students' lives. Everyone's strengths need to be used to create new possibilities in classrooms. The focus should not be on compromise or majority rule, but on attending to and acting on difference in order to build a true democracy that values everyone's contribution and supports each student in developing his or her own potentials.

Taking Control of Our Inquiry as Educators

These change stories about our inquiries as educators are not meant to reflect an either/or position of wrong versus right approaches to curriculum. We do not believe that we have "arrived" at some kind of superior understanding. Along with other educators, our understandings are always in process. We do not take the deficit view that educators must make changes in their teaching because something is wrong with that teaching. Change is the result of a stance of continuous inquiry, and we view ourselves and other teachers as professional learners.

For us, these change stories reflect the examination and transformation of beliefs and actions that are a constant part of our lives as teachers and learners. These stories are a reminder that we need to examine critically *both* our beliefs and actions. We need to pay attention to the tensions we feel about our teaching and take time to explore them. While most of our inquiry will involve examining our actions and exploring new potential actions based on our current beliefs, we remain open to the possibility that we may also need to explore different belief systems. We may need to take a leap to new beliefs and practices, so we continually critique our thinking and actions and acknowledge our feelings of tension and our sense that something is wrong.

There is great danger in believing that we have found the best way to teach and therefore becoming complacent. While most educators begin the change process by changing their teaching practice and noting what occurs, that change often leads to more substantial changes as their beliefs are challenged. If they believe that these first steps are all they need to take, they may miss the opportunity for inquiry that will lead them to even more powerful understandings. These change stories have made us more aware of where we are in our own thinking and provided us with strategies for continuing to push our thinking. By taking the perspective that curriculum is inquiry, we find ourselves in a state of continual learning and growth.

The stories of change also highlight the forces emanating from the publishing industry, from much of educational research, and from existing school structures to reform curriculum in ways that do not fundamentally change how schooling is done. These forces work hard to convince educators that adding a practice and a new set of materials constitute substantial change and reform in schools. The writing workshop is thus reduced to a set of precise steps for "how to do writing process." Literature approaches become a new set of literature anthologies with literature logs (workbooks in disguise) and cooperative learning groups or whole-class discussions. Literature circles become simply a replacement for reading-ability groups and a better way to teach reading, rather than collaborative inquiry by readers on life itself. Inquiry-based curriculum is reduced to asking students what they want to study and setting up a sequence of research steps while maintaining the dominance of traditional subject areas.

These forces make it easy to maintain the status quo and convince educators that they do not need to critically examine and question their beliefs as well as their practices. There is a need for teachers to seek wider options and not rely solely on the programs packaged and delivered to them. Many times the best of the current knowledge in the field is put together to create a set of procedures, activities, materials, and training workshops that is packaged for delivery. These programs are appealing because theoretically most educators agree with much of what they contain. The problem is that the packages close down alternatives—shut down the inquiry of educators. They represent a movement away from, not toward, difference. Educators need to control their own inquiry so that they can ask questions that really matter in their lives as educators, just as students need to ask questions that are significant in their lives.

We are incredibly nervous about inquiry. We have come to believe that curriculum as inquiry fundamentally questions how schooling is done. It changes our relationships with students, colleagues, families, the community, other educators, and society. It changes how we view knowledge and the role of knowledge systems and sign systems in schools.

Returning to Miss Elizabeth and her kite, we are convinced that we can't let go of that kite and go back to our comfortable rockers. We have to follow the kite to make sure we don't lose our vision of a democratic education. We have to act and work toward that vision, not release it and let it escape. Instead of letting go of her kite, Miss Elizabeth needs to learn to fly it.

References

Banks, J. (1991). *Teaching strategies for ethnic studies* (5th ed.). Boston, MA: Allyn & Bacon.

Berghoff, B. (1993). Moving toward aesthetic literacy in the first grade. In D. J. Leu & C. K. Kinzer (Eds.), *Examining central issues in literacy research, theory, and practice.* Chicago: National Reading Conference.

Calkins, L. (1986). *The art of teaching writing*. Portsmouth, NH: Heinemann.

Calkins, L., with Harwayne, S. (1990). *Living between the lines*. Portsmouth, NH: Heinemann.

Clyde, J. A. (1994). Lessons from Douglas: Expanding our visions of what it means to "know." *Language Arts, 71*(1), 22–33.

Copenhaver, J. (1993). Instances of inquiry. *Primary Voices K–6, 1*(1), 6–12.

Crawford, K., Ferguson, M., Kauffman, G., Laird, J., Schroeder, J., & Short, K. (1994). Exploring historical and multicultural perspectives through inquiry. In S. Steffey & W. Hood (Eds.), *If this is social studies, why isn't it boring?* York, ME: Stenhouse.

Dewey, J. (1938). *Experience and education*. New York: Macmillan.

Edelsky, C. (1994). Education for democracy. *Language Arts, 71*(4), 252–57.

Eisner, E. (1982). *Cognition and curriculum: A basis for deciding what to teach*. New York: Longman.

Freire, P. (1985). *The politics of education: Culture, power, and liberation*. South Hadley, MA: Bergin & Garvey.

Graves, D. (1983). *Writing: Teachers and children at work*. Exeter, NH: Heinemann.

Gray, L. (1993). *Dear Willie Rudd*. New York: Simon & Schuster.

Harste, J. (1993). Inquiry-based instruction. *Primary Voices, K–6, 1*(1), 2–5.

Harste, J., & Short, K. (with Burke, C.). (1988). *Creating classrooms for authors: The reading-writing connection*. Portsmouth, NH: Heinemann.

Leland, C., & Harste, J. (1994). Multiple ways of knowing: Curriculum in a new key. *Language Arts, 71*(5), 337–45.

Shannon, P. (1993). Developing democratic voices. *Reading Teacher, 47*(2), 86–94.

Short, K., & Armstrong, J. (1993). Moving toward inquiry: Integrating literature into the science curriculum. *New Advocate, 6*(3), 183–200.

Short, K., & Burke, C. (1991). *Creating curriculum: Teachers and students as a community of learners.* Portsmouth, NH: Heinemann.

Short, K., & Harste, J. (with Burke, C.). (1996). *Creating classrooms for authors and inquirers* (2nd ed.). Portsmouth, NH: Heinemann.

Chapter Three

The Journey from Pedagogy to Politics: Taking Whole Language Seriously

Susan M. Church
Halifax Regional School Board, Novia Scotia

It has been more than two decades since I first encountered the ideas that subsequently became associated with whole language. When Frank Smith turned conventional wisdom on its head in his keynote address at a reading conference in 1976, I guess I was ready to be convinced that what I was doing in the name of literacy instruction was not very helpful to many students. Smith's (1978) notions about the importance of nonvisual information in reading made sense to me, so, unlike many of my colleagues who resisted the message, clinging to their skills-based models of reading, I set out to find out more about these new and intriguing ideas. What I did not realize at the time was that I was embarking on a long journey, a journey that began with rethinking how I taught reading; changed direction slightly as I expanded my understanding of literacy learning to include writing, oral language, and other communication systems; and eventually evolved into an ongoing effort to advance the political agenda I now believe is inherent to whole language.

I have felt an increasing sense of urgency about that agenda for some time as I have observed what has been happening to literacy education in Nova Scotia, where I have lived and worked since 1979. Once an area that educators visited to learn about whole language, the province is caught up in conflicting and chaotic movements: back to basics, fiscal restraints, restructuring, site-based management, business and media attacks on education, national and provincial testing, and on and on. Demoralized by constant criticism, wage rollbacks, increasing class sizes, and ever more challenging students, many teachers have come to view whole language as a passing phenomenon, either too difficult to understand and implement or not compatible with the demands being made on them for greater accountability—especially calls for evidence that students have mastered "the basics."

Colleagues in other parts of Canada tell similar stories. Child-centered learning, a term widely used in the early 1990s to describe preferred practice, has now been expunged from the official discourse of curriculum documents. Even "process" has taken on negative connotations in this outcome-driven world. Several years ago, a publisher's representative told me that the editors in his company decided to delete all references to whole language and child-centered learning from manuscripts in an effort to gain acceptance in districts where those ways of talking about teaching and learning had fallen into disfavour. He also offered sobering statistics on the money the company had been making on the sale of spelling workbooks in many parts of Canada. How quickly we have slipped back.

Bringing whole language philosophy to life in the classroom, a difficult and complex task at the best of times, has become increasingly challenging within the current educational, social, and political context. Walmsley and Adams (1993) documented some of the realities of whole language for teachers in New York state where, like Nova Scotia, the movement has a relatively long history. In a series of interviews, teachers reflected on the complexities associated with implementing whole language in their classrooms, many expressing pessimism about the possibility that the philosophy would ever gain wide acceptance. There are a number of factors the teachers felt would inhibit its growth:

> The validity of teachers having different (even traditional) ideas about how to teach; lack of collegial, parent, district, even state support for whole language; the widespread misconceptions about whole language held even by teachers professing to practice it; the draining, time-consuming nature of preparing and managing a whole language program; the reluctance of schools to make systemic changes in their programs; the inability of whole language to guarantee satisfactory results in traditional assessments (or at least the perception that it cannot guarantee results); and

> finally, the threat posed by a traditional view of schooling that singles out whole language as one more reason to "get back to basics." (Walmsley & Adams, 1993, pp. 278–79)

One grade 4 teacher quoted in Walsley and Adams summed up the situation as follows: "I think that whole language will continue, but it will be a very small movement; and I think that the majority of teachers in the United States will never know what it is, much less learn to do it" (p. 272).

For someone like me, who has dedicated the better part of her career to promoting progressive and critical practices of literacy teaching and learning, that kind of remark is troubling. It is also remarkably prescient, given what has happened to whole language in the past five years. Her ideas are not unlike the ones I hear in my own community from equally perceptive teachers who themselves continually struggle to create whole language contexts in their classrooms. Many are saying, "How can we sustain what we have accomplished? How can we head off the seemingly inevitable shift back toward reductionist theories and practices? Where should we put our energies?"

For me, an even more basic question is, How and why did we get here? And following from that, Could we have done anything differently? Twenty years ago, as we found ourselves carried along with the excitement of new ideas and new ways of working in our classrooms, none of us could have imagined how much the context would change in a relatively short time. As I look back on that time, when small groups of Nova Scotian teachers first began working with Judith Newman, David Doake, Andrew Manning, and others from the local universities, it seems idyllic in comparison to today. I was fortunate to become associated with a community of learners, comprising university faculty and educators from the school system, who supported each other's ongoing inquiry into teaching and learning. We read, wrote, talked, and struggled toward new insights about literacy education and eventually about all education. For most of us, whole language has been about continually reinventing what we believe and how we teach; the prospect of going "back to the basics," or to anything else for that matter, is unthinkable.

I know, however, that the idea of returning to the past is

appealing, not just to the business and media critics of whole language, but to educators as well. The emphasis on "skills" and on the revival of practices, such as phonics first, that teachers perceive "worked better" than whole language provides ample evidence of the romance with the past. Several years ago (Church, 1994), I wrote about our propensity to see educational change as a series of pendulum swings, and offered some evidence that many parents and teachers are only too willing to swing back from what they see as a wrongheaded move toward whole language. That piece and earlier ones (Church, 1992; Newman & Church, 1990) represent my struggle to understand why the history of whole language in Nova Scotia, and I suspect in many other places, unfolded as it did. How did a generative theory of literacy learning become a divisive, polarizing force? Why is there such a widespread belief that whole language practices do not help children become skilled language users? Why did the growth of whole language seem to spawn camps, in-groups and out-groups, and endless orthodoxies about what teachers should and should not do in their classrooms? Some of the myths about whole language persist in beliefs such as that one should never tell a student how to spell a word; always have students work in groups; never teach directly; always give students choices; and many others.

Clearly there are no simple answers to these questions, but, as I have inquired into the Nova Scotia experience with whole language and have attempted to place it in the broader context of educational change, I have been able to make better sense of what has happened. First, I have come to see how attempts to implement whole language philosophy from the top down in hierarchical school systems have often been divisive and polarizing, largely because the approaches have been inconsistent with the learning beliefs that underlie whole language. Second, I have learned how essential it is that those of us who espouse whole language and other progressive practices look within for the source of many of the problems we face (Church, 1996). Arriving at these insights has been a sometimes painful process of confronting my own beliefs and practices as they have played out in my work. Learning for me has been a series of what Judith Newman calls "critical incidents" (1987, p. 727), those happenings (a few words spoken, a question asked, an unexpected reaction) that cause me to ask myself, What's going on here? Newman describes the incidents as "stories used as tools for conducting research on ourselves." I offer the following incidents as examples of the power of this process.

Becoming Political the Hard Way

My experiences of growing into whole language through involvement in a learning community were unusual. Most teachers in Nova Scotia came to it through district or provincial inservices developed as part of the implementation of a new curriculum guide, *Language Arts in the Elementary School* (Novia Scotia Department of Education, 1986, p. 1), which mandated programming consistent with "an integrated approach and a holistic perspective." At that time, most teachers developed their programs around one or more basal reading series, most of which reflected a skills-based model of literacy. Although some teachers had begun to incorporate more writing, drawing on the work of Graves (1983), in most classrooms reading instruction dominated. In my district, the inservice sessions revolved around introducing teachers to a theory of reading based on the work of Smith (1978, 1982), Goodman (1967), and others, and helping them explore an integrated model of literacy that included writing and oral language. Many of the sessions focused on new practices: brainstorming, semantic webbing, big books, reading and writing conferences, and so forth. Often presenters used comparison charts to show how the "new" approach differed from the "old" ways of teaching. The district also provided new resources in the form of literature-based, integrated language arts programs.

About the time I assumed responsibility for coordinating language arts for the district in 1988, it became obvious that the change effort was running into difficulties. After two years of district staff development, the responsibility for continued implementation had devolved to schools and individual teachers. While some continued to explore both theory and practice, ownership by schools of the new curriculum was tenuous. From the beginning, there were serious concerns about phonics, spelling, grammar, and other "skills" because many interpreted the comparison charts to mean that there should be no direct attention to language conventions. Many teachers struggled with how to move from fixed ability groups to the more flexible groupings described in the provincial guide. Parents raised concerns about invented spelling and memory reading, many expressing confusion and uncertainty about this radically different way of teaching. Teachers and administrators, themselves often confused and uncertain, frequently were unable to provide clear and convincing answers to parents' questions.

When the district determined that we needed to provide more guidance for teachers through a curriculum document for grades 4 through 9, I decided to take a different approach. It was clear that the top-down inservices had not been supportive of teacher growth. Convinced that more directives and teaching suggestions would only exacerbate the situation, I gathered a committee of teachers and administrators to help me think through the problem. During the next eighteen months, we met regularly to talk, read, and write our way to a publication we all thought would be an invitation to teachers. We created a learning context very much like a whole language classroom. We crafted our own classroom narratives, ones we felt demonstrated the principles of whole language in practice, and we invited students and other teachers to contribute their writing. We tried to demonstrate reflective practice in action by sharing not only the successes and certainties but also the problems and questions. We anticipated that our book, *From Teacher to Teacher: Opening Our Doors*, would generate useful professional conversations among other teachers. Committee members dreamed of starting their own small support or study groups within their own and neighbouring schools. I thought the committee work provided a powerful model for professional development through teacher inquiry that we could use to guide future change efforts.

How naive we were! The reactions of teachers and administrators were as far from what we had expected as they possibly could be. Our writing seemed to close more doors than it opened. Although the book helped to promote dialogue among some teachers, largely it was ignored, as most other system documents are ignored. In many schools, the principal handed the book out to teachers without comment. The authors became the object of sarcastic and critical remarks from colleagues: "Well, you're the expert, how would you get this student to write better?" or "What makes you such a super teacher, anyway?" Far more subtle and damaging was the unspoken negativity toward those who had been involved in the project. The authors felt alienated and upset when staff members dismissed their work and rebuffed their efforts to initiate interaction around the ideas in the book.

I felt great dismay and much guilt. After all, I had led the teachers into the situation by initiating the writing project and by publicly celebrating their accomplishments through the publication. I wondered why my attempt to move away from top-down implementation had actually made things worse for some of the best teachers in the district. What I came to understand, after I had some distance from the disappointment and anger, was how powerfully the social and political context shaped the experience for the administrators and teachers who were our audience. Because I was involved, and because many of those who contributed were associated with the whole language "camp," teachers and administrators interpreted the document as more of that "whole language being pushed down our throats." They reacted in a way that was quite predictable, given their acculturation in a hierarchical bureaucracy in which changes come from on high, rewards are few, and isolation is the norm. They resisted in the only way they knew how: they undermined and criticized the colleagues who had participated and who had seemingly garnered special status from that participation. A number of conflicting perceptions and expectations revolved around the project. We thought we were extending an invitation; they saw it as a directive. We thought we were sharing questions and inquiry; they saw us as self-appointed experts. We envisioned the book as a celebration of learning, our own and our students; they interpreted the book as privileging its authors as those in the district with the right answers.

For many teachers, the experience of curriculum change has been a series of "right" answers to questions they haven't asked. In the past several years, I have talked to many teachers about their experiences with the implementation of whole language. The following comments are typical:

> We felt everything we had done in the past was wrong.
>
> We were told not to teach phonics and spelling.
>
> We weren't allowed to question the change; we just had to go along with it and keep quiet.
>
> I was not at all sure what I was doing, but after a couple of years I was afraid to ask because I figured I should know by then.

The whole language experience in Nova Scotia is a case example of the kind of implementation that typically occurs in hierarchical systems. Constructing curriculum change within this kind of framework is especially problematic for whole language because it violates principles of learning inherent to the whole language philosophy. In Nova Scotia, teachers did not have opportunities to build on their prior knowledge and construct meaning in ways that made sense to them. For most, there were no supportive social contexts within which to learn. Those who had diverse perspectives and points of view felt silenced; there was no way for dialogue to occur. The inservices were too brief and disconnected; teachers had no opportunity to build a coherent theory on which to base their practices. If we believe in our own theories, we should not be surprised that many teachers adopted some of the practices without actually understanding the underlying theory. We should also not be surprised that teachers expressed resistance and often anger when subjected to learning experiences that left them feeling confused or incompetent in the classroom. In retrospect, I should not have been surprised that our document, however well-intentioned, was seen as just another directive from the bureaucracy, or that the authors, although peers, would become implicated in negative ways through their association. Other educators viewed them as somehow "moving up" in the power structure of the bureaucracy.

Surely we would hope that the situation would have improved as researchers (Barth, 1991; Fullan, 1991, 1993; Fullan & Hargreaves, 1991; Fullan & Miles, 1992) have offered alternative visions of educational change much more consistent with what whole language theory tells us about learning. Not so, if my experience at a conference several years ago is an example.

Two colleagues and I offered a session titled "Toward Whole Language: Collaborative Curriculum Change" in which we intended to share some of our concerns about top-down implementations and to invite participants to consider alternatives. Twenty minutes before the workshop began, the room was overflowing with teachers, some sitting on the floor, so anxious were they to hear what we had to say. Overwhelmed and surprised by the response, we spent a few minutes circulating in the room to find out why so many had chosen to attend our session.

The comments of a group of teachers from Texas were typical: "Our district has mandated whole language for the fall and we don't even know what it is. They've adopted a new whole language basal that we have to use, but we haven't had any inservice on it. We came to find out about whole language." Later in the conversation, we discovered that the teachers had been working with someone from the university to develop ways to address the needs of the many students in the school whose first language was not English. They were surprised to discover that much of what they had been doing was quite consistent with whole language and that they knew a great deal more about this innovation than they had thought. We tried as best we could during the session to demystify whole language, encouraging the teachers from Texas and many others not to abandon everything they were currently doing but to look for ways they might build on their current practices, incorporating new approaches that seemed to meet the needs of their students. We left them with a reading list and our hopes that they would be able to avoid the mistakes made in Nova Scotia. Given what they had told us about the planned district and school implementations and about their belief that they *must* follow the district directives, however, we did not feel optimistic.

Living with the Consequences of Our Own Demonstrations

While I have grave concerns about the ways in which institutional initiatives for change seem to distort whole language, perhaps more disturbing are the problems that emanate from within the whole language community. I have written (Church, 1994) about my experience at a workshop in which several colleagues and I led participants through a series of activities to illustrate how to address the "skills" within a literature-based program. I showed a videotape of a reading conference in which the teacher engaged actively with a student, challenging him to solve his own problems and to use the strategies she knew he had in his repertoire. Many participants objected to the way in which the teacher dealt with the student, despite the evidence that the student appeared relaxed and in the end quite pleased with his accomplishments. One woman commented, "I thought whole language was supposed to be warm and fuzzy!" It became obvious in the subsequent conversation that many in the audience shared that view. Several individuals who described themselves as experienced whole language teachers argued that this kind of instruction was not consistent with the philosophy. They maintained that the teacher had taken control of the learning and imposed her agenda on the student.

What bothered me most about this encounter was not so much the differing perspectives on the videotaped lesson but the zealousness with which the supposed whole language teachers defended their position. For me, the issue of the teacher's role in the whole language classroom is not so simple. Whole language instruction is not a clear-cut matter of supporting what students are doing, responding to their self-initiated attempts, and giving positive feedback on everything they do. I can see how that interpretation became so pervasive, given the way we often talk about learning in whole language classrooms. In my work with teachers, I know I have used words that imply a "hands-off" approach—for example, *"natural" learning, choice,* and *facilitation.* I have heard teachers tell students not to worry about spelling; I have said that to students myself. I now believe we must be much more explicit in helping students understand how, when, and why spelling and other language conventions are important as part of becoming an effective writer. It is not enough to hope that they will figure out intuitively that these conventions do in truth "count" both in school and in the world outside school.

Yet I also realize the hazards in using words such as *explicit* that smack of earlier versions of direct instruction and skills lessons. It can sound very much like a back-to-basics stance, especially in a world that seems most comfortable viewing teaching and learning in polarities: phonics versus whole language, student-centered versus teacher-directed, process versus product, and on and on. Appealing and pervasive as these categories are, it is essential to resist this polarized thinking and to articulate how complex and difficult it is to orchestrate the power relationships within a whole language classroom. As Field and Jardine (1994) express it:

> It is clear that whole language is not merely a shift in our language arts theories and practices. It is caught up in a nest of profound political, ethical, spiritual, and ecological orientations of our lives. It contains powerful notions: democratization, empowerment, ownership, choice, child-centeredness, authorship, silencing/voice, images of being public and being private, self-evaluation and self-expression, community and individuality. Given such an array, it is clear that the practice of whole language is a dangerous and risk-laden affair, full of implications and unforeseen consequences. We contend that these risks and dangers do not arise simply "from outside" but are part and parcel of whole language *itself*. The risks and potential dangers involved in handing over responsibility for writing to a group of eight-year-old children are not problems to be fixed. They are signs of the vitality and reality of the work we are doing. Even in the best examples of whole language theory and practice, these risks and dangers persist and require our interpretive caution and care. (Field & Jardine, 1994, p. 259)

There are no easy answers to how teachers can empower students and at the same time make aspects of their reading, writing, and talk problematic. There is always the risk of shifting into traditional teacher-pupil relationships in which students do what is expected of them because the teacher is in charge. Years ago, Smith (1981) wrote about the importance of "demonstrations" in the classroom: "Not only do we all continually demonstrate how the things we do are done, but we also demonstrate how we feel about them. What kinds of things are demonstrated in the classroom? Remember, children are learning all the time" (Smith, 1981, p. 109).

Our unintentional demonstrations are often much more influential than the ones we plan. Teachers are inherently powerful in the classroom because we are adults and hold positions of authority within the institution. It is only too easy, for both students and teachers, to unthinkingly perpetuate hierarchical patterns. Yet, even as we attempt to structure more democratic relationships, we also have the responsibility to create environments in which students become more informed and effective thinkers, problem solvers, and language users. We need classrooms in which teachers help students learn that not all their writing is wonderful, that some interpretations of texts are richer and more compelling than others, and that citizens in a democracy committed to social justice must name and confront sexism, racism, and classism. To suggest that negotiating complex power relationships and competing agendas within the classroom will ever be anything but fraught with tensions and contradictions is to misread whole language.

As a recognized "expert" in my area, I have become weary of defending whole language, usually by explaining how it really does include attention to the graphophonic system and to language conventions. While I understand the importance of providing a more informed perspective on those instructional issues, given the seemingly universal concern across North America, I worry about the consequences. I doubt that anyone who has taken a leadership role within the whole language movement ever intentionally sent the message that graphophonics, spelling, or grammar was not important in literacy learning. Most of us never meant that teachers should back out of the classroom. Yet there is overwhelming evidence that a large number of teachers brought that interpretation to the demonstrations we offered. Now, as we attempt to clarify how to incorporate these aspects of language into literacy instruction and to articulate a more active role for the teacher, what might be our new unintentional demonstrations? Are we making it seem as though teachers should once again take control of the students' reading and writing? Are we leaving the impression that there is a new right answer that teachers need to embrace? Are we implying that a better understanding of the theory and the practice will make whole language instruction "work" more easily? Or, as a colleague of mine put it after attending a session by one of the recognized leaders in whole language, "He makes it sound as though I wouldn't be struggling so much if I just believed a bit harder."

I have a strong sense that the way to sustain whole language is not through explaining it better but through engaging in conversations about the tensions and continual struggles of teaching within a whole language philosophy. Field and Jardine (1994) describe this as "owning our own shadow":

> The difficulties and tensions inherent in the relation between self-selected topics and pedagogical responsibility are not going to go away, even in *good* examples of whole language practice. Differently put, the appearance of such tensions is a sign that we are onto something *real*. Such shadows mean that the body of work we are involved in has real substance. (p. 262)

Inquiry into these kinds of difficulties and tensions seems to provide a potentially productive avenue of growth for the whole language community. Certainly, it promises to be far more fruitful than continually debating questions about the role of phonics and spelling in whole language classrooms.

Taking Up a Political Agenda

As I attempt to take up a political agenda in my own work, I find myself confronting tensions and contradictions not unlike the ones that continually emerge in a whole language classroom. At one point, I wrote rather glibly:

> I have come to the conclusion that I cannot advance a whole language agenda without also taking on a political agenda, one that entails profound changes in the way we view curriculum, leadership, school organization, our roles and relationships within the institution, and the change process itself. (Church, 1994, p. 369)

But what does that really mean for someone who has worked as a teacher educator and taken on a number of leadership roles in a school system? Some of those roles have brought me close to the top of an organization that is still very hierarchical despite small moves to flatten the structure and shift more decision making to the school level. How do I, from that position of relative power, advance an egalitarian political agenda? In truth, I have not found it easy (Church, 1999).

One major undertaking has been an ongoing effort to open up the conversation about literacy education within the district. Several years ago, I initiated dialogue with teachers and other professionals, primarily speech-language pathologists, about their perceptions of the difficulties we had been experiencing with whole language in the district. As we shared diverse perspectives on literacy learning, we found much common ground and developed several useful collaborative projects designed to help teachers explore language-literacy connections. We invited school staffs to revisit literacy teaching and learning through reflection on questions that emerged from their work with students. By opening the conversation, we have made it safer for teachers to discuss their beliefs and practices honestly. We have treated them as professionals and respected their opinions. The challenge for me, and for others in leadership roles, is to sustain this environment of trust and openness at the same time that we make certain practices problematic for the teachers. For example, everything I know about literacy learning suggests that phonics lessons in isolation do not help students use the graphophonic system effectively for reading and writing. Yet some teachers believe strongly in the efficacy of this approach, and, indeed, in many parts of North America these practices have been mandated. I believe that my responsibility to students obligates me to help teachers find new ways of teaching, but if I wish to sustain a more democratic relationship with them, I have to be careful about how I use my authority to try to bring about change.

To make the situation more complicated, this attempt to reshape relationships is taking place in a context in which teachers mistrust anyone in authority, having over the past few years seen several levels of administration and the provincial government make arbitrary and unilateral decisions about their working lives. Despite much rhetoric about shared decision making, empowerment, and site-based management, teachers and principals are wary; the demonstrations have carried a contradictory message. The necessity of making deep budgetary cuts may further damage the fragile sense of trust that currently exists across levels of the organization. The fiscal crisis has only intensified the isolation, competition, and individualism that are so characteristic of the culture of hierarchical school systems (Fullan & Hargreaves, 1991), as principals and teachers try to protect their own interests in a time of increasingly scarce resources.

The present economic and political context is not friendly to those of us who continue to promote the ideals of equity and social justice. Whole language principles and practices are not compatible with the corporate agenda for schools (Barlow & Robertson, 1994). As difficult as it sometimes is to sustain a sense of possibility under these circumstances, it is essential that we do so. We need to use our considerable language and literacy capacities to make ourselves heard. Those of us who occupy positions of relative privilege and power within our institutions should, I think, consider seriously what it would mean if we acted on the advice offered by Heilbrun:

> Many of us who are privileged—not only academics in tenured positions, of course, but more broadly those with some assured place and pattern in their lives, with some financial security—are in danger of choosing to stay right where we are, to undertake each day's routine, and to listen to our arteries hardening. I do not believe that death should be allowed to find us seated comfortably in our tenured positions. . . . Instead, we should make use of our security, our seniority, to take risks, to make noise, to be courageous, to become unpopular. (Heilbrun, 1988, p. 131)

Whole language has acquired a great deal of baggage over the years. I have contributed to an effort to recast it, to move beyond the obsession with phonics and spelling to focus on its potential to create more humane and democratic classrooms, schools, and school systems (Church, 1996). I continue to believe that critical whole language philosophy can help us learn to live and work more happily and productively with our differences. I was well along on my journey in whole language before I became aware that my pedagogical stance was also a political stance. Now it seems I devote most of my time and energy to exploring the potential of that political agenda. As a direct result of critical reflection on my experiences with whole language, the focus of my inquiry has shifted to rethinking leadership as it is constituted in the discourses of educational reform. As I observe the collective obsession with another set of right answers—guided reading, running records, phonics first, etc.—I attempt to use my "tenured position" as a place from which to contest these simplistic notions. Surely in the early twenty-first century we understand that literacy education for our increasingly diverse and challenging student populations cannot be captured in any set of right answers, no matter how compelling or well marketed.

References

Barlow, M., & Robertson, H. (1994). *Class warfare: The assault on Canada's schools.* Toronto: Key Porter Books.

Barth, R. S. (1991). Restructuring schools: Some questions for teachers and principals. *Phi Delta Kappan, 73,* 123–28.

Church, S. M. (1992). Rethinking whole language: The politics of educational change. In P. Shannon (Ed.), *Becoming political: Readings and writings in the policy of literacy education* (pp. 238–49). Portsmouth, NH: Heinemann.

Church, S. M. (1994). Is whole language really warm and fuzzy? *Reading Teacher, 47,* 362–70.

Church, S. M. (1996). *The future of whole language: Reconstruction or self-destruction?* Portsmouth, NH: Heinemann.

Church, S. M. (1999). Leadership as critical practice: A work-in-progress. In C. Edelsky (Ed.), *Making justice our project: Teachers working toward critical whole language practice* (pp. 286–302). Urbana, IL: National Council of Teachers of English.

Field, J. C., & Jardine, D. W. (1994). "Bad examples" as interpretive opportunities: On the need for whole language to own its shadow. *Language Arts, 71,* 258–63.

Fullan, M. G. (1993). *Change forces: Probing the depth of educational reform.* New York: Falmer Press.

Fullan, M. G., & Hargreaves, A. (1991). *What's worth fighting for? Working together for your school.* Toronto: Ontario Public School Teachers' Federation.

Fullan, M. G., & Miles, M. B. (1992). Getting reform right: What works and what doesn't. *Phi Delta Kappan, 73,* 744–52.

Fullan, M. G. (with Steigelbauer, S.). (1991). *The new meaning of educational change.* New York: Teachers College Press.

Goodman, K. S. (1967). Reading: A psycholinguistic guessing game. *Journal of the Reading Specialist, 6,* 126–35.

Graves, D. H. (1983). *Writing: Teachers and children at work.* Portsmouth, NH: Heinemann.

Heilbrun, C. G. (1988). *Writing a woman's life.* New York: Ballantine Books.

Newman, J. M. (1987). Learning to teach by uncovering our assumptions. *Language Arts, 64,* 727–37.

Newman, J. M., & Church, S. M. (1990). Myths of whole language. *Reading Teacher, 44,* 20–26.

Nova Scotia Department of Education. (1986). *Language arts in the elementary school.* Halifax: Author.

Smith, F. (1978). *Reading without nonsense.* New York: Teachers College Press.

Smith, F. (1981). Research update: Demonstrations, engagement and sensitivity: A revised approach to language learning. *Language Arts, 58,* 103–12.

Smith, F. (1982). *Understanding reading: A psycholinguistic analysis of reading and learning to read* (3rd ed.). New York: Holt, Rinehart and Winston.

Walmsley, S. A., & Adams, E. L. (1993). Realities of "whole language." *Language Arts, 70,* 272–80.

Chapter Four

What's It Going to Be?

Patrick Shannon
Pennsylvania State University

This book marks a major step in the development of the Whole Language Umbrella. *Critiquing Whole Language and Classroom Inquiry* continues the promotion of the universalized virtue of process through inquiry, yet it seeks to add principle or direction to the agency of our teaching. When coupled with the two questions from the last day of the 1994 San Diego Whole Language Umbrella of NCTE Annual Conference—*Has Whole Language Become Too Nice?* and *Should Curriculum Be Front Loaded with Issues of Justice and Equity?*—we're asked to consider the political interests of our work—and the consequences of our and our students' inquiry. What exactly are we critiquing or inquiring into—niceness or justice and equity? Although this choice captures some of the discussions within the Whole Language Umbrella, if not the movement, unless we are clear about what we mean by niceness, justice, and equity, it will do little to inform our decisions and actions.

Let me be clear. We cannot choose to act outside of politics, because all of our teaching is political. When you decide which books to have in your classroom or to read to your students, you make a political statement. When you decide how to relate with your students, their parents, or your peers, you make a political statement. When you arrange your classroom, you make a political statement. When you speak about the world to your students or choose to remain silent, you make a political statement. In

A version of this chapter was delivered as a speech at the Whole Language Umbrella Conference, Phoenix, Arizona, July 1994.

each case, within every act, we make decisions about whose stories will be told, who will do the telling, how the stories will be valued, and which symbols will represent what meaning. All of these decisions reflect and influence the power relationships among individuals and social groups within and outside of classrooms. In short, politics doesn't have to be brought to school, classrooms, or teaching because it's already there. We are all political agents, but just what types of politics do we practice through our work?

The Politics of Niceness

To my mind, inquiry into niceness is an attempt to ignore the politics of our work. According to this position, politics—issues of power—are considered "not nice": a dirty business that teachers and children should avoid. Rather, teachers should just "let children be children." In a way, advocates of this position echo Jean-Jacque Rousseau's negative education, in which children are kept from society until they have developed sufficient self-knowledge and love to enable them to be educated as caring, empathetic citizens. This is part of the rationale for separating primary from middle schools, rating movies, and regulating children's access to ideas through curriculum. Ironically, Rousseau considered literacy to be the catalyst for this transition from personal to social life, while many advocates of the "let children be children" philosophy see literacy as a primary way to explore the personal. Within this framework, student agency is limited to self-discovery and individual gratification without the attendant push toward any social understanding or civic responsibility beyond getting along with peers and sharing one's stories.

I question this fixed position about the nature of childhood as well as the consequences of the phrase "let children be children." Childhood is a social category, not a biological or even a psychological fact. (The contextualists tell us that young writers and readers have similar, but less sophisticated, intentions for their literacy as adults. We can't have it both ways, can we?) According to historians, the idea of childhood did not even exist before the fifteenth and sixteenth centuries. During the Middle Ages, children were mixed with adults as soon as they were considered capable of doing without their mothers. Although this may not seem to be the ideal circumstance for young people, it does attest to the historical relativity of the idea of childhood.

During the early seventeenth century, American children had a critical economic function: they were a vital part of the family labor force. While adults were deeply concerned about young people's religious and moral welfare, there were no institutions, except the church, designed to assist parents in these matters. With changes in commerce and industry, middle-class families began to view children as consumers rather than producers in the economy. Since not all men would be farmers and not all women would be wives, schools took a greater interest in young people's preparation for life. Children of lesser means, however, continued to enter the workforce as soon as they were able.

In cities it was not always possible to find work, and as families felt the economic and social strains of urbanization and industrialization, many urban families fell apart, leaving children homeless and destitute. As early as 1825, the New York House for Refuge provided the same services for children as the workhouse did for the adult destitute. (This "solution" has been reiterated recently; see Murray, 1984.) By 1850 the Children's Aid Society was sweeping children off city streets and shipping them off to waiting western families, in which they became vital parts of the family economies. During the twentieth century, changes in economic conditions warranted federal legislative answers to child labor, poverty, and homelessness. Yet, according to the Children's Defense Fund (1991), all three problems still exist for many U.S. children.

This evolution of the idea of childhood pertains only to white males. Females; immigrants; Native, African, Asian, and Hispanic Americans; and other children's lives were and are mediated by gender, race, and social class biases. For example, female children were only recently considered capable of socialization toward paid work. African and African American children endured two hundred years of slavery, and then an additional one hundred years of apartheid. Many Native American children still must separate themselves from their families in order to attend school, although now most often the curricula no longer attempt to forcibly suppress their cultures and languages. Even these qualifications disregard ethnic, language, or regional variations in the notion of childhood. In this historical light, what do whole language advocates mean by claiming that whole language should be nice and let children be children? I believe they are perpetuating a romanticized and nostalgic view of childhood, most notably a middle- and upper-class white male version in which children are all sweetness and light. While I can stretch my childhood into one of these fantasies, I now realize that it came on the back of my father, who started work in a lumber camp at eleven years of age driving draft horses, and of my mother, who was able to forego paid work to make a home by the time I was born. When I was a child, we had apples and grapes because migrant families came every September to pick them from orchards in our county and the counties to the west, and from vineyards in the counties south of us. We had milk and corn because farm families worked from early morning until after dinner in our township. We had clothes and heat because families worked in fields, mills, and mines in the states south of New York. Although the location of much of the labor has changed recently, it's often still children who are doing this work today.

To "remember" my idyllic childhood, I must forget the Korean and Vietnam Wars, bomb shelters, and reactions to the civil rights and women's movements. I must overlook the biases that led us to fight with children from other ethnic groups in and around our town. I must ignore the separation of the children whose families owned their houses from those that rented in our neighborhood, and the alcohol abuse of fathers, mothers, and teenagers.

To overcome such a childhood, I must deny what Walt Disney "told" me and what I saw on *Leave It to Beaver.* That childhood did not help me or others become caring, empathetic citizens, as we have witnessed during local, state, and federal elections over the last two decades. On whose back and through what amnesia shall we let today's middle- and upper-class young white people remain children? As journalist Alex Kotlowitz (1991) has suggested in the title of his book about two African American boys growing up in the Henry Holmes public housing projects in Chicago: *There Are No Children Here*. Because of the social consequences of difference in the United States, the lives of many children—in fact, of most children—are not as nice as "let children be children" advocates seem to imagine.

Politics of Justice and Equity

Issues of justice and equity that invite both understanding and action within a curriculum can help students and their teachers address those consequences of difference and, perhaps, alter the causes so that children's lives can be more humane and fair. This takes a certain kind of political agency because the relationship between being interested in justice and equity and effecting change in causes and consequences is not often straightforward. That is, if we are not careful, our actions can actually work against rather than for the justice and equity we desire for those outside the mainstream. This is particularly true when teachers and students blindly cede their agency to the modernist tools of the law, educational science, or the market without carefully interrogating just what benefits result and who receives them. Perhaps three extended examples will help make this point clearer.

Law

At the turn of the century, French critic and children's author Anatole France (1894) wrote, "The law, in its majestic equality, forbids the rich as well as the poor to sleep under bridges, to beg in the streets, and to steal bread" (92). France's remark makes the law and its implied neutrality problematic for me. Set in this context, equality does not seem to be the ideal toward which we should strive, because it leaves previous inequalities intact while at the same time frustrating any attempts to alter those inequalities by characterizing any such attempts as attacks on the ideal of equality. Requirements that we ignore the past and treat the have-nots the same as the haves means that we can never approach fairness among human beings through legal justice.

The rich sleep in their own beds, beg only for charities, and eat well. Their consuming, begging, and stealing are called "just good business." They can act this way, or have "lifestyles," because of past states of inequality and the ways in which the material consequences of that past pay out today. This unequal history means that substantial segments of our society and the world's population sleep where they are able (while banks build strip malls across the United States), subsist by their wits (while governments build, buy, and sell armaments), and are hungry (while farmers are paid not to grow crops).

Because in the United States not everybody is born into the same physical, economic, and social environments, people who apply the rubric of legal equality after the fact have an ironic sense of fairness. When you don't have to search for shelter or beg or steal to survive, it's much easier to feel justified in your enforcement of standards in life on which we may all agree abstractly and philosophically. When viewed from above, the law seems impartial, equality means that everyone is treated the same, and justice appears obvious. "Of course, squatting, begging, and stealing must be stopped," we tell each other. Yet the consequences of acting on these beliefs mean that the rich get richer while the poor get poorer—all in the name of the law and equality.

This unfair fact of our lives, I believe, makes Anatole France's use of the adjective *majestic* slightly cynical. Americans are often certain and complacent about the majesty of our laws, equality, and lives. "The system works," proclaimed George Bush just after the first Rodney King verdict, and just before the subsequent Los Angeles uprising. "That's how [the system]'s supposed to work," says Robert Dole after he championed a filibuster in the U.S. Senate to stop the 1993 Health Care Reform Bill. Yes, it works—it works to protect privilege and to prevent fairness, even in schools.

This is the fortieth anniversary of the *Brown v. Board of Education* Supreme Court decision that, according to Thurgood Marshall, was supposed to end apartheid in U.S. schools within six months. Prior to that ruling, schooling served as the deciding example in the *Plessy v. Ferguson* Supreme Court decision of 1896:

> The most common instance of social, not political, separation is connected with the establishment of separate schools for white and colored children, which has been held to be a valid exercise of legislative power even by courts in states where the political rights of the colored race have been longest and most earnestly enforced.

The first Supreme Court test case (*Cumming v. Richmond County Board of Education* [1899]) set limits even on the separate equality African Americans might enjoy by using the *Plessy v. Ferguson* ruling to majority advantage. The Supreme Court ruled unanimously that African Americans could not force school boards to open separate but equal schools if the board was acting on financial considerations and not according to open hostility toward African Americans. According to this ruling, schools would be separate—blacks could not attend white schools—and if the district could find the money to build a school for blacks, it had to be equal.

The *Brown v. Board of Education* decision seemed to change the meaning of equality in schools and in the United States. After 1954 every child in a neighborhood or centralized district would attend the same school. However, as Jonathan Kozol (1992) showed us, school districts have not acted with all deliberate speed to desegregate schools. And the "majestic" equality of the law has everything to do with this. For example, in the 1973 Supreme Court case *San Antonio Independent School District v. Rodriguez*, unequal funding among adjacent school districts was challenged under the equal protection clause of the Fourteenth Amendment of the U.S. Constitution. The Supreme Court decided five to four that the Constitution's equal protection clause does not require absolute dollar-for-dollar equality among districts and that equal schooling, like health care, is not an undeniable right protected by the Constitution. Children only get the schooling that their public can pay for, but they must get that. Rich and poor need not get identical schooling opportunities.

The 1974 *Milliken v. Bradley* Supreme Court decision denied the comparison of the racial balance between adjacent school districts. Lower courts ruled that because the Detroit school district had segregated schools, it and the suburban school districts should be combined and then divided into wedge-shaped districts to ensure racial balance. The Supreme Court overturned this decision, again five to four, reasoning that only Detroit schools were segregated, so only they must find a desegregation solution. This ruling encouraged further white flight from urban school districts to the suburban school districts, leaving urban schools without the possibility of desegregation.

Because children of color and white children do not start off equally distributed among the rich and the poor or the urban and the suburban, they do not attend the same schools. Towns and school districts segregated by income (and therefore by race in the United States) must be afforded the majestically equal treatment under the law. In this way, *Brown v. Board of Education* must be applied objectively in all cases, and therefore it has had the opposite effect of that which its originators intended. By not allowing the history and economics of segregation to be considered, *Brown v. Board of Education* and subsequent decisions meant that rich and poor, whites and people of color would not inhabit the same neighborhoods, or even the same school districts—leaving the poor and people of color to suffer savage inequalities while under the government's care at school.

Through this example, we can see that one putative tool of justice and equity—the law—is really a way in which past inequalities are preserved. Of course, it is not the case that we would be better off without the amendments to the Constitution or state and federal laws. Some, perhaps much, good can come from them, but we must also recognize the systematic limits of legal justice as an agent for bringing about the fair and rightful treatment of all people. Our faith in the illusion of the disinterest and neutrality of the law to solve our social, political, and economic problems ran—and still runs—afoul of powerful and material interests.

If the majestic equality of the law is blind, then so is our faith in it. If we are to achieve fairness in and out of school, we must take the blindfolds off our eyes so that we can read the ways in which the contradictions of majestic equality in the United States affect all our lives. Moreover, we must write new definitions of justice and equity rather than rely on those currently encoded in the law. This is what literacy is all about: reading the texts of our lives in order to learn about ourselves, our histories, and our cultures; to connect our lives with others and the social structure which surrounds us; to envision and believe that things could be different; and to act on that new knowledge in order to construct a more just future for others and ourselves. This recognition that the law does not work *for all* while it does work *on all* redirects our efforts from learning about the law and ensuring that the law is applied in our lives, toward discovering new ways of developing equitable social contracts among those with whom we are involved.

Educational Science

In the opening critical remarks of the book *Whole Language: The Debate* (Smith 1994), Michael McKenna, Richard Robinson, and John Miller suggest that negative consequences of civil rights legislation for schools was predictable because educational scientists have not used "valid measures of the worthiness" of school desegregation to make their argument. That is, science has not demonstrated beyond anyone's disbelief the necessity for students of color to sit next to white students in order to learn better. According to McKenna and his colleagues, if they had, all U.S. schools would be clearly and totally desegregated today. Because science hasn't proved this proposition to be true, however, there is no valid reason to disturb the status quo.

In fact, educational scientists have demonstrated that racially separate schools can be organized so that "validly measured" equality in educational outcomes can be produced for all races (see Comer, 1988). Students of color from these academies, schools, and preparatory programs receive scholarships to the best schools and colleges. This research shows that under scientifically tested conditions, when people of color are treated properly, racially separate schools work. That is, students of color score similarly to their white counterparts on standardized tests. Conversely, when a school system does not work—scores are low—it is solely because of the choices that school educators and community members have made for it. Apparently, they choose "failure" by ignoring the science of successful schools. For these researchers, then, the question is not about whether to integrate; rather, it is about why some segregated schools choose to act irrationally in the face of scientific findings. This example represents the position that citizens can transcend their personal interests only through the political neutrality of science. That is, educators and all other citizens should relinquish their political agency to science, which will then direct all human actions according to disinterested applications of natural laws.

This scientistic refrain is sung by many educational scientists—Jean Chall (Chall, Jacobs, & Baldwin, 1990), Michael Pressley (1994), Keith Stanovich (1994), Edward Kameenui (1993), etc. Each wants to know why educators keep debating about goals for schooling or literacy education and refuse to get down to the business of being scientifically successful with all students. Because they believe their findings to be politically neutral, objective, and disinterested, they want all other researchers and teachers to back off and let science make decisions for them. To a degree, whole language advocates make this claim when they begin to line up research results as primary support for their position (see Edelsky, 1990; Goodman, 1989; Stephens, 1991; Weaver, 1990).

Outside this instrumental logic, educational science can be understood as a human artifact which must encode the intentions of its originators and advocates. As an artifact, educational science cannot be "politically neutral, objective, or disinterested" unless these terms are limited to the application of means and not the goals or consequences of their use. Goals are always couched in some larger social project. Consequences always happen to real people with real lives and are not always directly within our control. Like the majestic equality of the law, science cannot lead us objectively toward justice, equity, or even good. The contradictions of unequal equality within educational science are perhaps best captured in two quotes from E. L. Thorndike at the turn of the century, but they are also imbedded in more recent comments:

> The judgments of science are distinguished from other judgments by being more impartial, more objective, more subject to verification by any competent observer and being made by those who by their nature and training should be better judges. Science knows or should know no favorites and cares for nothing in its conclusions but the truth. (Thorndike, 1906, p. 265)

> It may interest you to know that the first [postwar] problem chosen for investigation by the division of psychology and anthropology of the National Research Council is the problem of the mental and moral qualities of the different elements of the U.S. What does this country get in the million or more Mexican im-

> migrants of the last four years? What has it got from Italy, from Russia, from Scotland and Ireland? Who are the descendants of the Puritans and Cavaliers and Huguenots and Dutch; and what are they doing for America? Psychology will do its share in an inventory of the human assets and liabilities of the United States, whenever it is asked to do so. (Thorndike, 1918, pp. 280–81)

> I believe in letting scientific evidence answer questions about the reading process. . . . What science actually accomplishes with its conception of publicly verifiable knowledge is the democratization of knowledge, an outcome that frees practitioners and researchers from slavish dependence on authority. (Stanovich, 1994, p. 280)

> The focus of this book is the reading, writing, and language development of elementary school children from low income families. Such children have been referred to as "culturally deprived," "culturally different," "urban disadvantaged," or as living in inner cities. Occasionally, they have been referred to simply as the children of poor families. They are now increasingly referred to as "children at risk." No matter what the label, their educational problem is the same—they tend to perform below norms in literacy on national, state, and school assessments. (Chall, Jacobs, & Baldwin, 1990, p. ix)

> This means the average white person tests higher than about eighty-four percent of the population of black and that the average black person tests higher than about sixteen percent of the population. (Herrnstein & Murray, 1994, p. 278)

From its inception, then, and certainly into the present, educational science has projected the "back off" mentality that attempts to shame educators from exploring "subjective" reasoning. Moreover, it has intended to "discover" and "evaluate" the cultural differences among human beings, apparently holding white males as the norm. At school, teachers and students have suffered under these century-long political projects to make these discoveries and enforce these evaluations. Today we need not be as explicit as Thorndike was at the turn of the century, because those intentions are built into the tools of our trade: standardized tests, commercial textbooks, and classroom routines (Luke, 1988; Shannon, 1992). Thus, educational science is complicit in all types of school and societal segregation and inequalities. And by the design of educational science, schooling practices in their version of majestic equality treat rich and poor, women and men, white and people of color "objectively" using these tools of inequality.

Some researchers challenge the majestic equality of educational science and its consequent tools of modern schooling. Denny Taylor, Carole Edelsky, Luis Moll, Susan Lytle, Sonia Nieto, David Bloome, Linda Christiansen, Rita Tenorio, and others offer evidence that teachers' acknowledgment of historical inequalities leads to different results in classrooms and communities. Their work demonstrates how others might act when researchers refuse to remain disinterested in their subject or the people with whom they work and allow educational science and scientists to do business as usual. Rather, they roll up their sleeves to struggle for alternative practices directed toward fairness. In less overt ways, researchers such as Nancie Atwell, Susan Church, Karen Dahl, Heidi Mills, and others also challenge the status quo in educational science and schools.

Educational scientists' responses to these challenges have been instructive. While whole language advocates have found them useful, interactionists have been less receptive. For example, Steven Stahl (1994) referred to these challenges as "Coke ads," advertisements for personal interests that present unsubstantiated and biased information. Sticking to his metaphor, Stahl suggested that educational scientists offer *Consumer Reports* on all available alternatives on any subject. Although I believe that Stahl meant to discredit the challenges with these labels, his metaphor fails because his polar opposites—Coke ads and *Consumer Reports*—really work toward the same ends: preservation of historical inequalities and the protection of privilege.

On the surface, Coke ads seem simply to attempt to sell a soft drink. But because the competition among soft drink companies is fierce and the similarity of their products is great, Coke ads must sell more than their drink. In order to attract consumers, the Coca-Cola Company must sell a theoretical lifestyle in which their soft drink figures prominently. If you want the lifestyle, you need the soft drink. Accordingly, we find celebrities drinking

Coke, Coke available in exotic places, and Coke as an American symbol. This selling of a lifestyle influences our construction of our identity, our definitions of others, and our actions. It makes us want to buy the world a Coke to bring perfect harmony, despite having no clue about Coke's role in the real world. Perhaps this is what Stahl meant when he labeled as "Coke ads" the challenges to surrendering our agency to educational science: they offer teachers and students only a subjective lifestyle.

Yet his contrasting example, *Consumer Reports* (and its children's edition, *Zillions*), is also a shrine to the subjective lifestyle of consumerism. While that magazine and the technicians behind it may attempt to treat all current available commodities as majestically equal, as Stahl declares, they do nothing to illuminate the past inequalities which brought us to this historic juncture, when *things* seem to control our lives. For example, *Consumer Reports* may tell us which car it rates the highest, but it does nothing to enable us to read the social life of cars or their manufacture. That is, it doesn't explain or offer strategies to explore past inequalities which make cars necessary, expensive, exploitative, and dangerous. It doesn't speak about their pasts at all, telling us why they damaged community life, how their manufacture "tailor" our lives, and which alternatives might alleviate these problems. In short, *Consumer Reports* does nothing to educate us about ourselves, our histories, others, or the social structure. It leaves us illiterate and agents only of consumption. In fact, it tells us to buy more things, which simply preserves the status quo. Just as educational scientists' demonstrations that segregated educational experience can be successful do little more than send another poorly informed person into an unequal world, the *Consumer Reports* type of educational science sends teachers blindly into schools to maintain majestic equality. Both Coke ads and *Consumer Reports* sell the illusion that our lifestyles can be neutral, impartial, and disinterested in the world, while power and privilege, which defeat justice and equity, continue undeterred.

This illusion and illiteracy distort the meaning of justice and equity, making them synonymous with privilege and sameness. To reclaim justice and equity, we must affirm, advocate, and work to promote pedagogical actions which differentiate between the rich and the poor in order to diminish privilege in and out of schools. This inquiry will take us into homes, schools, hospitals, social service agencies, prisons, barrios, teacher groups, and welfare offices, not to find victims or to affix blame but rather to discover the capabilities, resilience, and agency of the people we find there. That is, we must record their ways and assist these people to resist the definitions and limitations that the law and science try to press on them in the name of justice and equity.

The Market

Informed consumers are supposed to make the marketplace a third tool for assuring equity and justice in the United States. According to capitalist logic, regardless of whether the market is the production of things or ideas, if left alone it will treat everyone the same, allowing everyone to compete for his or her rightful share of income and the good life. Accordingly, equality is the assumed starting point of all human beings—we all have the same chance to compete, and when consumers make informed choices, valuing the most worthy goods and services above all others, sellers of services, things, or ideas are treated justly. In the market, then, our energy and agency are devoted to these struggles because we must compete for our lives. The market requires economic natural selection, and advocates ask theoretically and rhetorically, "What could be more fair than that?" But in reality, the market, like majestic equality, meets the invisible hand.

Schools do provide goods and services, and they are infused with ideas from business and industry (Callahan, 1964; Shannon, 1989). Frederick Taylor's scientific management was translated for educators and schools during the turn of the century and has directed practice for better or worse since the 1920s. Economy of time and resources have long been the watchwords of school administrators; accountability in teaching and learning standards still drives many concerns about schooling, teaching, and learning; and the physical layout of schools and classrooms still mirrors the factory system. Only recently, however, have schools been measured according to the logic of the market (Hakim, Seidenstat, & Bowman, 1994):

> Each school district enjoys a monopoly position with its "consumers," the citizens who live within its boundaries. And the vast majority of school districts do not permit interdistrict transfers. In the parlance of business, that would be known as "conspiracy in restraint of trade." Like the teachers who work for schools, the students and families who are their customers must accept what the educational bureaucracy deigns to offer. (Kearns & Doyle, 1990, p. 81)

> The public school system is a rule-driven monopoly, like the post office and the Soviet Union. It's a failed concept. To run the most important function we have with a failed system is inexplicable. (Alibrandi, 1991, p. 52)

> The people who have money already exercise choice. It's time the rest of us have a way of forcing the regular schools to improve. (Williams, 1991, p. A10)

Although there has always been private education in the United States, public schools have not been asked to forego government subsidy and regulation in order to allow all interested parties to compete for a share of the profits of educating children. During the past decade, the call to make schooling a marketplace has been based on the assumptions that (1) public schools are failing to prepare graduates to enter the workforce because government sponsorship has given them a monopoly on education and they need not be responsive, and (2) teachers and support staff union contracts have allowed these educators to neglect their customers—business taxpayers, parents, and students (Chubb & Moe, 1990). On the other hand, certain types of private education *have* been successful for less money (Coleman & Hoffer, 1987; Hanushek, 1994). Therefore, according to market logic, if the public school monopoly can be dismantled and competition promoted in school, customers and society will be better served. "The lesson of public-private comparisons is not that private schools are better than public schools. It is that market pressures encourage the development of better schools more than political pressures do" (Chubb & Moe, 1990, p. 184).

One method of promoting competition is a voucher system, which puts a certain amount of money into the hands of each consumer of schooling (parents and their children) in order to allow them to make informed and free choice about which school the children will attend. Better schools (however defined) will gain attendance and funding, while poorer schools (however defined) will become poorer in enrollment and budget. Theoretically, this will provide incentive for the poorer schools to emulate the better ones. Of course, the good schools must have vacancies, and the parents must provide the transportation to and from the new school. In Minnesota, "choice" legislation allowed students to take their per-pupil allotment to any public school in the state that had room for them. When our family lived in Duluth, Minnesota, our children were too young for school. As Laura approached school age, we began to pay more attention to the neighborhood and city schools. Yes, the state offered us choice, but the infrastructure of Duluth was still crumbling from the first Reagan recession, which closed all of Duluth's factories and sent a third of the city's population elsewhere to look for work. At the same time, Duluth schools were under a court order to desegregate, and portions of all but one elementary school had been condemned by the fire marshal. That one school, nestled among the mansions of Duluth (yes, there are mansions in Duluth), was full beyond capacity. Our children had the illusion of choice without the actual possibility of attending classes in a physically safe environment. Just before we left the city, the remaining population voted down a tax levy to improve the schools.

The Republican National Committee proposed a plan to issue vouchers that would allow both public and private schools to compete for enrollments and state funding:

> No social experiment is more worthy than for an entire state [Florida]—with significant minority population—to embark on a true test of unrestricted CHOICE, complete with the participation of private, parochial, and for profit schools. The risks are grave, but so are the consequences of continued educational mediocrity. (*Time* Sept. 16, 1994)

From start to finish, however, the assumptions which underlie the market logic for schooling are questionable. First, the idea that schools are failing in their traditional goals is often overstated (Berliner, 1992; Carson, Huelskamp, & Woodall, 1991). Student learning is not decreasing; funding for schooling has not kept pace with other institutions, which does make a difference in what happens in schools; and students do seem prepared for the jobs that are available to them. In fact, the assumption that schools are tied directly to the United States' economic competitiveness in international markets is itself problematic (Noble, 1992). According to Cuban, "Schools are important but not critical to economic competitiveness in a global economy" (1992, p. 321). The need for market intervention in schools seems contrived at best, based more on corporations' interests in reducing social costs and, therefore, taxes.

Second, the market logic itself is flawed. Assuming at the outset equal resources, information, and opportunity skews any definition of justice in outcome toward a simple projection of privilege. Because of past inequalities in income and wealth, lack of access to information that matters, and/or denial of opportunity due to social and institutional biases, all citizens cannot compete equally to sell or buy goods and services. And because unregulated markets cannot take these past inequalities into consideration—they must treat all buyers and sellers equally—the market is another mask for the consequences of majestic equality. For this reason, governments of all countries regulate markets through tariffs and subsidies in order to protect their local privilege from global wealth. This is what saves General Motors from Toyota; it's what made Toyota in the first place; it keeps tobacco producers from extinction; and it allows baseball team owners to draft players and control their employment. As more multinational corporations are formed, however, such regulation will affect local and global interests in more complex ways (Barnet & Cavanaugh, 1994). Such "design flaws" in marketplace voucher plans are widely acknowledged but do not deter choice advocates:

> The better your specific proposal is designed, the less ammunition you give your opponents of school choice, and the better you are able to sell this exciting new idea. If your plan provides market incentives for private schools to meet the requirements of special needs children, including blind and physically handicapped children, you have anticipated an argument. If you provide relatively greater sums for "at risk" or inner city children, you dispel the notion that you are trying to create an "elite" private school

> system. If you phase in the costs of the programs of the mainstream students, you cushion the initial start up cost of school choice. Finally crafting your proposal to make certain that your natural allies (parochial schools, business leaders, parents, and inner city minorities) support the specifics of the plan, has insured the overwhelming grass roots support that you will need to overcome the entrenched government bureaucracy that has failed to meet the needs of so many of our American school children in the past generation. (Feeney, 1994, p. 55)

Finally, concern for the consequences of this majestic equality leads many to reject "choice" as a tool for justice and equity through schooling. All Americans do not have available to them the choices that will lead to distributive justice or equity in their academic or economic lives. Even informed consumers may not have the means or the opportunity to "choose" the better goods and services (however they may be defined). Certainly, they do not "choose" to be poor, unschooled, or powerless, as advocates of marketplace education imply. Given the opportunity, most of us would choose greater economic equity, fairer distribution of real information about the world and how it works, and more control over our lives. Whole language advocates' political agency in their teaching should be directed toward the struggle to expand membership in the group that gets that opportunity.

The Politics of Inquiry

The consequences of critique and inquiry are many for the Whole Language Umbrella and others interested in teaching according to whole language principles. We add principles to our promotion of process teaching. We see that all of our work is political. We reject the politics of niceness because it glosses over or deliberately suppresses important differences within our and others' lives. We seek justice and equity through our work, but with a new clarity about those values that warn us against surrendering our political agency to the law, educational science, or the market. Along the way to making these decisions, we discovered a role for critical literacy in our attempts to learn about ourselves, others, and the social structure, and we see how advocacy research can discover the problems inherent in and the barriers to the expansion of justice and equity within the choices available to us.

Underlying all our work is the belief that all people should be treated with respect, and that they should possess the freedom to live with dignity and to participate fully in the decisions which affect their lives. Moreover, we must be morally committed to act on that belief. The question, then, is "What do we do?" Although I do not have a blueprint for how others should act, I do think that the inclination of whole language advocates toward inquiry is useful because it stresses the connectedness of subject areas and human agency.

To work toward justice and equity, teachers and students must always keep clearly in view the connections between whatever they are studying and social life. Often these connections remain unexamined, leaving teachers and students with the notion that disciplinary knowledge can be brought to bear on an issue but without a theory of how things or ideas can domesticate or liberate us or do both at the same time for different groups. My earlier examples of the law, educational science, and the market show how this is possible. But it's also possible with any topic from the sensational to the innocuous that teachers or students might choose to study—that is, it's possible if teachers are ready to invite students to make such explorations (Shannon, 1995).

Take, for example, the apple included each day in my son's lunch box. That apple encodes a variety of hidden social relationships, all of which have something to do with justice and equity. So while we study how apples grow, why they are healthy for us, when Johnny Appleseed brought them to Ohio, or who grows them, we also want to consider who can afford them, where they come from at different times of the year, how they stay so red, and why they are so expensive or cheap depending on the consumer's economic location. Tim-Pat is seven years old, but he knows that the grocers don't pick the apples, nor do the farmers. He's seen the migrant workers who come to the farms around our town to pick fruit, and he's seen where and how they live during the harvest season. He's heard Woody Guthrie's "Deportee," a fitting anthem for the protesters of Proposition 187 in California, and he knows from listening to Sweet Honey in the

Rock's "Are My Hands Clean?" that he is part of the oppression of migrant workers. Even if he didn't eat an apple a day, he would still be implicated because he knows about the conditions of their work and lives. Yes, it's a big load for such a young boy, and he clearly doesn't understand the complexities of the social relationships. However, it's really quite a light load when compared to the (literal and figurative) loads for the children of migrant workers and the foreign fruit pickers who allow BiLo to keep apples stocked all year round. Issues of justice and equity require all of us to confront such issues in relation to whatever topic we select for inquiry.

I began this essay by stating that this book marks a major step for whole language educators. It challenges us to add principle to our love of process. Regardless of the topics we choose, if we are clear about our principles and the pitfalls of our political agency, we can help to redefine childhood as a time to learn about and act on justice and equity.

References

Alibrandi, J. (1991). The choice: Changing schools. *Fortune, 51,* 49–52.

Barnet, R. J., & Cavanagh, J. (1994). *Global dreams: Imperial corporations and the new world order.* New York: Simon & Schuster.

Berliner, D. (1992, February). *Educational reform in an era of disinformation.* Paper presented at the meeting of the American Association of Colleges for Teacher Education, San Antonio, TX.

Callahan, R. E. (1964). *Education and the cult of efficiency: A study of the social forces that have shaped the administration of the public school.* Chicago: University of Chicago Press.

Carson, C., Huelskamp, R., & Woodall, T. (1991). *Perspectives on education in America.* Albuquerque, NM: Sandia National Laboratories.

Chall, J., Jacobs, V., & Baldwin, L. (1990). *The reading crisis: Why poor children fall behind.* Cambridge, MA: Harvard University Press.

Children's Defense Fund. (1991). *The state of America's children.* Washington, DC: Children's Defense Fund.

Chubb, J., & Moe, T. (1990). *Politics, markets, and America's schools.* Washington, DC: Brookings Institution.

Coleman, J., & Hoffer, T. (1987). *Public and private high schools: The impact of communities.* New York: Basic Books.

Comer, J. (1988). Educating poor minority children. *Scientific American, 259*(5), 42–48.

Cuban, L. (1992). Are public schools to blame? *Phi Delta Kappan, 62,* 143–48.

Edelsky, C. (1990). Whose agenda is this anyway? A response to McKenna, Robinson, and Miller. *Educational Researcher, 19*(8), 7–11.

Feeney, T. (1994). Why educational choice: The Florida experience. In S. Hakim, P. Seidenstat, & G. W. Bowman (Eds.), *Privatizing education and educational choice: Concepts, plans, and experiences* (pp. 76–89). Westport, CT: Praeger.

France, A. (1894). *Le lys rouge* (Nouvelle ed.). Paris: Calmann Levy.

Goodman, K. (1989). Whole language research: Foundations and development. *Elementary School Journal, 90,* 207–21.

Hakim, S., Seidenstat, P., & Bowman, G. W. (Eds.). (1994). *Privatizing education and educational choice.* Westport, CT: Praeger.

Hanushek, E. (1994). *Making schools work: Improving performance and controlling costs: Concepts, plans, and experiences.* Washington, DC: Brookings Institute.

Herrnstein, R., & Murray, C. (1994). *The bell curve: Intelligence and class structure in American life.* New York: Free Press.

Kameenui, E. (1993). Diverse learners and the tyranny of time: Don't fix blame; fix the leaky roof. *Reading Teacher, 46,* 376–78.

Kearns, D., & Doyle, D. (1990). *Winning the brain race: A bold plan to make our schools competitive.* Lanham, MD: University Press of America.

Kotlowitz, A. (1991). *There are no children here: The story of two boys growing up in the other America.* New York: Doubleday.

Kozol, J. (1992). *Savage inequalities: Children in America's schools.* New York: Harper.

Luke, A. (1988). *Literacy, textbooks, and ideology: Postwar literacy instruction and the mythology of Dick and Jane.* New York: Falmer Press.

Murray, C. (1984). *Losing ground: American social policy 1950–1980.* New York: Basic Books.

Noble, D. (1992). Let them eat skills. *Rethinking Schools, 5,* 18–19.

Pressley, M. (1994). Commentary on the ERIC whole language debate. In C. Smith (Ed.), *Whole language: The debate* (pp. 372–97). Bloomington, IN: EDINFO Press.

Shannon, P. (1989). *Broken promises: Reading instruction in twentieth-century America.* Granby, MA: Bergin & Garvey.

Shannon, P. (1992). *Becoming political: Readings and writings in literacy education.* Portsmouth, NH: Heinemann.

Shannon, P. (1995). *Text, lies & videotape: Stories about life, literacy & learning.* Portsmouth, NH: Heinemann.

Smith, C. (Ed.). (1994). *Whole language: The debate.* Bloomington, IN: EDINFO Press.

Stahl, S. (1994). Is whole language "the real thing?" In C. Smith (Ed.), *Whole language: The debate* (pp. 352–71). Bloomington, IN: EDINFO Press.

Stanovich, K. (1994). Romance and reality. *Reading Teacher, 47,* 280–91.

Stephens, D. (1991). *Research on whole language: Support for a new curriculum.* Katonah, NY: Richard C. Owen.Thorndike, E. L. (1906). *The principles of teaching based on psychology.* New York: A. G. Seiler.

Thorndike, E. L. (1918). Fundamental theories of judging men. *Teachers College Record, 19,* 278–88.

Weaver, C. (with Stephens, D., and Vance, B. J.). (1990). *Understanding whole language.* Portsmouth, NH: Heinemann.

Williams, B. (1991, May 3). School choice and choices. *Wall Street Journal,* p. A10.

Chapter Five

Critical Inquiry or Safe Literacies: Who's Allowed to Ask Which Questions?

Barbara Comber
University of South Australia

What Counts as Inquiry in School?

In this chapter, I raise the possibility that inquiry approaches in schools often depoliticize the topics of study. Through examining an incident with my son, I discuss the limitations and possibilities of school inquiry. Have you ever tried to help your children with their school homework only to be told, "That's not the way our teacher does it!"? You might have thought you knew how to do long division, or a book report, or a project, or a history essay, but your children know otherwise. The logic of parents' help does not necessarily match your child's experience of the phenomenon by the same name at school. At school there are teachers' ways of doing things, and as my children tell me, that is what counts. "Your way is great, Mum, and thanks for trying to help me, but that's not what we're meant to be doing. Thanks anyway. Don't feel bad. Your way may even be better, but it's not what I have to do." A recent example of parent-child homework negotiation between fourteen-year-old Tom and me highlights this common but revealing scenario:

Tom: Was the Iron Cross a Nazi symbol?

Barbara: I don't know. Well, let's find out. Have you looked in the encyclopaedias? What makes you think it might have been?

TOM: Don't get carried away, Mum. I just need to know whether I can put it on my Nazi propaganda leaflet. I've already drawn it. I don't want to rub it out. I just thought you might know. Don't go getting out the encyclopaedias. They won't have that in there anyway. It doesn't matter.

I resist the opportunity for a full-scale lecture on why in fact it does matter. I have learnt, with some frustration, that Tom is unlikely to listen to my treatises on racism and history. His concern is to get the homework done. Yet I slink off to check out the encyclopaedia and find this information about the Iron Cross, which I read to Tom as he moves around the house collecting food for an after-school snack. Instead of a lecture, I demonstrate (I hope) by reading the following text that it is worth checking these things—that there is much to be learnt, and that what can be learnt has important social consequences:

> Prussian Military decoration instituted in 1813 by Frederick William III for distinguished service in the Prussian War of Liberation. Use of the decoration was revived by William I for the Franco-Prussian War of 1870, recreated in 1914 for World War I, and was last revived by Adolf Hitler on September 1, 1939, the same day that German forces invaded Poland. (*Encyclopaedia Britannica, Micropaedia* [15th ed., 1990], Vol. 6, p. 388)

The text goes on to explain in some detail how the grades for the award were expanded in World War II from three to eight, and how "the World War II badge also had a swastika, which replaced the previous symbols of the crown and royal cipher," and also that "since 1957, a West German statute permits the Iron Cross to be worn only if the swastika is removed" (6:388).

The situation I've described is an occasion with unlimited potential for teaching and learning about the ways in which history, language, symbols, and the law interconnect. It is, if you like, a critical literacy teacher's dream, but Tom is back with his homework, content that he will not have to rub out the Iron Cross. Although he remembers in some detail now how the Iron Cross was changed in Nazi Germany and since, he tells me that the symbols are not important, but what happened is. As I reflect on this incident, I consider how his history might have been different:

What kinds of history is he learning and what else might he be learning?

What kinds of inquiry is he engaged with?

What kind of token literacy is required by his propaganda leaflet?

What kind of learning opportunity might this assignment represent if it were altered slightly?

I bet his teacher would be fascinated with the details we have discovered, but will Tom think it appropriate to tell him? What might Tom and his classmates learn if they had the opportunity to trace the history of the various symbols rather than just use them as decoration for their work? Why is Tom constructing a Nazi propaganda leaflet without investigating the effects of the symbols and the language of propaganda? Why does Tom have the message that such investigation doesn't matter? His energies tend to be tied up in completing the product and getting a good mark for it, rather than considering why the words and symbols of Nazi propaganda really matter and how they still matter; he doesn't connect his history assignment to the neo-Nazi rally which was due to occur in our suburb around that time and receiving much local media attention.

When I think about Tom's experience, I see how schools limit students' opportunities to engage in critical literacies. Setting the task of writing a propaganda leaflet reflects his teacher's awareness of the power of language in historical movements, but by stopping short of analysis of specific instances, it fails to help students understand how language works. They role-play themselves as writers for the Nazi Party, ignorant of the ways in which language and symbols construct realities, where millions were murdered. It's not that they don't know what happened in Nazi Germany. It's not that they don't know how propaganda was used in the process of genocide. My problem is that this knowledge is treated as a history of what happened as if it is over, as if it's just this week's history topic, and next week we'll do the Vietnam War. Writing and drawing leaflets could be the beginning of inquiries about symbols and politics. They could have considered how a symbol of liberation was appropriated by the Nazi Party and made to represent something else; they could have looked for other symbols of liberation which have been colonized by new regimes. School literacies or histories often replace inquiry with productivity. But it doesn't have to be this way. Kutz and Roskelly (1991) report on a history curriculum that "uses the Holocaust to foster students' understandings about history and cultural difference" (p. 88).

Tom's propaganda assignment is not an isolated incident. My daughter Laura, in grade 4 at the time, used the same notebook for a subject called Aboriginal Studies and a subject called Australian History (at the other end of the notebook). Aboriginal Studies is intended to provide a view of history from the points of view of Indigenous people, who see the white "settlement" as colonization. Yet her first entry in the Australian History side reads, "The first people to discover Australia were the Dutch." Students still copy lies into notebooks as if they are truths, even as teachers try to attend to minority histories and antiracist curricula. Our versions of what counts as knowledge need radical examination before inquiry learning approaches can produce the kinds of culturally and politically aware learners that our educational discourses proclaim. These traditional approaches to learning occur frequently enough in schooling that students may become convinced that the object of study is irrelevant; all that matters is getting the task done, getting the questions answered, getting the work finished.

It might be argued that these problems do not arise when students construct their own questions. I want to argue, however, that students are just as likely to reduce and depoliticize topics as their teachers. It doesn't take long before students know that when they do a project on a country, they are meant to have headings such as Population, Capital City, Industries, Language, Natural Resources, Geographical Features, and so on. This Western capitalist way of "knowing" about other countries is the dominant discourse of school textbooks and encyclopaedias. Students quickly learn to ask the questions that are answered by their textbooks and modeled by their teachers. The questions that need to be asked are constrained by what teachers and textbooks answer. (See Robyn Jenkin's essay in Chapter 11 of this volume for an account of this problem.) The headings and subheadings which organize school knowledge construct particular kinds of inquiries and not others. In this chapter, by examining approaches, techniques, and sources of inquiry, I continue to argue why and how schools need to politicize topics of inquiries beyond the safe assignment.

Inquiry Techniques

One of the most popular techniques used to organize students' inquiries was developed by Yetta Goodman and Carolyn Burke (1980): the What I Know/What I Want to Know procedure. As a classroom teacher, I used this approach on numerous occasions with my students and found that it was a great way to mobilize their current knowledge and generate lists of questions. More recently, teachers have combined this approach with semantic webs to help students organize information (Harste & Short, 1988). Students can identify different kinds of knowledge before they begin their inquiries. These approaches claim to generate cycles of learning rather than sequential question-answer models. What is absent from this version of inquiry, however, are questions about how people come to know; questions about why certain kinds of knowledge are more important than others; and questions about whether there are different versions of knowledge on this topic. Prior questions might include: "How do they know that?" or "Who knows that?" or "What other kinds of knowledge are there about that?" As Harste and Short (1988, p. 370) note, this kind of inquiry can be used to have students explore political realities in their own lives. I agree. What are urgently needed are accounts of inquiry in which the objects of study include social, cultural, and political life and the methods of inquiry are not restricted to school texts (see, for example, Singh, 1989; Moll, Amanti, Neff, & Gonzalez, 1992.)

Topics such as plants, dolphins, and dinosaurs should not be thought of as neutral. Texts always involve decisions about what will count as knowledge. No topics are innocent or sacred. Through their readings of such topics, students read versions of science and versions of history. They learn what will count as a good question. We should also not assume that simply by making the topics of study political or cultural in nature that the inquiries students pursue will be political or cultural. As my discussion of Tom and Laura's schoolwork on history and race shows, it is possible for schools to depoliticize the objects of inquiry for student consumption. A kind of "safe literacy" is produced in which topics are covered, not uncovered. Students can examine the language use in a hierarchically organized workplace and find the differences interesting but not problematic. Students can say, "We did Aboriginal Studies last year," or "We did Nazis in grade 10," in the same breath as "We did dinosaurs in grade 2." Contradictory histories are left intact. Science still reigns. Capitalist discourses still frame the atlas and the encyclopaedia. The move to new topics does not necessarily guarantee new forms of critical inquiry.

Schoolbooks as Sites for Inquiry

Schoolbooks, from the atlas to the encyclopaedia to the picture book, produce versions of the world for the child reader. In so doing, they construct a particular kind of child learner, child reader, child inquirer. Often the child inquirer is assumed to be more curious about the natural world than the social world. In sales of nonfiction big books, science-related texts far outstrip the cultural or people-related books. Space, animals, and dinosaurs are bestsellers even though school library shelves are already overrepresented in these areas. "New-age" children are also interested in ecology. Books about rain forests, endangered species, or the Antarctic sell to ecologically responsible teachers and parents. Book clubs and publishers working the market respond to current hot topics by promoting versions of the ideal child/reader/learner/future citizen. I would argue that in the case of inquiry learning, the generic child is still the male infant of child development studies, ever curious about his world. As Jenkin's study (Chapter 11) shows, even when a topic appears gender neutral or gender inclusive, female students and male students read the text differently. They engage in different kinds of inquiries. Thus, in thinking about inquiry learning, topics need to be examined in terms of gender. Books are written for gendered readers. My argument is not that we need to cull suspect texts. No texts are neutral. We need to provide opportunities for students to read contrastive texts critically and to compare the wisdom of texts with their own experiences.

Books are written for particular versions of the developing child and are selections of what is considered appropriate for the target age group. Producers of informational texts work from the prevailing view of the ideal school student at that stage of development. For example, producers of texts for young readers make a number of problematic assumptions: that young children prefer to read stories; that stories are easier to read than nonfiction texts; that young children aren't capable of learning about complex information; that young children require simple language. Until the last decade, these assumptions led to the limited production of informational texts for young readers. Often what was produced was inaccurate, patronizing, conveyed in watered-down language, and about kiddy topics. As Unsworth (1993) has pointed out, a "childist" view has dominated many publications for children, particularly on science topics.

Consider the following extracts from two factual texts about penguins produced for use in junior primary classrooms:

Text A

> This is a penguin. Have you ever seen a picture of a penguin? The penguin looks as if it dressed for a party.

The illustration shows a penguin next to a mirror with a backdrop of patterned wallpaper. The next few pages explain that the penguin is a bird but that it cannot fly, and the illustrations show three rather sad penguins watching a seagull fly over head. One penguin flaps its nonflying wings hopefully. The writer then explains how penguins "get around." This is followed by the question:

> What does the penguin eat? Penguins love to eat fish. Look at this penguin swim after its dinner.

The accompanying illustration shows a penguin swimming after some tropical fish. The next page explains that penguins have babies by laying eggs, that they feed their babies, and that they are good parents. The next page deals with where penguins live:

> Where do penguins live? Penguins live in ice and cold. They live near the South Pole. And they don't need a house to live in or a fur coat to wear.

The accompanying illustration shows six penguins upside down on an unlabeled globe of the world with four of them clustered around the South Pole and two on other unlabeled locations. The final page shows a penguin next to a mirror with the wallpaper backdrop. This penguin is wearing a party hat and winking. The text reads:

> Is the penguin real? Is the penguin make-believe? What do you think? (The penguin is real.)

Text B

> Fairy penguins belong to a small group of penguins and a big group of birds.
>
> Fairy penguins are blue and white. Other penguins are black and white. Fairy penguins are 35cm tall. They have webbed feet. Fairy penguins have a blue back and a white chest. That is why they are called little blue penguins.
>
> Fairy penguins eat fish, squid, shrimps. Their enemies are sharks, seals, sea-lions, dolphins, hawks, eagles and seagulls. . . .

This was followed with a description of penguin "habits," including hunting for food:

> Other penguins live in Iceland. Fairy penguins live in burrows, under rocks. . . .

The text concluded with some physical features of fairy penguins such as their poor eyesight, how they use calls to help them find their way, and how their oily skin helps them to float. No illustrations accompany this text.

Drawing on questions developed by Freebody and Luke (1990), we can consider the kinds of readers, writers, and knowers that are produced in the construction and use of these texts.

Who could have written each of these texts?

What can you guess about the age and role of each writer?

Who are the intended readers for each of these texts?

For what purposes might the texts be used?

Text A consists of eight pages. Published in 1984, it was written by Dr. Alvin Granowsky (though what he is a doctor of is not stated) and illustrated by Lulu Delacre. Granowsky is a regular presenter at International Reading Association meetings and is obviously committed to children's literacy. The text includes a "words to study" list inside the back cover, and it is Book 1 in a "real or make believe" series. Only adults could have produced a text such as this. Who else would think of putting a penguin next to a mirror in a wallpapered room to help someone else understand that the penguin is real? But books such as *The Penguin* sell. The production of this text is based on certain assumptions about the child reader/knower. One assumption seems to be that inaccurate illustrations do not matter for young readers. It is not considered important to mention that there are different kinds of penguins that live in different kinds of places. It is also assumed that comparing penguins' lives with the human world (which are represented as separate worlds) will help the child understand penguins. This is done explicitly in the text and quite problematically through the illustrations, which could be intended to "trick" the child reader (in the nicest possible way, of course). In fact, a child may well find the question about whether a penguin is real or make-believe difficult to answer when the penguin in question is wearing a party hat and standing next to a mirror hanging from a wallpapered room. The penguin is also depicted as standing in midair—a slight problem for a flightless bird. No wonder the editor decided to put the right answer—that the penguin is real—in brackets as the final sentence! The use of question and answer format provides the novice reader with a model of inquiry in itself. It is interesting to consider what the publishers intended to achieve with this text and how it might have been written differently if the writer had understood his child readers and knowers differently.

Text B was written by a grade 2 student after an excursion to an island in South Australia (nowhere near the South Pole), where there is a nesting ground of fairy penguins. The excursion was led by the teacher and a Parks and Wildlife officer, and the students were given detailed information, using specialized language, about this particular group of penguins. The teacher, Sandra Naismith, had been working with the students on writing reports on other topics. They had spent time deconstructing many factual texts in order to work out how they were structured. It is interesting to imagine what this child inquirer might do with the other published penguin text.

These texts about penguins have some things in common; they are produced for school use. In the case of Text A, an adult writes for emergent readers who, it could be argued, are assumed to know little or nothing about penguins. The child is also assumed to have a problem with distinguishing what is real from what is make-believe. It is also assumed that the kind of knowledge a child reader might want depends on it being related to what children already know—wallpaper, mirrors, party hats, tropical fish, good parents, and globes of the world. It is salutary to read this text produced for the five- to eight-year-olds market in light of what these child writers and knowers produce based on experiences of the topic and a knowledge of how texts work.

The published penguin text takes for granted a young reader who doesn't know much and who will tolerate inaccuracies and illogical representations unproblematically. If this text is read against those produced by young children, it exposes some of the contradictions which occur when adults try to simplify for children—when knowledge is reproduced in a cute fashion to make it more palatable. This example suggests the need to look closely at the kinds of texts children are reading and how they are being read, and to consider how school experiences with reading and writing construct the literate child.

Across a term or a school year, what kinds of knowledge, content, topics, and texts do students deal with, and what does this say about what we think is important for them to be doing? If students read enough of *The Penguin* genre, what kinds of inquirers might they become? The point is not that texts such as *The Penguin* should not be used, but that they need to be used in ways that give students an opportunity to read them critically and to read them against other texts about penguins and against their own experiences. Students can consider why this text is written in this way for them and how it might have been written differently. Students in the early years of schooling can discuss the proposition that some writers seem to think that children know nothing, and can enjoy engaging with texts by listing the things they didn't know and the things they already knew (Comber & O'Brien, 1993; also see Jennifer O'Brien's essay in Chapter 8 of this volume).

The problem is not restricted to basal readers or to simple reading materials such as *The Penguin*. School and public libraries are full of such texts, and publishers are still producing them. Teachers need to look closely at texts that are produced for young children to help them learn to read, because it is through these texts children learn what counts as reading. If the books they read have little to offer, then why read? Students are still learning the capital cities of countries that no longer exist because class sets of an out-of-date atlas are available for use. The problem is not just one of poor or inaccurate resources. There will always be poor and inaccurate resources, and students will always need to use them. Instead, we require pedagogical approaches through which students inquire about the resources they use to make their inquiries. Students need to interrogate the texts they use in their inquiries: Who wrote the text? What authority does this person have for producing this book? Are the illustrations and diagrams accurate? What other books are there about this topic? In what ways do these texts differ? What questions does the book not answer? How else could this book have been written? Who else might have written it? In this era of information, in which texts confront us almost continuously, students need to become "text-proof"—they need to see texts as particular kinds of cultural artifacts produced to do certain kinds of cultural work.

Who Has Access to Which Forms of Inquiry?

When I conducted research in the late eighties about students' questions and requests for help during literacy time, I found that students' questions differed (Comber, 1988). Analysis of students' questions showed that middle-class Anglo students asked questions that gave them access to lengthy teacher explanations and extra resources and ideas, whereas working-class non-Anglo students asked questions that related to completion of task. In other words, students' questions determined their access to different kinds of help. At issue here is the need to look closely at who is asking what and what the effects might be? In this classroom, the result was that some students learnt how to proceed with tasks and others engaged in extended conversations with the teacher about issues and possible projects they might do next. The questions students were able to ask depended on what they already knew, and the way they asked depended on the discourses to which they had access. This investigation was a case study of the students at one site, and I do not wish to make generalized arguments about these observations. But it does raise questions that require further study. Who benefits from inquiry learning and in what ways? What different kinds of inquiries do students make? How and why do different students engage in different types of inquiries? Inquiry learning needs to be examined in terms of what it offers different groups of students. If students' learning depends on the questions they generate, then they will learn different things. How this different learning is assessed and valued requires scrutiny.

Material and human resources dramatically influence the kinds of literacies that are offered in schools. In 1992 I worked with a group of high school teachers in an industrial town where a high percentage of the school community was living in poverty. The teachers had been enthused by a recent workshop on resource-based learning, which is a text-based inquiry approach. The aim was to put students in the position of information hunters, gatherers, and users rather than providing them with synthesized texts. These teachers saw inquiry learning as an important literacy orientation for their students and more motivating than using textbooks or copying notes from the chalkboard. They reframed their curriculum activities so that students could operate as inquirers. They quickly discovered, however, that the school library was not equipped for this approach, and neither were the local community libraries or the students' home libraries. There simply were not enough recent, accurate texts available, and the teachers could not assume that students would have access to other resources at home. Resource-based learning was one kind of literacy they were not going to have the opportunity to practice. I am not suggesting that this pedagogy should be abandoned at such sites, but clearly the resource implications for inquiry pedagogies will have a different impact in a poor school than in a wealthy school. Political action to increase the resources of schools serving poor communities is urgent. Educators need to address major questions about who has access to what kinds of literacies and who is privileged when the assessed curriculum depends on accessing multiple resources. In relation to inquiry learning, the kinds of resources available to different schools, families, and communities need to be taken into account.

Another key equity issue for educators advocating inquiry approaches is the use of technology. The advertising of technology centers in schools in order to attract student enrollments is becoming common practice. Yet promises of "computers on every desk" are still restricted to wealthier schools—schools where the average student is likely to have both a computer and a desk at home. As access to information networks becomes easier and more available, the need to consider the impact on schools serving poorer communities is crucial. Thus the formation of new literacies and new forms of inquiry are particularly vulnerable to class-related differences. In our excitement to move to inquiry pedagogies, we must attend to equal distribution of the tools and resources such inquiries demand.

Critical Inquiry

The first part of this chapter raised questions about inquiry approaches. But inquiry methods in school literacy programs can construct students and teachers as critical inquirers without ignoring the experiences and knowledge of students who are traditionally disadvantaged by schooling (Bigelow, 1992; Janks, 1993b; Luke, O'Brien, & Comber, 1994; Moll et al., 1992; O'Brien, 1994; Singh, 1989; Jongsma, 1991). Shannon (qtd. in Jongsma, 1991) reviews key historical examples of critical literacy teaching in the

United States, showing the potential of school literacy for social and political inquiry about genocide, community health, organized labor, homelessness, war, and apartheid. In the following section, I briefly describe a selection of contemporary work which explores critical inquiry in the language classroom. To conclude, I draw out key challenges this work raises for inquiry pedagogy.

School Life as a Site for Student Inquiry

Singh (1989) explains a project undertaken by a group of high school students and their teachers in a working-class community. They investigated the problem of truancy amongst themselves and their peers, particularly how it was experienced by students who spoke English as a second language. Thus the object of their inquiries was directly related to their own lives as students and to questions of educational disadvantage that emerged from not being native English-speakers. Students conducted interviews and a survey, wrote autobiographies, and wrote a formal report to the sponsoring agency on the research team's findings. Singh explains this work as a form of critical literacy: "These non-Anglo students were active agents engaged in producing new knowledge through collaboration with others in a socially significant task—rather than the passive recipients of trivial, vague or superficial information" (1989, p. 37).

The work Singh describes goes well beyond safe school literacies. Here, students work on a social problem which directly involves their school communities. They explore the construct of educational disadvantage and how it connects with language and power, and how it makes an impact on their lives at school.

Communities as Sites for Teacher Inquiry

Family and community life are often scrutinized through the institutional work of schools. Schools provide a form of surveillance on the family as teachers and administrators record and monitor the student population, looking for signs of abnormality and deviance. This need not be so. In an innovative research project reported by Moll (Moll et al., 1992), a team of university researchers and school-based teachers studied working-class Mexican American communities in Tucson, Arizona. Unlike some investigations of minority groups, this work was based on the assumption that households and communities have accumulated "funds of knowledge" which are essential to their survival and well-being. According to Moll et al. (1992), "this view of households . . . contrasts sharply with prevailing and accepted perceptions of working-class families as somehow disorganized socially and deficient intellectually" (p. 134).

Funds of knowledge included agriculture and mining, economics, religion, and medicine. Within these broad areas, specific knowledges such as construction, repairs, household management, folk cures, loans, labor laws, child care, and numerous others were identified. Rather than teachers and researchers searching for sets of assumed deficiencies or problems, their intentions were to learn about community strengths in order to build them into the school curriculum. Students' out-of-school knowledge rarely gains a place in official school curriculum. Yet researchers found that these students' out-of-school experiences had prepared them to explore topics such as the study of other countries, different forms of government, and economic systems.

In this research, the focus of teacher inquiries was different from that of most such studies. One teacher explains that instead of being concerned with whether parents read to their children or how many books were in the home, the broader anthropological approach meant that she learnt about how the families organized their lives between two countries and about the sophisticated skills children had developed as a result. Moll and his colleagues (1992) explain how the teachers' inquiries into community funds of knowledge led them to reframe their classroom approach so that students could "use their social contacts outside the classroom to access new knowledge" (p. 138).

Children's Literature as a Site for Inquiry

> Children's biographies of Christopher Columbus function as primers on racism and imperialism. They teach youngsters to accept the right of white people to rule over people of color, of powerful nations to dominate weaker nations. (Bigelow, 1992, p. 112)

With these hard-hitting statements, Bigelow confronts his readers with the problems of histories of colonization written for children. He goes on to critically read eight children's biographies of Columbus as the curious adventurer who wanted to discover lands just because they were there. Bigelow shows how these texts portray Columbus as a man of deep religious faith, thereby excusing his stealing from and physical maltreatment and murder of the Indigenous peoples, who are constructed as heathens. As he puts it, "The reader is practically strangled by Columbus's halo" (1992, p. 114).

These books, Bigelow argues, train young people to think that the oppressed deserve to be oppressed and should remain that way. These texts produce their own pedagogy, in which the child reader is constructed as passive. No dilemmas, questions, or problems are posed. Thus history is made innocent. Heroes tell the story, and victims are kept in their place, as nonhuman, through a religious discourse. As students read school history, modern-day politics of exploitation are preserved. Books are constructed to sanitize, purify, or make superheroes out of murderers of the past. Students' inquiries are cut short by books that have it all sewn up:

> Each biography is constructed as a lecture, not as a dialogue or problem-posing. The narratives require readers merely to listen, not to think. The text is everything; the reader, nothing. Not only are young readers conditioned to accept social hierarchy—colonialism and racism—but they are also rehearsed in an authoritarian mode of learning. (Bigelow, 1992, p. 119)

The questions Bigelow asks of these biographies are not restricted to historical literature, but can be extended to the contents of big books, poetry, songs, anthems, social studies texts, mathematics books, and science charts. Bigelow (1991) offers detailed suggestions for critical exploration of history through dramatic play, through problem solving concerning questions of justice, and by reading counterhegemonic texts. Bigelow's work highlights the need to ask what school inquiries are about. What kinds of young people are produced by classroom texts? What kinds of worlds are preserved, venerated, or obliterated in the texts students use every day? In what ways do such books position themselves as beyond question for young inquirers and teachers alike?

Textbooks as Sites for Critical Inquiry

Educators have rightly criticized textbooks as productive of limited literacies incorporating mainstream, capitalist, and patriarchal ideologies (Shannon, 1992; Luke, 1991). Whole language teachers have resisted the de-skilling of teachers that textbooks and kits produce (Apple, 1993). In a politically oppositional project in South Africa during the apartheid regime, however, Janks and her colleagues (1992, 1993a, 1993b) found ways of rewriting textbooks as sites of resistance and critical inquiry at a time when political action in school curricula was almost impossible. Janks (1993b) explains:

> Materials are perhaps not the most effective way of transforming classroom practice, but in South Africa there were few options available at the time. Student and teacher organizations had been banned, the State had, and still has, a monopoly on in-service training and discussion pertaining to People's Education had been criminalized. (p. 28)

Writing texts constituted one form of possible political action. Using insights from critical linguistics, Janks and a team of writers including school and tertiary teachers developed a series of workbooks for tertiary and secondary school students titled *Critical Language Awareness*. The books require students to examine the ways in which language produces power relations in selected texts. In this way, texts are not treated as neutral accounts of facts but as socially and politically constructed. Students explore topics such as language and position; language and the news; language and advertising; languages in South Africa; language, identity, and power; and words and pictures. The workbooks include numerous questions which ask students to read critically. For example, an excerpt from a history textbook used in South African primary schools is analyzed using questions such as the following:

> Why is this information placed at this point in the passage? What are the effects of these words? How does the writer convey the impression that the trekkers are civilized? How does the writer give the impression that God is on the side of the trekkers? Why is that important? Give reasons other than God's intervention to account for the trekker victory. Use information in the passage. Why is this information kept in the background? How is it kept in the background? (Janks 1993c, p. 12)

Each of the workbooks is richly illustrated with examples of different kinds of texts and ways of analyzing them. The explicit agenda is for students to practice critical and oppositional readings of texts which they may have previously taken as uncontested truth. As Janks (1993b) explains:

> All the workbooks attempt to raise awareness of the way in which language can be used (and is used) to maintain and to challenge existing forms of power. In any unequal relation of power there are top dogs and underdogs. (p. 30)

The work of Janks and her colleagues makes an important contribution to the knowledge of language and literacy educators globally. It shows what can be achieved even in highly controlled states; demonstrates explicitly how insights from critical linguistics and poststructuralist theories can be applied in school literacy curricula; and illustrates how textbooks are potentially sites of critical inquiry. The authors attempt to open up their own text to inquiry by inviting readers to critically analyze the workbook as a text that has worked on them. The books are excellent models for teacher-writers who want to produce classroom materials that help students investigate how language and power work together to produce advantage and disadvantage.

Community Texts as Sites for Inquiry

In the early years of schooling, teachers are often preoccupied with socializing students into school and the demands of the institution. Literacy lessons often emphasize listening to, enjoying, and producing stories. But children are surrounded by a multiplicity of texts before they begin formal schooling, and many of these texts are "free"—from billboards to direct mail advertising. Jennifer O'Brien, a teacher of a composite grade kindergarten-1-2 (five-, six-, and seven-year-olds in Australian classrooms), decided to use the material that overflows mailboxes in capitalist societies. In particular, she investigated the junk mail surrounding the celebration of Mother's Day. Drawing on insights from feminist poststructuralist analysis, O'Brien (1994) worked to help her students become critical text analysts from the beginning of their school literacy instruction.

> My overall aim was to set tasks that would give students a chance to think about the version of reality constructed by the text and to think about different possibilities for constructing reality. In other words, to consider the broad question, What sort of world is constructed in and by this text; what other possible worlds could have been constructed? (p. 44)

Students were asked to draw and label what they expected to find in Mother's Day catalogs and the kinds of things they wouldn't expect to find in these texts. O'Brien asked students to compare their drawings and discuss where their expectations came from or why they had made the choices they had made. Next, students were asked to look through a selection of Mother's Day catalogs and record through writing and drawing the kinds of gifts that were pictured. Thus even students who could not yet decode were actively reading. O'Brien asked the students to draw, write, and talk about other issues too: Which groups of people get the most out of Mother's Day? How are the mothers in the catalogs like real mothers? How are the mothers in the catalogs not like real mothers? Notice the words used about mothers. Notice the words placed near the word *mother.* Students were positioned from the start as critical inquirers in regard to texts.

Not totally satisfied with her study of the Mother's Day catalogs, the next year O'Brien (reported in Luke, O'Brien, & Comber, 1994, pp. 144–47) decided to involve the parent community as well and to look explicitly at issues of race and class as well as gender. O'Brien and her class designed and conducted a survey of mothers, grandmothers, and female caregivers about their interests and preferred ways of celebrating Mother's Day. Their findings foregrounded "the gaps between the constructed world of commerce and the students' worlds." The class tallied which groups of mothers were represented and which groups were left out of the catalogs, immediately becoming aware that people of color were missing. Students were also able to notice the representation of wealth associated with such advertising.

From the beginning of schooling, then, these students inquired into the ways in which language and power work together, how particular worlds are constructed in the everyday texts which confront them daily, and how gender representation forms possibilities for who they can and cannot be.

Inquiry about What?

There is potential for critical inquiry in all that students and teachers do in schools. Even in poorly resourced communities, educators have been innovative in pursuing social analysis in the literacy classroom. But still there is much that works against inquiry and prevents students from interrogating fictional histories or resisting restricted versions of identity. Many forces continue to maintain schools as sites of noninquiry, or as one high school student put it, as a place where "literacy non-events" are the norm. As a starting point, we may need to examine what isn't asked about in school; what cannot be talked about; which questions are excluded from children's literature; which texts are ignored in the classroom. By considering what we have failed to question, what we have taken for granted as unquestionable or beyond question, we may gain some insights into the boundaries which have marked out appropriate school inquiries. Through critical inquiry, students and teachers can collaboratively produce countertexts that tell different stories and build on community knowledge. To do this, teachers need to recognize teaching as political and cultural work. The interests of schools and their communities must intersect as students work in and on the texts of their worlds. In pursuing inquiry-based curricula, educators need to develop an ethical stance about which knowledges will count and whose questions will be pursued. Literacy teachers are in an ideal position to change the questions from which inquiries proceed. For this to happen, teachers will need to take up ongoing critical inquiries about the role of schooling in global societies that comprise diverse communities.

References

Apple, M. (1993). *Official knowledge: Democratic education in a conservative age*. New York: Routledge.

Bigelow, B. (1991). Rethinking Columbus: Teaching about the 500th anniversary of Columbus's arrival in America [Special issue]. *Rethinking Schools.*

Bigelow, W. (1992). Once upon a genocide: Christopher Columbus in children's literature. *Language Arts, 69*(2), 112–20.

Comber, B. (1988). Any questions, any problems? Inviting children's questions and requests for help. *Language Arts, 65*(2), 147–53.

Comber, B., & O'Brien, J. (1993). Critical literacy: Classroom explorations. *Critical Pedagogy Networker,* 6(1/2), 1–11.

Freebody, P., & Luke, A. (1990). Literacies' programs: Debates and demands in cultural context. *Prospect: A Journal of Australian TESOL, 11,* 7–16.

Goodman, Y., & Burke, C. (1980). *Reading strategies: Focus on comprehension.* New York: R. C. Owen.

Granowsky, A. (1984). *The penguin.* London: Macmillan Education.

Harste, J., & Short, K. (with Burke, C.). (1988). *Creating classrooms for authors: The reading-writing connection.* Portsmouth, NH: Heinemann.

Janks, H. (1993a). *Critical language awareness series.* Johannesburg, S. Africa: Hodder & Stoughton/Witwatersrand University Press.

Janks, H. (1993b). Developing critical awareness. *Opinion: Journal of the South Australian English Teachers Association,* 22(2), 2733.

Janks, H. (1993c). *Language and position.* Critical language awareness series. Johannesburg, S. Africa: Witwatersrand University Press/ Randburg, S. Africa: Hodder & Stoughton.

Janks, H., & Ivanic, R. (1992). Critical language awareness: Perspectives for emancipation. In N. Fairclough (Ed.), *Critical language awareness* (pp. 305–31). London: Longman.

Jongsma, K. S. (1991). Critical literacy (Questions and answers). *The Reading Teacher, 44*(7), 518–19.

Kutz, E., & Roskelly, H. (1991). *An unquiet pedagogy: Transforming practice in the English classroom.* Portsmouth, NH: Boynton/Cook.

Luke, A. (1991). The secular word: Catholic reconstructions of Dick and Jane. In M. Apple & L. Christian-Smith (Eds.), *The politics of the textbook* (pp. 166–90). New York: Routledge.

Luke, A., O'Brien, J., & Comber, B. (1994). Making community texts objects of study. *Australian Journal of Language and Literacy, 17*(2), 139–49.

Moll, L., Amanti, C., Neff, D., & Gonzalez, N. (1992). Funds of knowledge for teaching: Using a qualitative approach to connect homes and classrooms. *Theory into Practice, 31*(2), 132–41.

O'Brien, J. (1994). Show Mum you love her: Taking a new look at junk mail. *Reading, 28*(1), 43–46.

Shannon, P. (1992). Commercial reading materials, a technological ideology, and the deskilling of teachers. In P. Shannon (Ed.), *Becoming political: Readings and writings in the politics of literacy education* (pp. 182–207). Portsmouth, NH: Heinemann.

Singh, M. G. (1989). A counter-hegemonic orientation to literacy in Australia. *Journal of Education, 171*(2), 35–56.

Unsworth, L. (1993). *Literacy learning and teaching: Language as social practice in the primary school.* S. Melbourne, Australia: Macmillan.

CHAPTER SIX

Writing for Critical Democracy: Student Voice and Teacher Practice in the Writing Workshop

TIMOTHY J. LENSMIRE
Washington University

A central theme within writing workshop approaches to writing instruction is increased student control over writing processes and texts. Students have wide powers to determine the topics, audiences, purposes, and forms of their writing. Such control is in the service of student voice. With the support of the teacher and numerous opportunities to collaborate and share texts with peers, students are supposed to gradually become more and more adept at expressing themselves in written text.

Like advocates of writing workshop approaches to the teaching of writing, I think that the idea of voice—especially student voice—should be an important part of our plans and efforts to improve the education of our children. In what follows, I explore and critique the conception of voice put forward by writing workshop advocates (e.g., Atwell, 1987; Calkins, 1986, 1991; Graves, 1983; Murray, 1985). I also critically examine the conception of voice put forward by advocates of critical pedagogy (e.g., Aronowitz & Giroux, 1991; Freire, 1970, 1985; Giroux, 1988; Giroux & McLaren, 1989; Simon, 1987).[1]

The main title of my chapter—Writing for Critical Democracy—is also the working title of a larger book project I am pursuing. My goal in this project—a goal that has not, for the most part, been taken up by workshop advocates—is to link the teaching and learning of writing in schools more closely to a critical democratic vision of schools and society. In this chapter, I summarize what I have learned so far in my work on the concept of student voice. First, I characterize and contrast writing workshop and critical pedagogy versions of voice. Then I examine a serious weakness shared by both workshop and critical pedagogy treatments of voice. Finally, I point to several aspects of teacher practice in the writing classroom that will need to be rethought, given new understandings of student voice.

Voice in the Workshop and Critical Pedagogy

Workshop approaches emphasize the students' work of finding their own voices in their writing. Finding their voices involves looking to their own experiences for what it is they have and want to say. Calkins (1986), for example, asserts that we write in order to "turn the chaos into something beautiful" and "to uncover and to celebrate the organizing patterns of our existence" (Calkins, 1986, p. 3). The image is one of burrowing deep into subjectivity to discover our authentic, unique nature and a voice that expresses who we are.

Workshop advocates do not assume merely that it is a good thing for students to tap into and express their real, authentic selves in their writing. Advocates also assume a particular conception of the "self" to be tapped: a traditional Enlightenment conception, in which the self is imagined to be stable, unitary, and autonomous.[2] Thus far workshop advocates have paid little attention to the serious criticisms this conception of self has received from, among others, psychoanalytic and feminist theorists (see Flax, 1990). As Willinsky (1990) has noted: "The self, as that pure and singular essence of our being, is no longer a reliable figure in the psychological or literary landscape" (p. 220). This unreliable figure carries workshop advocates' conception of voice.

Advocates of critical pedagogy assume no such self. For them, the self is a social one, created out of the cultural resources at hand. This does not mean they envision the self as determined by these cultural resources; the passive individual does not simply become whatever is dictated by an overpowering social context. Although the resources available—the experiences, languages, histories, stories—obviously constrain the possible selves an individual can become, they also provide possibilities, possibilities that can be more or less consciously worked in the creation of a self. As Emerson (1986) expressed it, "One makes a self through the words one has learned, fashions one's own voice and inner speech by a selective appropriation of the voices of others" (p. 31).

The space for choosing, for fashioning the self out of the words of others, is enlarged by the complexity and plurality of the social contexts of our lives. No environment, as Dewey noted, is "all of one piece" (1983, p. 90). Instead, society is marked by a multiplicity of cultures, meanings, and values. Advocates of critical pedagogy would have us pay attention not only to this plurality, but also to asymmetries of power across this diversity—asymmetries of power that enable powerful groups to define their own particular meanings, experiences, and forms of writing and reading as *the* valued ones in society (Aronowitz & Giroux, 1991).

For critical pedagogists, dominant groups determine dominant meanings, but not without a struggle and never once and for all. In fact, the larger educational and political project of critical pedagogy is exactly to empower students to engage in this social struggle over meaning. The conception of voice in critical pedagogy is linked to this project.

For advocates of critical pedagogy, voice signals *participation*, an active part in the social production of meaning. If the workshop sense of voice is evoked with the contrast, "my words versus someone else's words," then the contrast to voice within critical pedagogy is silence, where silence points to oppressive conditions that keep certain people from speaking and being heard. Rather than emphasizing the attempt to distinguish oneself from others, voice here emphasizes inserting oneself and one's texts into public spheres.

Another way to contrast writing workshop and critical pedagogy versions of voice, then, is through their relations to democratic theory. If we think of democracy in terms of liberty and popular sovereignty, then the workshop commitment to voice is concerned primarily with liberty, especially freedom of thought and expression. Voice in critical pedagogy is chiefly linked to the goal of popular sovereignty, to making power "accountable . . . to those affected by its exercise" (Bowles & Gintis, 1987, p. 4). Critical pedagogy is concerned with having students be active participants in the construction of their worlds, rather than trapped in the meanings, subjectivities, and forms of authority determined by powerful others.

Voice also serves different functions within the pedagogical schemes of writing workshop approaches and critical pedagogy. For workshop advocates, voice is a goal, an endpoint, a criterion with which to judge the success of the writing and instruction. Without that stamp of individuality—without, as Graves (1983) put it, "the imprint of ourselves on our writing" (p. 227)—the writing and teaching have failed. Within critical pedagogy, however, voice is less a goal or endpoint in itself and more a starting point for collective work to be done by the classroom community.[3]

Student voices are a starting point in that they make available a multiplicity of texts that can be examined, learned from, and criticized. Critical pedagogy's emphasis on voice, then, is very much in the spirit of Dewey's (1980) call for a transformed recitation. In the traditional recitation, individual students answered teacher questions for the purpose of displaying what they had memorized from the textbook in a competition for teacher rewards. Dewey imagined a different sort of recitation, one in which the recitation "becomes the social clearing-house, where experiences and ideas are exchanged and subjected to criticism, where misconceptions are corrected, and new lines of thought and inquiry are set up" (Dewey, 1980, p. 34).

Advocates of critical pedagogy and writing workshops also embrace contrasting teacher stances in relation to student voice. Within critical pedagogy, individual students' voices are assumed to arise from a social self, shaped and created in social contexts of great diversity. These voices—like the voices of teachers, curriculum developers, novelists, and scientists—are assumed to be necessarily partial, to express a particular position on the world that will make possible certain understandings and constrain others. Consequently, critical pedagogists say, again and again, that student voices must not only be affirmed, but also *questioned*. As Giroux put it:

> It is not enough for teachers merely to dignify the grounds on which students learn to speak, imagine, and give meaning to their world. Developing a pedagogy that takes the notion of student

> voice seriously means developing a critically affirmative language that works both *with and on* the experiences that students bring to the classroom. This means taking seriously and confirming the language forms, modes of reasoning, dispositions, and histories that give students an active voice in defining the world; it also means working on the experiences of such students in order for them to examine both their strengths and weaknesses. (Aronowitz & Giroux, 1991, p. 104)

Nowhere do workshop advocates even hint that teachers should take up a critical position vis-à-vis reports of student experience and the meanings students make with their texts. Workshop advocates point to a stance that has the teacher intervene, strategically, in the technique of students' writing processes and texts. But writing teachers are to ignore the intentions and meanings of students' work except to help students pursue them more effectively (Lensmire, 1993).

Gilbert's (1989a, 1989b, 1994) work helps us understand this lack of critical attention to meaning. She argues that the notion of personal voice in workshop approaches ties student-written text and student tightly together. One consequence of this merging of text and student is that student texts "are seen to be so closely aligned to the individual child and that child's original making of meaning that they are 'beyond criticism'" (Gilbert, 1989b, p. 198). In other words, any criticism of the meanings students make with their texts can be interpreted as a disparagement of or attack on the student personally.

Gilbert also points to some of the difficulty this notion of personal voice gets us into. For what if the authentic student voice is, say, a sexist one, as in an example Gilbert (1989b) provides from a year 5 writing workshop in Australia? Gilbert tells of the collaborative effort of four nine-year-old boys who wrote themselves into their own fictional story of war and destruction. They made themselves heroes, of course. They also wrote seven girls from the class into their tale. Six of these girls were given stereotypical roles in the story—"having 'affairs,' holding hands with boys, getting married, saying 'I love you'"—before becoming victims of war, disposed of in "reasonably ugly ways" (Gilbert, 1989b, p. 200). The one girl to escape the textual fate of stereotype and death happened to be the biggest girl in the class.

In the story, she jumps on top of the enemy and scares them off for a while. She also gets called "Super Blubber." As Gilbert notes, "No need to kill off this female: her size and aggression have effectively excluded her anyway (what worse fate for a girl than to be called Super Blubber?)" (Gilbert, 1989b, p. 200).

Are we, as workshop advocates seem to suggest, to marvel at this exploration of the world by these young boys and help them make it work even more effectively?

It should be obvious that I find much about critical pedagogists' treatment of voice attractive and persuasive. I value their assumption of a social self-development within multicultural contexts. I affirm, in general, the critical democratic project they are pursuing. Within this perspective, voice is conceived of in terms of participation in the construction and reconstruction of the world and the ways we make sense of it. And advocates of critical pedagogy avoid an uncritical stance in relation to student meaning-making.

But writing workshop and critical pedagogy versions of voice also share important similarities (Giroux, 1987). Both would have student voice flourish in the classroom. Both seek to humanize teaching and learning in schools through the acceptance and affirmation of student voice. Both encourage the active exploration by students of their worlds, rather than passive submission in the face of teacher control and knowledge.

Unfortunately, critical pedagogy and writing workshop conceptions of voice also share at least one serious weakness: Neither has come to grips adequately with what *conflict* among voices—conflict generated among students, between teacher and students, and within individual students—means for the actual production of speech and writing within classrooms. In the end, neither workshop advocates nor advocates of critical pedagogy embed student voice in the immediate social context of the classroom, and consequently, they ignore important problems and issues attending the speech and writing of students there. Writing workshop advocates embed voice in the inner context of the author's intentions, desires, dreams, and experiences; when the social context of the workshop is considered at all, it is only as a friendly one that supports individual students' expression. Critical pedagogy advocates embed voice in politics and history writ large, rather than within the local meanings, values, and relations—the micropolitics and microhistories—of particular classrooms.

Voice and Classroom Conflict

In my own teaching and research in a third-grade writing workshop—work influenced by both writing workshop and critical pedagogy perspectives—I found that the local peer relations among students were extremely important influences on their activities and texts in the classroom, and not always in positive ways (Lensmire, 1993, 1994a, 1994b). Students used the relative control they exerted over their own movement and writing processes within the workshop to divide themselves up along gender and social class lines. Girls conferenced and collaborated with girls, and boys with boys. And middle-class students tended to work within shifting groups of middle-class friends and to avoid association with the working-class students who lived in a large trailer park in the middle of the mainly suburban community this school served.

Karen, for example, spoke for both boys and girls when she stated that "the boys like the boys, but the girls like the girls" for peer conferences (personal communication, May 21, 1990). In Mary and Lori's interview, Mary was quite explicit about whom she did and did not want to work with: "I like working with Carol, Lisa, Marie, Sharon, Emily, Julie, and Suzanne. And I don't like working with the boys." Mary's list of girls, except possibly for Emily and Julie, was a fairly complete naming of the most popular girls in the class. She also was forthcoming about girls with whom she did not want to work and why. Mary said that "some of them have lice, they stink"; she did not like their "styles" or their personalities.

> MARY: Most of them, and some of them are from the trailer park and I don't like working with people who are from the trailer park. . . . Like at first I thought that Lori was from the trailer park before I went over to her house the first time.

LORI: Thanks a lot.

MARY: Well I did. (personal communication, May 31, 1990)

Instead of the uniformly supportive workshop context that workshop advocates imagine, individual students felt they were confronted with multiple peer audiences that they judged to be more or less supportive, *and more or less hostile*, to their attempts at expression. In other words, students, especially unpopular students, felt there were serious risks involved in writing for peer audiences—risks to their sense of self, to what they valued and cared about, and to their social standing in relation to others. Robert, one of the boys from the trailer park, said in his interview that he liked to conference with Leon, his friend William, and Rajesh. When asked why he conferenced with them, he responded:

ROBERT:	Well, I know they wouldn't like tell everybody, you know?
INTERVIEWER:	No, tell me. Tell everybody what?
ROBERT:	Well, they wouldn't tell, they wouldn't go off telling everybody what you wrote.
INTERVIEWER:	Yeah. Is that important to you?
ROBERT:	Yes it is.
INTERVIEWER:	Why is that?
ROBERT:	Well, because, sometimes they laugh at you, they tease you.
INTERVIEWER:	What do they laugh or tease you about?
ROBERT:	Well, what you didn't write and what they didn't write, like the same, like, they would think that theirs, theirs was better than the others. (personal communication, May 24, 1990)

Students' responses to risks associated with writing for peers included seeking out certain classmates for writing conferences and avoiding others. In their writing, students avoided genres and topics that they felt involved too much exposure of self. Some students chose not to insert themselves and their texts into public spaces within the workshop, spaces such as sharing time and the workshop library—spaces created specifically to allow all students' voices to sound and be heard within the classroom community.

Unpopular students (mostly from the trailer park, a few not) felt these risks most keenly. The upshot is that students—not just teachers—can silence students' voices in classrooms. Jessie, one of the most unpopular students in the class, summarized it this way. When asked why most students felt comfortable sharing their work during sharing time and she didn't, she replied: "Because they have lots of friends" (personal communication, May 30, 1990).[4]

If possibilities for conflict and risk attend peer relations in classrooms, they also attend relations between teacher and student, even when the teacher rejects traditional practices and embraces workshop or critical pedagogy approaches to teaching and learning in classrooms. McCarthey (1994) provides a worthy example in her story of Anita, an eleven-year-old girl in a fifth/sixth-grade writing class in New York. Anita's teacher, Ms. Meyer, was inspired by Calkins's (1991) discussion of writers' notebooks to have her students keep notebooks of their own. When it came time for Anita to write a piece developed from her notebook, she thought she might write about her experiences at camp. Her teacher, however, worried that such a topic lacked impact and focus, and that Anita would be unable to write about these experiences with the sort of powerful, personal voice workshop advocates call for. After an examination of Anita's notebook, Ms. Meyer thought that material concerning Anita's relationship with her father could be developed into a strong piece, and she encouraged Anita to write about that.

Ms. Meyer was in good workshop form. She carefully read Anita's notebook and tried to help Anita identify a topic—within the realm of Anita's own experiences—worthy of Anita's attention and effort. She didn't demand that Anita write about her father, but did *encourage* her to do so.

Now Anita had a problem, for she didn't want to write about her father. Anita hadn't spelled it out in her notebook, and Ms. Meyer didn't know: Anita didn't want to write about her father because he physically abused her and her brother. But how can she not write about this topic and still please her teacher? And if she doesn't want to tell Ms. Meyer about her relationship with her father, she can't even reveal her real reasons for avoiding this topic.

Eventually, Anita came up with a fairly ingenious solution to her writing problem. She wrote about someone who was close to her but not abusive—her grandfather. This allowed her to fulfill Ms. Meyer's seeming desire that she write about her relationship with an important person in her life, without exposing certain facets of her personal life to public scrutiny.

Let me draw one moral from this story: given unequal power relations among teachers and students, encouragement is sometimes not far from coercion in the classroom. The institutional authority of the teacher in school does not just go away when that teacher chooses to engage in alternative teaching practices; it remains for the student to negotiate with the teacher, or work through, or (as in Anita's case) work around. It's a complicated business.

It's a complicated business that is passed over too quickly in critical pedagogists' calls for the questioning of student voice in the classroom. Anita and Ms. Meyer's story suggests that simply supporting student voice in classrooms may be hard enough to accomplish.[5] Advocates of critical pedagogy ask teachers to support *and question* student expression. In questioning student expression from their position of authority in the classroom, teachers once again run the risk of silencing student voice in the classroom. Rather than pushing classroom participants' thought and action forward to increasingly critical evaluations of their world, such questioning could encourage students not to speak their mind, or to look for the correct thing to say to please the teacher. Although advocates of critical pedagogy recognize asymmetries of power in the classroom, they have, as Ellsworth (1989) asserts, "made no systematic examination of the barriers that this imbalance throws up to the kind of student expression and dialogue they prescribe" (p. 309). At times, critical pedagogists seem overconfident that student voice will flourish in the face of questioning.

In addition to conflict among peers and between teacher and student, advocates of writing workshops and critical pedagogy have largely ignored the inner conflict and struggle students often face when speaking and writing in classrooms. Workshop advocates recognize that the writer faces difficulties in capturing complex experiences in words, in finding words to express inner meanings. But their conceptions of self and writing make it difficult to address the inner conflicts inherent in having to use *others'* words when those others are different from, opposed to, and more powerful than the student writer or speaker.[6] Bakhtin (1981) noted that

> the word in language is half someone else's. It becomes "one's own" only when the speaker populates it with his own intention, his own accent. . . . And not all words for just anyone submit easily to this appropriation, to this seizure and transformation into private property: many words stubbornly resist, others remain alien, sound foreign in the mouth of the one who appropriated them and who now speaks them. . . . [I]t is as if they put themselves in quotation marks against the will of the speaker. (p. 294)

Stephen Dedalus, the young Irish protagonist of James Joyce's (1916/1976) *A Portrait of the Artist as a Young Man*, expresses this problem in his inner reflections on a conversation he is having with an English priest (who is also a dean at his school).[7] Their discussion is moving, somewhat haphazardly, through questions of esthetic theory and how to light fires and lamps, when the two discover that they use different words to name the same object—Stephen calls the priest's "funnel" a "tundish." The priest, with a courtesy that Stephen thinks rings false, calls *tundish* "a most interesting word" and repeats it several times to himself. For Stephen, this "little word seemed to have turned a rapier point of his sensitiveness against this courteous and vigilant foe," the priest. Although English is the shared native tongue of both Stephen and the English priest, Stephen believes that

> the language in which we are speaking is his before it is mine. How different are the words *home*, *Christ*, *ale*, *master*, on his lips and mine! I cannot speak or write these words without unrest of spirit. His language, so familiar and so foreign, will always be for me an acquired speech. I have not made or accepted its words. My voice holds them at bay. My soul frets in the shadow of his language. (p. 189)

Advocates of critical pedagogy, with their assumption of a multiple, social self, certainly are in a better position than workshop advocates to recognize the inner struggles of people like Anita and Stephen. When Giroux writes that one's voice "constitutes forms of subjectivity that are multilayered, mobile, complex, and shifting" (Aronowitz & Giroux, 1991, p. 100), he is pointing to a conception of voice that is not far from acknowledging inner conflict in the production of speech and writing in schools. Unfortunately, critical pedagogists have not usually pushed this far. Their conception of voice, as Ellsworth notes,

> does not confront the ways in which any individual student's voice is already a "teeth gritting" and often contradictory intersection of voices constituted by gender, race, class, ability, ethnicity, sexual orientation, or ideology. . . . It is impossible to speak from all voices at once, or from any one, without traces of the others being present and interruptive. (1989, p. 312)

I should take care here. I am not saying that classrooms are always and necessarily places hostile to student voice. Teachers and students can work together in ways that reduce risks and address the conflicts they confront. Classrooms can be better places, learning places. Many already are, and sometimes they are supported by the visions of workshop and critical pedagogy advocates.

Classrooms can be better places, and as educators we have a moral obligation to make them so. But just because we are working to make them better doesn't mean that students don't continue to confront problems in expressing themselves in classrooms, problems originating in conflicts with peers and teachers, and in the difficult choices they are making about who they will be in relation to school and a larger, heterogeneous social world. I am not trying to be a glass-half-empty person; I am arguing that if our ideas of something better are linked to the flourishing of student voice in classrooms, then our theorizing and efforts to make things better have to account for the risks and problems students face in expressing themselves there.

Stated a little differently: We work for something better; as we do, our students still confront what is not yet better. We have to acknowledge this in ways that workshop advocates and critical pedagogists have not.

Obviously, the situation I have described calls out for an alternative conception of voice, one that draws on the strengths of previous work by workshop and critical pedagogy advocates but that locates voice more firmly in the immediate social context of the classroom. This is what I am in the middle of trying to do, with the help of Bakhtin (1981, 1986) and others who have used Bakhtin's work to inform their own writing on voice (e.g., Dyson, 1992; Kamberelis & Scott, 1992; O'Connor, 1989; Ritchie, 1989).[8] Instead of providing a beginning sketch of that work here, however, I conclude with some comments on teacher practice in the writing classroom, for conceptions of teacher practice are bound up with conceptions of student voice. If we see voice differently, then we will have to imagine teacher practice differently as well.

Student Voice and Teacher Practice

At least two aspects of teacher practice are in need of further examination and development. First, more attention needs to be paid to the immediate classroom community within which students speak and write. If, as Harris (1989) asserts, we "write not as isolated individuals but as members of communities whose beliefs, concerns, and practices both instigate and constrain, at least in part, the sorts of things we can say" (p. 12), then we had better pay attention to the classroom communities we create. Future work will need to explore both what sorts of classroom communities we think would be desirable, and what sorts of actions we can take as educators to create and sustain such classroom communities within schools.

In previous work (Lensmire, 1994a), for example, I proposed that workshop teachers and students be guided by a vision of what I called an engaged, pluralistic classroom community. An engaged, pluralistic classroom community is one that recognizes and affirms differences among students and encourages students to learn from and be enhanced by those differences. I adapted this vision of classroom community from Bernstein (1988), who identifies what he calls the "ethos of pragmatism" in the writings of Pierce, James, Dewey, and others. An important theme of the pragmatist ethos, for Bernstein, is the vision of a community of inquirers that supports critical thought and action by its members.

A shortcoming in my work, however, was that I did not take up in any detail the issue of how we might actually promote such classroom communities. Paradoxically, the writings of workshop advocates are filled with concrete suggestions for how to help teachers and peers interact in helpful ways around text, but their work does not connect these suggestions to a vision of community. Workshop approaches have aligned their goals with individual students' intentions without considering that the ends some students pursue may not be beneficial for other students, or even themselves (remember the young boys in Gilbert's example discussed earlier). Consequently, when things don't go as planned—when students don't act the way they are supposed to according to writing workshop scripts—teachers are left to their own resources and visions in adapting workshop procedures and suggestions to local circumstances. Certainly, many teachers adapt in ways we would applaud. But our work could certainly benefit from careful explorations of what sorts of classroom communities we want, and how we might create and sustain them.

A second aspect of teacher practice in writing classrooms that is in need of revision is teacher response to student writing. The workshop conception of teacher response—what Graves (1983) calls "following the child"—emphasizes following and supporting students' choices of topic and purpose for writing. Such a conception, however, ignores the problem of students pursuing questionable intentions and material in their texts, such as when students' texts affirm—even if unintentionally—gender, race, and social class stereotypes and boundaries.

In response to such problems, I developed a second conception of response that draws heavily on the work of critical pedagogy advocates (Lensmire, 1993). I also looked to psychoanalysis, especially the simultaneously accepting and critical stance that the analyst takes in relation to patients' narratives, and began thinking of teacher response as a type of analysis. This is not one supported by Freudian theories of the unconscious, repression, and resistance: I looked to the "socio" rather than the "psycho," to the workings of language, culture, and power in the lives of speakers and writers, and conceived of teacher response as "socioanalysis." Response as socioanalysis assumes that traces of racial, class, and gender oppression will, at times, find their way into the stories students tell.

There are, however, problems with this conception of response. The critical teacher stance I created with the notion of socioanalysis proposed reading and responding to student texts as abstracted artifacts of an oppressive larger society. This sort of response is important if we want to help our students avoid modes of thought and action that perpetuate these aspects of our society. But in the end, socioanalysis, like following the child, is inadequate because it does not concern itself with local politics, the micropolitics of the classroom, or how students' texts might operate there.

In my thinking about teacher response to students' texts, I had realized that students in writing workshops made important curricular decisions for themselves, and that some of the material they might work with required their critical evaluations with my help. But I had thought of students' decisions about curriculum as private ones, affecting only individual students' work for the duration of individual projects. I had not considered how students' stories *became curriculum for other students* in teacher-sponsored events and classroom practices that encouraged (and required) students to listen to and read carefully the texts of other students (Gilbert, 1989b). With the help of critical pedagogy advocates, I had thought of "questionable" material in students' texts as the unfortunate traces of societal politics of class, race, and gender. And with the help of critical pedagogy advocates, I had ignored how students' stories participate, for better and for worse, in the micropolitics of the classroom.

It is disturbing enough to realize that students' texts can reflect, in some way, differences in status and power among groups in society and among groups of students in the classroom. But we must also consider the active role texts play in producing and maintaining these relationships. Texts are rhetorical—they have effects in the world. They can influence others' conceptions of themselves and their worlds, make them laugh, make them hurt, make them feel connected to others, make them feel safe or unsafe, encourage them to speak and write or remain silent. Such is some of the work students' texts do in our writing classrooms.

Future work on teacher response will have to confront the rhetorical play of students texts within the classroom community.[9] If it is to intervene helpfully in the production of student voice in classrooms, teacher response will have to concern itself with the consequences of students' texts, both for the students who write them and for those who read them.

Notes

1. My own work and thinking have been most concerned with elementary schools. So for me the writing workshop advocates who have been most influential are people such as Donald Graves, Lucy Calkins, and Nancie Atwell. Donald Murray, though more closely identified with college composition, has also been important because his work introduced me to workshop approaches. As for advocates of critical pedagogy, Paulo Freire, Ira Shor, Henry Giroux, Roger Simon, and bell hooks have probably been most influential. It seems, however, at least in my reading of these writers, that Giroux has given the most explicit attention to the idea of voice, and consequently my comments on voice in critical pedagogy are based largely on his work.

2. According to Berlin (1988), workshop advocates embrace an "expressionistic rhetoric" that is the descendant of both Rousseau and Romantic responses to nineteenth-century capitalism. This rhetoric assumes an autonomous, stable self who takes up relations with the world in order to make sense of it and her- or himself, and is characterized by a radical individualism that portrays the individual as the source and final arbiter of what *is*, of what is *good*, and of what is *possible*. It is not that the reality of material, social, and linguistic aspects of the world is denied, but that "they are considered significant only insofar as they serve the needs of the individual. All fulfill their true function only when being exploited in the interests of locating the individual's authentic nature" (Berlin, 1988, p. 484). Expressionistic rhetoric's critique of society emerges from this demand that the material and social contexts of the individual support the pursuit and discovery of personal meaning. Berlin argues that this rhetoric has been closely tied to psychological theories that assert the inherent goodness of the individual, and that within expressionistic rhetoric, this inherent goodness is, of course, "dis-

torted by excessive contact with others in groups and institutions" (p. 484). That is, all too often social relations and institutions (such as schools) corrupt human nature and demand conformity to petty social convention, rather than provide the supportive backdrop for a flourishing individuality.

3. I am simplifying a bit here with the characterization of voice as endpoint in writing workshop and voice as starting point in critical pedagogy. Workshop advocates will sometimes talk of voice as a driving force or essential ingredient in the writing process itself (Graves, 1983). Thus, voice is linked not only to a quality of the text produced, but also to the assumed natural desire to express the self. Within critical pedagogy, voice is sometimes used to suggest a desired endpoint in the development of the individual, as when Giroux calls for "a voice capable of speaking in one's own terms, a voice capable of listening, retelling, and challenging the very grounds of knowledge and power" (1988, p. 71).

4. With the help of the regular classroom teacher, I tried in a number of ways to make the workshop a safe, supportive place for all students, with limited success. I examine in detail students' responses to peer relations in this workshop in Chapter 4, "Peer Audiences and Risk," and Chapter 5, "Fiction, Distance, and Control," of Lensmire (1994a).

5. See Florio-Ruane (1991) and Ulichney and Watson-Gegeo (1989) for helpful discussions of the difficulties teachers and students face when they try to transform traditional teacher-dominated talk in writing conferences.

6. Soliday (1994) provides a solid overview of research and an excellent account of the inner struggles students face in working across cultures in their school writing.

7. I got this Joycean example of inner conflict over language from McDermott's (1988) wonderful piece on "Inarticulateness."

8. I expect that a recently published book, *Voices on Voice: Perspectives, Definitions, Inquiry* (Yancey, 1994), will also help me in my work to develop an alternative conception of voice (as well as provide complications, challenges, and inner struggles I could probably do without).

9. See Lensmire (1993) for an alternative conception of teacher response to both following the child and socioanalysis, based on the work of critical pragmatists such as Cherryholmes (1988).

References

Aronowitz, S., & Giroux, H. (1991). *Postmodern education: Politics, culture, and social criticism*. Minneapolis: University of Minnesota Press.

Atwell, N. (1987). *In the middle: Writing, reading, and learning with adolescents*. Portsmouth, NH: Boynton/Cook.

Bakhtin, M. M. (1981). *The dialogic imagination: Four essays*. Austin: University of Texas Press.

Bakhtin, M. M. (1986). *Speech genres and other late essays*. Austin: University of Texas Press.

Berlin, J. (1988). Rhetoric and ideology in the writing class. *College English, 50*(5), 477–94.

Bernstein, R. J. (1988). Pragmatism, pluralism, and the healing of wounds. *American Philosophical Association Proceedings, 63*(3), 5–18.

Bowles, S., & Gintis, H. (1987). *Democracy and capitalism: Property, community, and the contradictions of modern social thought*. New York: Basic Books.

Calkins, L. M. (1986). *The art of teaching writing*. Portsmouth, NH: Heinemann.

Calkins, L. M. (with Harwayne, S.). (1991). *Living between the lines*. Portsmouth, NH: Heinemann.

Cherryholmes, C. (1988). *Power and criticism: Poststructural investigations in education*. New York: Teachers College Press.

Dewey, J. (1980). *The school and society*. Carbondale: Southern Illinois University Press. (Original work published 1899)

Dewey, J. (1983). Human nature and conduct. In J. Boydston (Ed.), *The middle works of John Dewey, 1899–1924* (Vol. 14). Carbondale: Southern Illinois University Press. (Original work published 1922)

Dyson, A. H. (1992). The case of the singing scientist: A performance perspective on the "stages" of school literacy. *Written Communication, 9*(1), 3–47.

Ellsworth, E. (1989). Why doesn't this feel empowering? Working through the repressive myths of critical pedagogy. *Harvard Educational Review, 59*(3), 297–324.

Emerson, C. (1986). The outer word and inner speech: Bakhtin, Vygotsky, and the internalization of language. In G. S. Morson (Ed.), *Bakhtin: Essays and dialogues on his work* (pp. 21–40). Chicago: University of Chicago Press.

Flax, J. (1990). *Thinking fragments: Psychoanalysis, feminism and postmodernism in the contemporary West*. Berkeley: University of California Press.

Florio-Ruane, S. (1991). Instructional conversations in learning to write and learning to teach. In L. Idol & B. Jones (Eds.), *Educational values and cognitive instruction: Implications for reform* (365–86). Hillsdale, NJ: Lawrence Erlbaum.

Freire, P. (1970). *Pedagogy of the oppressed*. New York: Continuum.

Freire, P. (1985). *The politics of education: Culture, power, and liberation*. South Hadley, MA: Bergin & Garvey.

Gilbert, P. (1989a). *Writing, schooling, and deconstruction: From voice to text in the classroom*. London: Routledge.

Gilbert, P. (1989b). Student text as pedagogical text. In S. de Castell, A. Luke, & C. Luke (Eds.), *Language, authority, and criticism: Readings on the school textbook* (pp. 195–202). London: Falmer Press.

Gilbert, P. (1994). Authorizing disadvantage: Authorship and creativity in the language classroom. In B. Stierer & J. Maybin (Eds.), *Language, literacy and learning in educational practice: A reader* (pp. 258–76). Clevedon, UK: Multilingual Matters/Open University.

Giroux, H. (1987). Critical literacy and student experience: Donald Graves' approach to literacy. *Language Arts, 64*(2), 175–81.

Giroux, H. (1988). Literacy and the pedagogy of voice and political empowerment. *Educational Theory, 38*(1), 61–75.

Giroux, H., & McLaren, P. (Eds.). (1989). *Critical pedagogy, the state, and cultural struggle*. Albany: SUNY Press.

Graves, D. (1983). *Writing: Teachers and children at work*. Portsmouth, NH: Heinemann.

Harris, J. (1989). The idea of community in the study of writing. *College Composition and Communication, 40*(1), 11–22.

Joyce, J. (1976). *A portrait of the artist as a young man*. New York: Penguin. (Original work published 1916)

Kamberelis, G., & Scott, K. D. (1992). Other people's voices: The coarticulation of texts and subjectivities. *Linguistics and Education, 4*(3-4), 359–403.

Lensmire, T. (1993). Following the child, socioanalysis and threats to community: Teacher response to children's texts. *Curriculum Inquiry, 23*(3), 265–99.

Lensmire, T. (1994a). *When children write: Critical re-visions of the writing workshop*. New York: Teachers College Press.

Lensmire, T. (1994b). Writing workshop as carnival: Reflections on an alternative learning environment. *Harvard Educational Review, 64*(4), 371–91.

McCarthey, S. (1994). Opportunities and risks of writing from personal experiences. *Language Arts, 71*(3), 182–91.

McDermott, R. (1988). Inarticulateness. In D. Tannen (Ed.), *Linguistics in context: Connecting observation and understanding: Lectures from the 1985 LSA/TESOL and NEH institutes* (pp. 37–67). Norwood, NJ: Ablex.

Murray, D. (1985). *A writer teaches writing* (2nd ed.). Boston: Houghton Mifflin.

O'Connor, T. (1989). Cultural voice and strategies for multicultural education. *Journal of Education, 171*(2), 57–74.

Ritchie, J. (1989). Beginning writers: Diverse voices and individual identity. *College Composition and Communication, 40*(2), 152–74.

Simon, R. (1987). Empowerment as a pedagogy of possibility. *Language Arts, 64*(4), 370–82.

Soliday, M. (1994). Translating self and difference through literacy narratives. *College English, 56*(5), 11–26.

Ulichney, P., & Watson-Gegeo, K. (1989). Interactions and authority: The dominant interpretative framework in writing conferences. *Discourse Processes, 12*, 309–28.

Willinsky, J. (1990). *The new literacy: Redefining reading and writing in the schools*. New York: Routledge.

Yancey, K. B. (Ed.). (1994). *Voices on voice: Perspectives, definitions, inquiry*. Urbana, IL: National Council of Teachers of English.

Chapter Seven

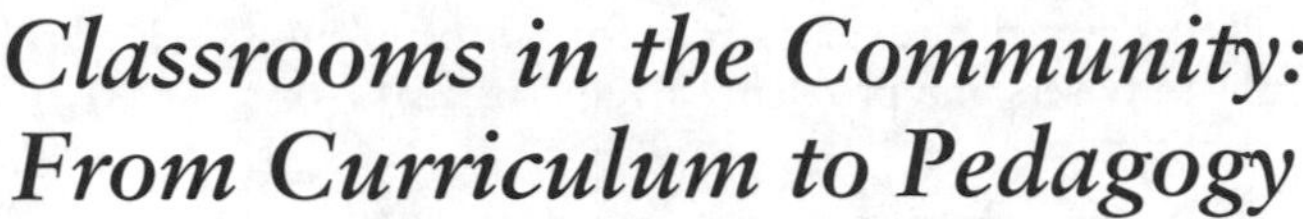

Classrooms in the Community: From Curriculum to Pedagogy

Timothy Shannon
Janesville Central School District, Janesville, California

Patrick Shannon
Penn State University

Progressive educators have been vocal during recent debates about literacy education curricula in the United States. In response to twelve years of federal and corporate assaults on schools and teachers, progressives have criticized the rhetoric of "what works" (Bennett, 1986) and "what every American needs to know" (Hirsch, 1988) and declared sound principles for curriculum development and practice. Rather than algorithms for how to teach regardless of content or context (Hunter, 1982) or a course of study based on selected readings of European experience (Bloom, 1987), progressives have offered risk taking, reflection, and collaboration as the basis for teacher-developed curricula in classrooms and schools. And, apparently, important constituencies have listened. Professional organizations (e.g., the National Council of Teachers of English [NCTE]), state departments of education (e.g., Pennsylvania), and thousands of individual classroom teachers have produced guides and practices to facilitate the realization of what has come to be known as *curriculum as inquiry*.

Defined as the self-selection of questions and the struggle for answers, inquiry is said to drive learning, teaching, and curriculum development. Short and Burke (1991) explain:

This chapter was written in 1994 when Timothy Shannon was a graduate student at Penn State University.

> If a curriculum is truly learning centered, then that curriculum is based on inquiry and the search for questions that matter to us, whether we are adults or children. . . . We learn to search for problems as well as explanations for our problems. We are both problem posers and problem solvers. (p. 55)

Such a curriculum requires active participation from students and teachers; opportunities for students to construct reality through play, the arts, and language; support for students' and teachers' risk taking; a print-rich environment; and frequent observation of good role models:

> Teachers should plan a reading curriculum which is broad enough to accommodate every student's growth, flexible enough to adapt to individual and cultural characteristics of pupils, specific enough to assure growth in language and thinking, and supportive enough to guarantee student success. (Harste, 1989, p. 49)

To accomplish this, progressive educators offer opportunities for students to continue their natural learning processes while at school. Such invitations to inquire affirm students' motivation to learn, helping them to develop a generative habit of identifying and addressing new questions, and providing a sense of empowerment that assures students they have the ability and the right to use that habit. Together as curriculum inquirers, teachers and students form a community of learners that is prepared to support its members as they push past their current understandings of themselves and their experiences. Together, they prepare for future demands by learning how to make sense of their current experiences and lives. "The curriculum, then, must always be connected to as well as go forward from students' life experiences," according to Short and Burke (1991, p. 35). (Thus, "What has already happened to us is our invitation to the future" (p. 34).

Curriculum as inquiry, then, is both a statement of process (ask questions, take risks, ask more questions, etc.) and a product (a vision of the present and the future). Through it, progressive educators attempt to consider what types of individuals they hope to live and work with in the classroom now and later in society. "Our hope is that when children leave elementary school, they will be well on their way to full participation as citizens" (Lloyd-Jones & Lunsford, 1989, p. 3). Advocates of curriculum as inquiry assume a free market of ideas in which all participants feel equally empowered to inquire into whatever questions each may find most pressing. Such an assumption, however, requires progressives to separate their classrooms from the politics and problems of everyday life in a way reminiscent of Rousseau's negative education (Rousseau, 1762/1972). Like young Emile, students in progressive classrooms are to be protected from the temptations and threats of a social life in their community beyond the classroom door. But this supposed separation is artificial at best and mythical at worst. Regardless of the teacher's theoretical perspective, classrooms exist in a larger social context and are subject to the same contradictions and political issues as the rest of society.

A negative education—one that seeks to shelter students from social controversy until they develop sufficient self-love to weather social temptation—is impossible because students bring with them to school the politically and socially charged voices of their communities and social groups. Even under the direction of the most remarkable educators, the classroom is unlikely to become a free market of inquiry because the discourses students and teachers bring to school are inscribed with differing amounts of cultural and economic capital, privileging some and silencing others. Without careful analyses of these differences and how they might affect student and teacher inquiry, progressives employing curriculum as inquiry are likely to reproduce a stratified community in and out of the classroom. This is what Lisa Delpit (1988) has struggled to articulate. Unless progressive educators are willing to engage the larger social context of their classroom and curriculum, the democracy they seek is impossible on anything more than a limited and artificial scale.

A step toward this analysis can be facilitated by including pedagogy when thinking about inquiry and empowerment. Pedagogy is a view of how people within a specific context articulate a particular vision of what knowledge is of most value, what it means to know something, and how we might construct representations of ourselves, others, and our physical and social environment (Simon, 1992). Pedagogy requires an integration of particular curricular content and design, strategies, and techniques, and a time and space to practice those strategies, techniques, and evaluative purposes and methods: "In other words, talk about pedagogy is simultaneously talk about the details of what students and others might do together and the cultural politics such practices support. To propose a pedagogy is to propose a political vision" (Simon, 1992, p. 140).

If progressive educators seek a pedagogy of inquiry and empowerment, then they must articulate explicitly their political vision as well as their concerns for curricula and practice. To do so, they must elaborate on what they mean by inquiry and empowerment in society, not just the classroom. Inquiry means more than posing and solving problems: it means having an inquisitive nature. Inquirers are skeptical about the world as it is presented to them. They doubt their own and others' current knowledge and understanding of any topic and seek to uncover more new information to help them understand why things are the way they are. At times this skepticism may seem overly critical as students inquire about rules, mores, or traditions that even few adults can explain. But inquirers are also hopeful as well as critical. If they were not hopeful about a better understanding and a better future, then why ask questions at all? If we cannot ameliorate our present circumstances, then what's the point of inquiry?

Empowerment means to give, permit, or enable some ability or right to someone or somebodies. It assumes unequal power relationships among members within some social organization—after all, one "permits" others to do something—and it implies some structure which protects this differential power. To value empowerment, then, is to take the side of the powerless because the structure of privilege is unwarranted or unjust. When combined with inquiry, empowerment becomes a critical act in identifying and resisting the unequal and unjust past and present, and a hopeful act in bringing about a more equal and just future. Working toward empowerment and inquiry is more than establishing a free market of ideas or ensuring equal opportunity among classmates to inquire. Rather, empowerment and inquiry require progressives to question the status quo and to advocate for the powerless in school and society.

Since students and teachers bring the inequalities of our society and their communities with them to class, a progressive pedagogy of inquiry and empowerment must not restrict itself to classroom relations. Instead, progressive educators must push past the classroom and school doors to inquire about the community which surrounds and informs them. Most progressives acknowledge this need to reach out:

> Effective programs of change work under the assumption that curriculum and curriculum development take and are enhanced by partnership. Joint school and university research projects that extend over time and community programs such as Literacy Day, Reading in the Mall, Young Authors Conferences and the like, are signs that this assumption is being practiced. (Harste, 1989, p. 55)

Although these programs may be a start toward pedagogies of inquiry and empowerment, they lack a political imagination sufficient to help progressives realize their hopes for the future. Fortunately, we have many theoretical and practical examples from the last one hundred years to stimulate progressive imaginations and actions (Shannon, 1990).

Pedagogies of Inquiry and Empowerment

> We are, then, concerned in our curriculum to make sure that it affords the kind of experiences and the kind of activities which will help children to grow normally and naturally. The old-line pedagogue was continually asking, What must a child know, what knowledge is of most worth? We ask instead, What should a child be like, what ways of acting and what habits of response are most worth while? But we do not consider the child alone, for naturally the individual is part of a larger group and this group part of a wider community. Our school is neither child-centered nor society-centered. Rather we take the child as he is and where he is, try to understand him, and then seek to help him understand the kind of world in which he lives and the part he is to play in it. (De Lima, 1942, p. 17)

In this description of the work at the Little Red Schoolhouse, Agnes De Lima foreshadows the current concern about pedagogy. Deeply embedded in the philosophy and activities of the progressive education movement, she explains the curricular thinking and practice in the struggle for curricular innovation and change that began in earnest with John Dewey and the teachers at the Laboratory School in Chicago and has never ended.

Dewey believed in schools driven by philosophy rather than by intellectual abstractions, by social and emotional experiences that tested philosophy pragmatically. The philosophy that drove the Laboratory School was an attempt to understand the everyday social experiences students brought to the classroom and to develop hypotheses for appropriate curricular activities that were testable against social events. The curriculum, then, became the scrutiny and scientific evaluation of all aspects of human life. Recognizing that "life" did not treat everyone equally, Dewey set the school's first priority—to work toward equality and justice in school and community: "Until there is something like economic security and economic democracy, aesthetic, intellectual, and social concern will be subordinated to an exploitation by the owning class which carries with it the commercialization of culture" (Dewey, 1928, p. 270).

Schooling, then, was to be the institution through which social knowledge, memory, thought, and habit could be developed in order to reach democratic ideals. Because the ideals were to be achieved through individuals' experiences, the task of educators was to develop within students scientific thinking and malleable habits that would allow them to make sense of the current social order and to remake school and community life according to these ideals. In this way, Dewey's educational theory was really a political theory.

In the Laboratory School, students, teachers, and parents planned school programs and curricula together in order "to harmonize" the children's interests and lives with adult ends and values. Throughout its history, the school was community centered rather than child centered (Dewey, 1934). The projects always began with the students' interests, and the object of each activity was to connect those interests with the world outside the home and school and to consider the academic, moral, and civic principles extending from those activities. The teacher's role was to facilitate the activities and to recognize when the students were ready to take the next step intellectually or socially.

For example, several eight-year-olds decided to study weaving as a means to connect school and community. The students built looms, interviewed immigrant weavers in the surrounding community, and began to consult books to determine how weaving was conducted in different parts of the United States and the world. This domestic work also led to the guided activity of exploration of different methods of spinning and weaving in the American colonial period: "They learned that the invention of machines had brought many improved ways of living, had changed the organization pattern of many industries, and had left many industrial and social problems for later generations to solve" (Mayhew & Edwards, 1936, p. 194). Students found enjoyment and experienced physical development in the activity while they applied principles of physics, literacy, history, geography, mathematics, and art, all as extensions of domestic science. They also examined social relations through collective work and inquiry:

> The children realized somewhat the position of the spinner and weaver, the beginnings of organization in several branches of the industry, the misunderstanding of the value of machines and the benefit of machine work to the community, and the riots which followed any invention replacing hand-work. (Mayhew & Edwards, 1936, p. 194)

Albion Small, a colleague of Dewey's, described the scope of Dewey's and all teachers' work during an address to the National Education Association in 1896:

> Educators shall not rate themselves as leaders of children, but as makers of society. Sociology knows no means for the amelioration or reform of society more radical than those of which teachers hold the leverage. . . . [When teachers] begin to recognize and accept their social function, rather than thinking of themselves merely as providing tonics for various kinds of mental impotence . . . they will begin to fulfill their vital role in making a better future (qtd. in Kliebard, 1986, p. 184)

William Kilpatrick (1918) sought to popularize Small's and Dewey's ideas through a more accessible, systematic means of curriculum development. To do so, he sought to make pedagogical thought less explicitly political but nonetheless based on student inquiry. His solution, called the "project method," was based on four interrelated ideas:

> 1. *The pupils must propose what they do.* The pupils choose the next "project" they are to work on.
>
> 2. *Actual learning is never single.* Learning in addition to the matter at hand has many concomitant learnings perhaps building attitudes toward various other life interests involved in what is going on.
>
> 3. *All learning encouraged by the school is so encouraged because it is needed here and now in order to carry on better the enterprise now under way.* When the activity (project) is first chosen, the learning and subject matter are henceforth subordinate to it. If, for example, arithmetic or history were needed for the better doing of an enterprise under way, the children learned then and there exactly what was so needed for that specific purpose.
>
> 4. *The curriculum is a series of guided experiences so related that what is learned in one serves to elevate and enrich the subsequent stream of experience.* The principle of activity leading to further activity. (qtd. in Collings, 1923, pp. 18–20)

Following Dewey's example, Collings sought to test Kilpatrick's philosophy in an experiment conducted in three rural public schools in McDonald County, Missouri, from 1918 to 1921. The experimental schools were organized around conversation in which students could raise points and questions vital to them and could benefit from their peers' opinions and suggestions. These conversations provided students with a forum to express, reconsider, and reformulate their understandings and misconceptions about their community and academic work. That is, students talked their way to more sophisticated understandings of themselves, their relationships with others, and the social structures and practices of their communities. Through these conversations, curricula were generated, experienced, and evaluated, while students learned to ask and seek answers to their own questions (Collings, 1923).

An example of a project proposed by members of the intermediate group (ages nine to twelve) was an investigation of a repeated outbreak of typhoid at a classmate's house. After a visit to the classmate's home, significant "book work," and consultation with experts at a regional university, the class built a flycatcher, wrote a letter apprising the classmate's father of ways to prevent reinfection, and surveyed the community about the prevalence of other communicable diseases. The class's advice solved the family's problem, and they presented the results of their survey at a parents' meeting, prompting the establishment of a community health care service (Collings, 1923, p. 54). Through this and other projects, these students and their teachers brought the community directly into the classroom and the classroom into the community. And the students fared very well in later comparisons on standardized tests.

Caroline Pratt (1924) argued that play is the primary means through which young children make sense of their social experience and bring their community to school. In the City and Country School, play was the catalyst for investigation and further study. During outings from the classroom, students were encouraged to notice the events, objects, and interactions of their community:

> They have been engaged in the whole thing without much particularizing. Now they become interested in the details. What part of the engine makes the whistle? what makes the movement? who pulls the throttle? Children are not interested in these as facts, but as facts to be used in play; or it would be more correct to say that what the information does to the play is to keep it going and help it to organize as a whole, to raise new inquiries, and above all to offer opportunities for new relationships. (p. 3)

For example, the "Sevens" [seven-year-olds] at the City and Country School developed a play city which was left intact and worked with throughout the year. During this year, these young students dealt with many of the same issues as their parents:

> There was also a great deal of work to be done in cleaning the yard and the cement river bed. . . . Douglas and Roger kept on steadily with their sweeping of the cement river bed. They said, "We should be paid for this by the City." Jenny, overhearing them, answered, "We must have taxes." (Pratt, 1924, pp. 236–37)

In a passionate speech to the Progressive Education Society in 1932, George Counts asked educators to reinstate explicit politics in their work. He criticized members who

> are rather insensitive to the accepted forms of social injustice, who are content to play the role of interested spectator in the drama of human history, who refuse to see reality in its harsher and more disagreeable forms, and who, in the day of severe trial, will follow the lead of the most powerful and respectable forces in society, and at the same time, find good reasons for so doing. (Counts, 1932, p. 259)

Thinking that politics would not find its way into classrooms without appropriate curriculum materials, Harold Rugg created some success in schools with large-scale adoption of his overtly political social studies textbooks. Beginning in 1926, Harold and his brother Earle produced two editions of an elementary and secondary social studies text series. The textbooks were originally in pamphlet form to allow for frequent, inexpensive updating and offered an activity format (Nelson, 1978). Rugg proposed that the conventional subject matter be swept away by a new curriculum, which would be developed strictly on the criterion of desired social outcome. The Ruggs felt that their social science curriculum should be based on "dealing with the diversity of life among peoples of the earth; crucial facts in one's own community; the problems of human migration, interdependent civilizations, various governments and issues in modern life" (Rugg, 1926, p. 7). The diversity of the subject matter as well as the fusing of all the disciplines of the social sciences made these textbooks unique and nationally appealing. Over 2.5 million were used in schools until 1941 (Shannon, 1990).

Working in a homestead community built with federal funds to attract families out of the hills during the Great Depression, Elsie Clapp had one mission in mind: she hoped to create a public school in Arthurdale, West Virginia, that would bring the entire community into the classroom in order to create a reciprocal teaching relationship between children and adults. Ethel Carlisle was the first-grade teacher at Arthurdale School at the time. She wrote in her diary:

> *September 29, 1934.* This morning we discussed the kind of potatoes grown here. They saw trucks taking bags of potatoes that had been dug, so they were eager to go to the patch. It was down at the new school site, and was the community potato patch.
>
> Down at the potato patch, the children immediately began to pick up potatoes and put them in a bag. Fern's father was working there and he isn't at all well, so he was very grateful for their help and sat down and rested for a few minutes. There was a team of horses there, too, which pleased the children. Several of the children's fathers were there and they were eager to answer any questions. (qtd. in Clapp, 1940, p. 133)

Thus, when the community could not come into the classroom, the classroom went into the community. The adults taught their children about life and work, and the children taught many of their parents more about academic subjects and literacy. In this small rural area, the school was the center of the community.

Although elementary school teachers attempted to use the community as their curriculum, secondary schools remained bastions of the university-dominated, discipline-oriented, or scientifically processed, socially efficient curriculum. In 1932 the Progressive Education Association began an experiment in thirty high schools with the assurance from over three hundred colleges that they would waive traditional entrance criteria. These high schools made modest to dramatic changes in their curricula. In the Denver high schools:

> With the growing interest toward giving young people an opportunity to supplement their school experiences with firsthand knowledge of the community, closer understandings are sought

> between those who work in the schools and the men and women who carry forward the life of the city as a whole. Factories, retail stores, newspaper plants, public service companies, and others are making it possible for young people to study the productive life of the city. Federal, state and municipal institutions, such as the Denver Water Works, the State Legislature, law courts, the city jail, and the Colorado General Hospital are open to visitors from the schools. (*Thirty Schools,* 1942, pp. 148–49)

Eight years later, after one group of students had graduated from college, the experimental results suggested that students from the progressive high schools were better college students than their counterparts from traditional high schools (Chamberlin et al., 1942).

Today, views of possible relationships between schools and communities are often called critical pedagogies. Although previous advocates often conducted too simplistic analyses of social issues, modern

> reconceptualized reconstructionism would aim at the realization of the basic human interest in practical competence and the sociocultural conditions necessary for praxis. . . . Through a pedagogy of hope in the face of the very formidable barriers to critical analysis, we can gain a sense of human interests. (Stanley, 1992, p. 221)

To previous concerns about social class, critical pedagogists add sensitivity to issues of race, linguistic differences, gender, and culture:

> There is a need for the continued development of theory and research that emphasizes social justice and emancipation. Such theory must, however, see race, gender, and class as equally important and as enduring forms of oppression that are interrelated but not reducible to one form. (Sleeter & Grant, 1988, p. 145)

Critical pedagogists ask teachers to develop a curriculum which does more than simply further legitimate shared assumptions, agreed on proprieties, or established convention, and to recognize that the foundation for all human agency as well as teaching is steeped in a commitment to the possibilities of human life and freedom. Teachers must recognize the political nature of their jobs when deciding what knowledge is of most value, who is considered knowledgeable, and how teachers' decisions and actions can create a democratic community built on a commitment to equality and justice (McLaren, 1989).

Linda Christensen (1991) teaches English at Jefferson High School in Portland. In *Rethinking Columbus*, a teacher resource for critical pedagogy, she explains her efforts to advance the natural inquiry of children:

> To help Justine and her classmates dismantle those old values and reconstruct more just ones, I have two goals when we study children's culture: first, to critique portrayals of hierarchy and inequality; second, to enlist students in imagining a better world, characterized by respect and equality. (Christensen, 1991, p. 54)

Christensen's class has written several analyses of cartoons and submitted their work to the PTA as a report: "Importantly, students saw themselves as actors in the world; they were fueled by the opportunity to convince some parents of the long-lasting effects cartoons impose on their children or to enlighten their peers about the roots of some of their insecurities" (Christensen, 1991, p. 55).

Jesse Goodman has worked with the teachers of Harmony School in Bloomington, Indiana, to create a curriculum he calls critical democracy. He claims that today's schoolchildren demonstrate "personal freedom" through antisocial, egotistical posturing because our cultural values favor the individual and self-development. Goodman argues that in democratic schools, students' individuality can grow only within a community structure in which restrictions and expectations are placed on the individual by the community. Although teachers retain their authority in these schools, there can be no authoritarianism if teachers and students are to make human and academic connections. With this concept as the driving force, cultural differences are recognized as a strength of democratic pedagogy, and a shared language of cooperation develops to direct all learning. Goodman and the teachers at Harmony believe students' inquiries should be collaborative efforts and that criticism can be turned into possibility for a truly democratic future:

> Collective learning is an essential characteristic of a connectionist curriculum. Resisting and offering alternatives to the competitiveness in our schools and society is crucial for establishing critical democracy. Although it is essential that students' sense of uniqueness and creativity are preserved, engaging children in cooperative activities and, more important, providing them with a genuine sense of shared learning are a necessary foundation for the type of education envisioned. (Goodman, 1992, p. 141)

Discussing his national survey of progressive schools and teachers, George Wood (1992) explains that by having students do "real things," schools can develop students' sense of agency. They can learn to make a difference. The classrooms described in *Schools That Work* reach well beyond the classroom door. Wood chronicles the curriculum, the life, and the activities of teachers and students who are trying not only to understand, but also to make a difference in their communities. For example, in Winchester, New Hampshire:

> the faculty at Thayer have decided to challenge the conventional ways of thinking about preparing students for the world after school. Rather than seeing their mission as primarily vocational, preparing kids for either college or a job, they see their work as primarily civic, preparing kids to make a contribution to the world around them. They believe the best way to do this is to engage students in exploring that world while they are in school, not only with an eye toward the curriculum or services, but with a focus on who they will become as members of the community. (Wood, 1992, p. 221)

An Invitation to Act

Pedagogies of inquiry and empowerment ask teachers to recognize and act on the power that lies in their hands to encourage social betterment. Such pedagogies require theories of learning, teaching, and curriculum which value and develop not only students' cultures and intellects, but also their civic leadership and social agency. Besides theory, pedagogies of inquiry and empowerment require appropriate action that places students and teachers squarely in the specificity of the communities which surround their schools, as preparation for later action in larger social units. To understand themselves and their communities, teachers and students venture from the classroom to investigate the issues they find most interesting, worthwhile, or pressing. At times they bring their understandings of those issues and the community back into their classroom through role-play and curricular materials in order to examine their usefulness for them. These adventures require that teachers and students take seriously the social wonders and problems that pervade every community and that they work diligently to challenge those aspects which impede the social development and political rights of all or some community members.

The examples we offer from our past and present are both exhilarating and paralyzing. On the one hand, they suggest that many educators practice pedagogies of inquiry and empowerment that take the community as the curriculum. Yet because some of these examples seem distant from teachers' everyday concerns, they can inhibit us from taking that first step toward broadening curriculum into pedagogy. Progressive educators must take that step, however, if we value inquiry, empowerment, and democracy. And perhaps a personal example will prove the best.

Feather Falls School is a small rural public school in northern California where Tim was superintendent, principal, and intermediate and junior high teacher simultaneously for eleven years. It is safe to say that the town would not exist without the school and that the school could not function without the direct assistance of the townspeople. They have a truly symbiotic relationship. For example, the town's recycling program began when Judy, the primary grade teacher and now the superintendent, asked her students to bring their recyclable waste to school on Mondays so she could drive it down the mountain to the recycling center. Each spring, the upper-level students walk "the road" (the only road to anywhere) to pick up garbage, cans, paper, and car parts in order to make the drive up to Feather Falls as aesthetically pleasing as possible. They bring the waste to the school, where Bob, the maintenance person, takes it to the recycling center.

The school attempts to teach compassion and civic responsibility through example. Nancy, the school secretary, has the staff and students assemble Thanksgiving and Christmas baskets each year for families who need them. The volunteers for the fire department and the staff of the health center help identify the needy and distribute the baskets. When the Shasta Fire of 1992 burned the school library and many houses in a neighboring town, Feather Falls students brought food, clothing, books, and "something that someone their age would like" to that community. In remembering the fire of 1987 that nearly burned Feather Falls, these students learn early that communities must look out for each other.

Because the school is literally and figuratively the center of the community, many organizations share the facilities with the students. Such use takes its toll on the buildings and the grounds, but the budget for repairs is low. This past spring break, Eileen, the school librarian, her husband, Steve, and the new upper-division teacher, Galen, resurfaced the basketball court and painted new lines to surprise the basketball team, the Skyhawks, and to prepare for the "end of the year community lunch," which Joyce, the school cook, prepares every year for the entire town. It's held on the basketball court—weather permitting.

Each year, the older students take a camping trip to the Pacific Ocean because many of them have never seen it before. The members of the school board and the community fund the trip privately, and the entire town comes alive with conversation when camp-out time approaches. Galen; Bill, the bus driver; Cooky, LaDonna, and Ginger, classroom aides; and Louise, the special needs teacher, leave their homes and families for a week to accompany the students on this annual adventure. They go to a different place every year to experience new things. Days are spent tidepooling, hiking, exploring the coastal mountains, and body surfing in the Pacific. More than one adult has overheard a student claim that this is the most memorable time he or she had at school; it broadens their conceptions of community to include society.

Together, the faculty, staff, students, and adults of Feather Falls have built a humane community in and out of school. The students have become concerned about the millpond in town. They have organized an action committee to test the toxicity of the water and posed questions about the cleanup. They have questioned the local lumber company about clear-cutting the forests which surround their school, and developed strategies to avoid clear-cutting and yet still continue to be able to remove the timber for lumber. The lumber company has stopped clear-cutting and left smaller trees to begin reforestation. Parents who work for the company are proud of the students' work.

The students, teachers, and community members, in this and the examples offered earlier, are attempting to develop pedagogies of inquiry and empowerment in the hope that together we can all build a more humane society. Inquiry in school is the catalyst for empowerment and hope, as well as offering the possibility of student contribution to a democratic society. This work in the specificity of a particular community is our best chance to prepare students for a larger social context that crosses borders of nations, races, and genders. Inquiry begins the process that results in broader understanding of the possibility of one humane society.

References

Bennett, W. (1986). *What works: Research about teaching and learning*. Washington, DC: U.S. Department of Education.

Bloom, A. (1987). *The closing of the American mind: How higher education has failed democracy and impoverished the soul of today's students*. New York: Simon & Schuster.

Chamberlin, D., Chamberlin, E., Drought, N., & Scott, W. (Eds.). (1942). *Did they succeed in college? The follow-up study of the graduates of the thirty schools*. New York: Harper and Brothers.

Christensen, L. (1991). Unlearning the myths that bind us. In B. Bigelow, B. Miner, & B. Peterson, (Eds.), *Rethinking Columbus* (pp. 56–59). Milwaukee, WI: Rethinking Schools.

Clapp, E. (1940). *Community schools in action*. New York: Viking.

Collings, E. (1923). *An experiment with a project curriculum*. New York: Macmillan.

Counts, G. S. (1932). Dare progressive education be progressive? *Progressive Education, 9*, 257–63.

De Lima, A. (1942). *The little red school house.* New York: Macmillan.

Delpit, L. (1988). The silenced dialogue: Power and pedagogy in educating other people's children. *Harvard Educational Review, 58,* 280–98.

Dewey, J. (1928). The house divided against itself. *New Republic, 56,* 268–70.

Dewey, J. (1934). *Education and the social order.* New York: League for Industrial Democracy.

Goodman, J. (1992). *Elementary schooling for critical democracy.* Albany, NY: SUNY Press.

Harste, J. (1989). *New policy guidelines for reading: Connecting research and practice.* Urbana, IL: National Council of Teachers of English.

Hirsch, E. D. (1988). *Cultural literacy: What every American needs to know.* New York: Vintage Books.

Hunter, M. (1982). *Mastery teaching.* El Segundo, CA: TIP Publications.

Kilpatrick, W. (1918). The project method. *Teachers College Record, 19,* 319–35.

Kliebard, H. M. (1986). *The struggle for the American curriculum 1893–1958.* Boston: Routledge & Kegan Paul.

Lloyd-Jones R., & Lunsford, A. (1989). *The English coalition conference: Democracy through language.* Urbana, IL: National Council of Teachers of English/New York: Modern Language Association.

Mayhew, K., & Edwards, A. (1936). *The Dewey school: The Laboratory School of the University of Chicago, 1896–1903.* New York: Appleton-Century.

McLaren, P. (1989). *Life in schools: An introduction to critical pedagogy in the foundations of education.* New York: Longman.

Nelson, M. R. (1978). Rugg on Rugg: His theories and his curriculum. *Curriculum Inquiry, 8*(2), 119–32.

Pratt, C. (Ed.). (1924). *Experimental practice in the city and country school.* New York: E. P. Dutton.

Rousseau, J. J. (1972). *Emile, or Treatise on education.* W. Payne (Trans). London: Everyman's Library. (Original work published 1762)

Rugg, H. O. (Ed.). (1926). *The foundations of curriculum-making: Part 2. The foundations and technique of curriculum-construction. Twenty-sixth yearbook of the National Society for the Study of Education*. Bloomington, IL: Public School Publishing.

Shannon, P. (1990). *The struggle to continue: Progressive reading instruction in the United States*. Portsmouth, NH: Heinemann.

Short, K., & Burke, C. (1991). *Creating curriculum: Teachers and students as a community of learners*. Portsmouth, NH: Heinemann.

Simon, R. (1992). Empowerment as a pedagogy of possibility. In P. Shannon (Ed.), *Becoming political: Readings and writings in literacy education* (pp. 139–51). Portsmouth, NH: Heinemann.

Sleeter, C. S., & Grant, C. A. (1988). A rationale for integrating race, gender, and social class. In L. Weis (Ed.), *Class, race, and gender in American education* (pp. 87–103). Albany, NY: SUNY Press.

Stanley, W. B. (1992). *Curriculum for utopia: Social reconstructionism and critical pedagogy in the postmodern era*. Albany, NY: SUNY Press.

Thirty schools tell their story. (1942). New York: Harper & Brothers.

Wood, G. H. (1992). *Schools that work: America's most innovative public education programs*. New York: Plume Books.

"I Knew That Already": How Children's Books Limit Inquiry

Jennifer O'Brien
University of South Australia

Anthea's Text

> Kate Petty wanted me to know Cleopatra was an Egyptian queen. I already knew that. She fell in love with Mark Antony who died in a battle. Here is the story: Cleopatra was an Indian queen who fell in love with Mark Anthony. Mark died in a battle. So one night when everyone was sleeping she got out of bed and got one of the cobras and put [it] against her chest. The cobra bit her. She died. Anthea, 7

In this piece of writing, seven-year-old Anthea takes an inquiry approach to *My First Book of Knowledge*, a general knowledge text produced specifically for young readers (Petty, 1990). She first focuses on the relationship between herself as a young reader and the information offered by the text: "I already knew that." She then goes on to construct an account of the Antony and Cleopatra story. In writing about the text, she draws on class discussions and written activities I had introduced during regular shared book sessions. When we read together from a shared text (perhaps an enlarged print "big book," or a narrative, or a poetry book, or an informational school text), I encourage students to make *critical readings* of the texts.

Critical Text Inquiry

A critical orientation is based on an understanding that all texts work to produce authority relations between themselves and their readers. Critical readers analyze the work the text does, making the text an object of inquiry. When working with informational texts written especially for five- to eight-year-olds, I explore the idea that factual books do more than simply provide information. Texts frequently fail to take young readers seriously as researchers and knowers, positioning them instead as having little capacity to engage in inquiry and as having little or no prior knowledge of the subject. In other words, the authority to know about a topic and to construct a particular version of it for young readers is claimed by the text. In this chapter, I demonstrate how I have introduced a pedagogy that encourages students to conduct a critical inquiry into texts written for them.

Despite their central role in defining students' reading and research practices, texts have not themselves been objects of critical classroom inquiry. How they work to produce students as specific kinds of readers and inquirers has only recently been considered a suitable topic for classroom investigation (Baker & Freebody, 1989; Luke, 1993; Gilbert, 1989; Freebody, 1993). Students have been encouraged to question some aspects of informational texts: Is this text up to date? Does it have an index, table of contents, page numbers, appropriate terminology and illustrations? What are the credentials of the writers? Such questions, though important to readers and researchers, fall far short of any sort of critical inquiry. They fail to challenge the text's claims to be taken for granted as a source of information, not just about the topic but also about the child reader.

Inquiry approaches in schools are likely to be limited to the sorts of questions modelled by teachers and answered by textbooks. They are likely to be tied to topics deemed "suitable" for student investigation and to be restricted by the kind of child inquirer produced by school informational texts (for more on this topic, see Barbara Comber's essay in Chapter 5 of this volume, as well as Robyn Jenkin's essay in Chapter 11).

Comber argues for the politicization of the topics into which students conduct their inquiries. It is essential, she claims, that teachers show students how to ask "prior" questions about inquiry topics, questions which probe how people come to know why certain kinds of knowledge are more important than others, and whether there are different versions of knowledge on this topic.

I claim, in addition, that teachers need to introduce students to a politicized use of the texts they consult in the course of inquiry—that they need to be introduced to the position that far from being neutral, innocent sources of information, texts written for them offer selected, partial versions of the social, physical, and political world. I swing the spotlight away from inquiry into topics based on the physical and social worlds outside the classroom and turn it instead onto questions and activities designed to make classroom informational texts themselves into a topic for student inquiry. I refer to this orientation as "critical text inquiry."

I have chosen to demonstrate critical text inquiry using episodes revolving around three different kinds of factual texts written especially for young students:

- *My First Book of Knowledge* (Petty, 1990), a general knowledge text written for reading at home rather than at school.
- *Amazing Landforms* (Brian, 1992), an enlarged print informational "big book" designed for classroom inquiry approaches.
- *Sunshine Books: Science* (1992), a series of short books written to accompany a school science course for five- to eight-year-olds.

These three factual text types are likely to be encountered by young readers at home or at school.

How Do Texts Position Readers?

I encourage students to bring readily available books such as *My First Book of Knowledge* from home so that they can be included in regular language lessons. Texts like this may not be commonly found at school, but they are often an important part of children's leisure reading as well as a source of information for research conducted outside school. Like all other texts, they position readers in particular ways.

Writers, illustrators, and publishers of children's books select from available knowledge to produce versions of the physical and social world designed for children's consumption. Text features—such as linguistic forms and the categorization, description, placement, illustration, and layout of the concepts and knowledge selected as suited to young readers—produce particular kinds of relationships between text and reader, and produce specific kinds of child readers and child inquirers. School texts and the discourses surrounding texts in classrooms together construct relationships in which students' knowledge is subordinate to text knowledge (Baker & Freebody, 1989). Students are positioned by school texts and by the inquiry practices of teachers to take up specially constructed views of the world and of themselves as readers, as researchers, and as knowers.

My usual practice with classroom texts is to implement a pedagogy which makes it possible for students to change their relationship with texts. I frame questions and activities so that students can inquire into a particular topic using the texts I read in shared book sessions. At the same time, I show students how to challenge the way they are treated as readers, inquirers, and knowers by these books.

Using the Text as a Source of Information

When we first looked at *My First Book of Knowledge,* I guided students with suggestions about what to look for: "Let's see if these drawings on the cover give you an idea of the topics covered in the book"; "Let's read the list of contents together and you can choose a section that you'd like me to read aloud"; "Talk about the drawings. Do they illustrate information in the printed text? Are they related to the printed text as far as you can tell? Do they provide extra information?"

I led them through activities designed to demonstrate a metalanguage for the ways informational texts are organized: "Read out the main heading of this section: Find the sub-headings and read them aloud." Other activities encouraged students to listen to and retell information couched in book language: "Ask some questions about how people lived in ancient Egypt and we'll listen for the answers"; "Tell the person you're sitting next to one piece of interesting information from that paragraph"; "Tell the person you're sitting next to one thing you heard that you didn't know"; "Tell the person you're sitting next to some information that interested you." Students identified text features, listened for the answers the text provided to their questions, interpreted the text, and retold remembered facts.

Questions and activities such as these make it possible for students to use the text as a source of information but not to consider the text itself as a topic for inquiry. These questions and activities position students to accept the text's authoritative voice. Often inquiry stops here. As I argued earlier, teachers need to frame questions and activities that position students to be critical readers of their texts, to challenge the limitations to inquiry that are frequently constructed by children's factual texts.

Challenging the Text's Position of Authority

Next, I encouraged students to investigate the roles of writer, illustrator, and publisher in producing a children's factual text and to contribute their own knowledge to the discussion of the topic. When adults produce factual books for children, they have ideas about what children should know, based on presumptions about things like age, gender, life experience, and authority relations. In my talk about *My First Book of Knowledge,* I drew students' attention to the central role these people play in defining and limiting student knowledge in this way: "I notice that the writer's name is on the cover. I wonder what Kate Petty and the other people who produced this book decided to put in this book for you to read about?"

In this early stage of their experience as inquirers into texts, student talk was limited to statements that began, "I notice that Kate Petty thinks we should read about . . . ." While this inquiry went no further at this time, the talk I initiated challenged the usual practice of taking for granted the content of children's books.

Illustrations play an especially important part in limiting or extending how children operate as researchers. On this occasion, I started with a conventional inquiry into the use of cover drawings as a guide to the contents: "Let's find out if these drawings on the cover are meant to give you an idea of the topics included in the book." Following this question, the inquiry took a critical turn. One drawing was so poorly executed that students were misled about one of the topics. An illustration purporting to be a fan but actually looking very much like pink fairy floss (cotton candy) became a topic of discussion. I then framed an investigation into how the text positioned young readers: "The people who have produced this book don't seem to care whether or not they give young readers accurate information about the contents of the book. Let's look out for other examples of not taking the trouble to get things right for young readers." Even though students found no other examples of misleading drawings, I had given them permission to be critical not only of illustrations, but also of the assumption on the part of the text producers that misleading drawings were appropriate for a children's factual text. Later in the lesson, Nicole's written response drew on this brief inquiry: "Kate Petty made us think the fan looks like fairy floss but it is really a fan."

Teacher talk plays an important role in challenging instructional practices that ignore children's knowledge of a topic in the face of textual authority. When students selected ancient Egypt as one of the topics they wanted to follow in *My First Book of Knowledge*, I invited them to add what they already knew about this topic to what the book told them. This move produced extended contributions. Anthea fleshed out the brief reference to Cleopatra and explained how cats were mummified. When Ben told us in some detail about his mother's interest in the special properties of pyramids, I explained that that was a different kind of information, not included in this book.

At the same time that I encouraged students to consider the role of text producers in defining what they should know and how this knowledge should be presented, I authorized students to add other kinds of information. An investigation like this is only a start, however. A broader inquiry might include comparing a number of general knowledge texts, with students keeping records of the topics considered suitable for young readers; rating the illustrations, the design, and the layout; speculating about the uses to which the books might be put; and sending the results to the respective publishers with suggestions for future publications.

Writing about the Text

Young students' written responses to factual texts have typically been in the form of learning log entries, often requiring them to play the part of the curious and fascinated young inquirer. Tasks and instructions have included:

- Write down one interesting piece of information you remember from the book.
- What were the most interesting things you read about?
- Write down something you learnt from that section.
- Write down something new that you found out.

Tasks such as these induct students into a view of inquiry as a search for enlightenment. They construct an almost personal relationship with a text, as if it exists to entertain, inform, or fascinate the reader.

In the case of *My First Book of Knowledge*, however, I wanted to design different kinds of writing tasks. We had already talked extensively about the information provided about ancient Egypt; several students had contributed knowledge from other sources. We had talked about Kate Petty's role in selecting information in order to construct a version of ancient Egyptian history suited to child readers. Now I asked students to consider the following question:

> What does Kate Petty, the writer, want you to know about the ancient Egyptians?

The following three pieces of writing were produced by students in response to this question. These writers used the question as a springboard into brief inquiries into the relationship constructed between them as knowers and the text, *My First Book of Knowledge*. These responses illustrate the kinds of writing that can emerge from a pedagogy which demonstrates to students how they can operate as critical inquirers into their own texts.

Anthea's text

Kate Petty wanted me to know Cleopatra was an Egyptian queen. I already knew that. She fell in love with Mark Antony who died in a battle. Here is the story: Cleopatra was an Indian queen who fell in love with Mark Anthony. Mark died in a battle. So one night when everyone was sleeping she got out of bed and got one

> of the cobras and put [it] against her chest. The cobra bit her. She died. Anthea, 7

Of the three young writers, Anthea's rejection of textual authority is most comprehensive. She deals with the inquiry I posed in a perfunctory sentence, acknowledging that the writer has selected information about Cleopatra suited to her as a young reader:

> Kate Petty wanted me to know Cleopatra was an Egyptian queen.

Having nodded to *My First Book of Knowledge* and to my question, Anthea goes on to carve out for herself a position as critical inquirer into this text, basing her writing on two questions she had encountered previously in shared book sessions:

> What does Kate Petty tell me that I already know?
>
> What do I know about this topic that Kate Petty doesn't tell me?

She first asserts her prior knowledge of the topic ("I already knew that"). Next she recounts her version of the Antony and Cleopatra story, thereby interrupting the usual assumption in texts for young readers that all knowledge resides with the text. By taking up two additional lines of inquiry for herself, Anthea has found a way to approach the text and to make meaning from it that is not commonly encouraged by classroom language activities nor by the texts available to young students.

Writing this has caused me to think about how I might deal with Anthea's version as an alternative to the text's version. The issue is not so much one of authority; Anthea's text clearly does not embody the sort of unproblematic authority assumed by children's books. It is rather that, along with *My First Book of Knowledge*, Anthea contributes one version among many possibilities. At the same time that I invite and celebrate Anthea's knowledge, I need to acknowledge the partial nature of her information and, if factual accuracy is an issue (and it most often is), probe her sources.

Nicole's text

Kate Petty wants us to know that the kings died. They get their

> bodies wrapped in special bandages to preserve them. They make the graves look fancy and decorate them. Kate Petty made us think the fan looks like fairy floss but it is really a fan. Nicole, 8

Nicole uses the question "What does Kate Petty, the writer, want you to know about the ancient Egyptians?" in a slightly different way. She starts with an extended retelling of the text's version of ancient Egyptian history. She then uses the question to critique a text that seems to care so little for its child readers that the illustrations of fans look like fairy floss. Nicole rejects the assumption that it doesn't matter if the illustrations aren't quite right in a children's book. She has conducted an inquiry into the text's positioning of child readers and found it wanting.

Mark's text

> Kate Petty wants us to know that they wrap mummies in bandages. Anthea said that they cut off cats' heads and put bandages on the cats' heads. They draw some eyes and a mouth. Mark, 7

Mark draws on both my critically framed question and on Anthea's account of the mummification of cats in ancient Egypt. He constructs a position that acknowledges Petty's role in selecting information and Anthea's as an additional source of information. His explicit naming of his sources ("Kate Petty," "Anthea") can be seen as the beginning of an understanding that information is not just there waiting to be used, but has been produced in social contexts.

In this brief survey of some aspects of critical inquiries into factual texts, I have not been arguing that young readers and researchers should necessarily learn to reject textual authority. After all, it may well be appropriate to follow carefully the instructions on a medicine bottle. My point is rather that an inquiry into how a text accomplishes its positioning of readers is always in order.

What Kinds of Child Inquirers Does This Text Produce?

I now turn from a general knowledge text that students are likely to have at home to two kinds of informational texts designed specifically for classroom use: a factual big book and a science series (*Sunshine Books: Science*). Enlarged-print nonfiction "big books," written especially for young readers and teachers to share, have in the last few years found an important place in elementary school language lessons. One of the editors of several series of big books explains that she and her colleagues surveyed young students to find out what they wanted to learn about. These publishers aims to produce books that

> provide young children with fascinating information on a variety of topics using appropriate genres to convey it: for example, children are introduced to scientific vocabulary, scaled diagrams, charts, realistic photographs, contents, indexes, colour coding, headings and sub-headings. Such texts do not patronize young readers. . . . [They] have been designed and written to mirror the devices, language, and information used in non-fiction texts for adults. The writers, editors and publishers shared a very strong belief that young children would enjoy non-fiction texts as much as narrative if they were offered texts with compelling information. (Badger, 1990, p. 215)

These texts are clearly designed to produce serious researchers who also enjoy their investigations. In the light of these aims, I now examine briefly *Amazing Landforms* (Brian, 1992), an informational big book that is part of the *Sunshine Books: Science* series. I ask, "What kinds of inquirers does this text encourage students to be?" I then take a look at some classroom questions and activities teachers can use to add to the possibilities offered by texts like this.

Amazing Landforms: The Text

Amazing Landforms contains brief physical descriptions of fourteen "strange and amazing" landforms from around the world. The page dealing with each landform contains a sentence or two describing physical aspects of the landform:

> **Wave Rock**
> Rainwater flowing over this granite cliff slowly shaped it like a wave.

> **Devil's Marbles**
> These granite rocks were once shaped like boxes. The wind and weather made them round.
>
> **Mt. Everest**
> Mt. Everest is the world's highest mountain above sea level.

For most landforms, these sentences are followed by another sentence or two of some sort of physical, social, or linguistic information:

> **Wave Rock**
> Wave Rock is only one side of a bigger rock called "Hyden Rock."
>
> **Devil's Marbles**
> The Australian Aborigines of the area believe the rocks are the eggs of the Rainbow Serpent, a Creator Ancestor from their Dreaming.
>
> **Mt. Everest**
> The word "Himalaya" means "home of snow."

The location and the dimensions of each landform and a coloured photograph taking up one-third to one-half of each page are included.

The entry for Uluru (until recently known to non-Aboriginal Australians as Ayers Rock) is as follows:

> Uluru
> This sandstone rock is one of the biggest in the world.
> [Full colour photograph, one-third of the page.]
> Place: Northern Territory, Australia
> Height: 348m (1142 feet)
> Perimeter: 9km (5-1/2 miles)
> [Diagram showing Uluru alongside a 90-storey building.]
> The rock changes color during the day (see cover and title page).
> It is also called "Ayers Rock."

Amazing Landforms assumes that young students are serious researchers. It provides glossary; index; table of contents; page numbers; large, clear, coloured photographs; and big print.

Information is clearly set out, making use of a number of methods of presentation including connected prose, photographs, diagrams, and embryonic charts. The credentials of the text producers are listed.

The print material and photograph on each page work together to produce readers with an interest in the physical attributes of these landforms. The text promotes questions of this sort: What does it look like? Where is it found? How big? Which country? What is it made of? How was it formed? Questions about how people relate to the landforms make up only a small part of the inquiry prompted by these texts.

The minimal print and the use of charts and labeled diagrams interrupting the prose suggest at least a couple of different ideal readers. One is an inquirer in a hurry, requiring a functional source of information that is efficiently displayed. The spare, open layout and large font promote easy assessment of the usefulness of the information to the researcher. The other is a very young reader who finds inquiry facilitated by a text that promises there isn't too much to read.

The large size and clarity of the photographs extend the possibilities of the text. They suggest other kinds of readers: those who use the photograph and text in conjunction, perhaps checking information from the two sources, and those who pour over photographs rather than over print.

But *Amazing Landforms* offers itself as a text that provides more than information. The cover hails young readers curious about the physical environment. The book's potential to be used by a child reader as a source of wonder is suggested by a number of features: the huge colour photograph of Uluru on the cover; the use of "amazing" in the title and the evocation of the mysterious in the terms "strange and amazing" in the introduction; and the inclusion of landforms, suggesting the sensational or perhaps quirky (Giant's Causeway, Devil's Tower, Grand Canyon, Camel Rock, Pancake Rock). Children can indeed use it in this way. I've listened as small groups of boys lie on their stomachs in front of this book, chanting the written text together; I've watched them use the table of contents to locate potentially exciting landforms; I've observed a couple of boys of Chinese background use the map on the back and the index so they can read about Camel Rock in China.

I promote all of these uses of *Amazing Landforms* through the classroom language program. But the photographs, minimal prose, and charts together produce an extremely functional text, leaving little room for maneuvering; the efficient presentation of facts reduces options for young readers. The relationship between child and text involves essentially an exchange of information; it is not a book that encourages contemplation. It assumes and produces specific reading, instructional, and research practices. Therefore, I deliberately experimented with a set of questions that I hoped would produce a very different way of reading this book, an experiment I discuss in the following section.

This analysis is not intended as a negative review of the text. The point is that while texts position students to read in specific ways and to make inquiries of specific kinds, they rarely announce this explicitly. In addition, few informational texts written for children—or texts of other kinds, for that matter—show any signs of unease about their contradictions or limitations. *Amazing Landforms* does not invite young readers to speculate about why, for example, a book that offers so limited a view of landforms should use the terms "strange" and "amazing." Cynical adults might have some suggestions here, along the lines that a book titled *Amazing Landforms* might have a wider market than one titled *Landforms of the World*.

It is interesting to speculate how this text could have suggested extra meanings to its readers. Of course, the potential to do this is limited by the text producers' notions of which sorts of factual texts are appropriate for very young readers, by the exigencies of modern global publishing and book distribution, by the size limitations imposed by big book technology, and by the uses to which big books are put. Still, I offer some possibilities for additional features:

- The facts about one landform presented in a variety of different ways; a commentary explaining the sorts of readers aimed at; a set of questions inviting readers to consider how these differences might change the way they use the text

- Variation from page to page of the relative size of photographs, tables, print, and so on; a set of questions encouraging readers to consider the difference these changes might make to the way they use the text
- Annotations placed next to items of information explaining their selection; questions inviting readers to consider how placement and size of items determine their relative importance
- A list of other texts providing similar information
- Acknowledgment that the information provided is partial and that readers might know other information about the landforms; space where readers can add to what is presented in the text

Critical inquirers do not take a text's assessment of itself at face value. The reality is, however, that few texts offer readers the opportunity to consider how texts work to produce specific kinds of readers. What is more, *Amazing Landforms* and texts like it are widely used with young children as sources of information. As I argued earlier, through the pedagogy they employ, teachers are implicated in students' relationships with informational texts. And as long as students use texts as a resource in an inquiry approach, it is essential that classroom language discussion and activities draw attention to how the texts work to make meanings.

Amazing Landforms: Making Different Meanings

Texts not only position readers in specific ways, but they also suggest a range of appropriate classroom activities. Anyone who has tried to read aloud to a class a text like *Amazing Landforms* knows that students can readily engage with it as seekers of fast facts. Answers can be found to questions such as: What is another name for Uluru? Which country is it found in? What sort of rock is it made from? How tall is it? How far around? Discussion of the devices used on each page to display information and of the terminology (height, perimeter) used to convey this sort of information extends the possibilities. Questions about the photographic representation of Uluru might move students into the realm of speculation, thus producing a different kind of inquiry:

What colours are shown in the photograph? What shape is it? What does it make you think of?

But the text itself is not the only factor determining how it is used. I took a different set of questions and tasks—this time inviting speculation into how the book could have been written, how a different view could have been taken of one landform—and used these questions and tasks to produce new ways of making meaning from an informational text. The switch to a focus on the text as an object as opposed to its content and design shows young readers that the relationship of information receiver and information provider between child and text is not the only one possible.

Amazing Landforms offered an opportunity to consider the relative usefulness of photographs, tables, charts, diagrams, and prose for conveying particular kinds of information. Having done this, I returned to a topic I had raised in the past. I formulated it in this way:

> We've had a detailed look at how the people who produced this book have chosen to present the information about Uluru to you, and we've talked about what information they decided to include. And we've talked about how readers can use a book like this. But they didn't have to write about Uluru in this way. They could have written a different kind of book about Uluru.

I then began to shape speculation about a different kind of text with these observations and discussion starters: "The writer, illustrator, and publisher of this book have been very serious about Uluru, haven't they? They haven't made room for you to have any fun with this book, have they? Let's make some suggestions about what they could have said about Uluru if they had decided to produce a fantasy about Uluru."

The talk was lively. Students wove local current events and familiar elements of childhood stories into their suggestions. There was a moment, very telling for me, when the glances I exchanged with a couple of the older students seemed to sum up the position we were sharing: "This is all very well, and it's a lot of fun, but there must be limits to it, and those limits will be evoked by the teacher." I went on, however, to set a writing task that encouraged students to play with the idea that the text could have been written differently, that a different view of Uluru could have been constructed for young readers.

Writing Different Texts

As preparation for their writing, I asked students to focus on the photograph of Uluru (deep orange with dark slanting shadows) and to speculate about how the sentence "This sandstone rock is one of the biggest in the world" might have been different if Uluru had been treated as an object that could be made ridiculous and if the producers of *Amazing Landforms* had made young readers their partners in a fantasy world.

As the following examples demonstrate, this new set of classroom activities produced student inquirers who could talk and write about texts in a variety of ways. At the beginning of the lesson, they had dealt with *Amazing Landforms* on its own terms, as a source of information and some wonder. During the lesson, I had consciously encouraged students to change their relationship with the text so that they could talk and write about it speculatively and imaginatively. Most of the writing took narrative shape, and as was my usual practice, I asked the younger students to draw and the older students to help them with captions:

> Once upon a time there was a dancing rock called Uluru. Uluru ate five state bank[s], six cupboards and ten children.

> The mountain ate some clothes. The mountain turned into a purple mountain. The mountain can eat you up. The mountain ate coloured food. It turned into a yellow mountain. Then he got fat.

> The Ayers rock has a secret door. The more he eats the wider the door opens.

> Once upon a time there was a zoo called Uluru. It was a red hot zoo rock and lots of animals lived there.

A couple of pieces formed a loose collection of metaphors:

> Ayers Rock has got a big door where you go and sing a song of a kangaroo. Ayers Rock has got a closet full of clothes. Ayers Rock is a bank for the Aboriginal people. Ayers Rock is a castle in the Northern Territory.

> It is a ballet dancer with chicken pox. It is a gymnastics rock.

One student created a riddle:

> What did Ayers Rock say to Ayers Rock?
> Hi! I am Rocky

One took up the notion of interrupting the expected sort of text and produced a very unexpected piece:

> Once upon a time there was a dancing rock. It had a friend. Hold it! I forgot the title. The end.

I do not claim that texts of this kind are in any way preferable to *Amazing Landforms;* rather, my argument is that had texts like these been available as classroom reading material, they would have produced very different readers. Students playing with texts in this way are engaged in a form of critical text inquiry in which they investigate other possible versions of the topic "Uluru."

Again, not only are these pieces of writing unlike those that might usually be produced, but they also work to produce different kinds of inquirers and readers. During the course of the lesson, I consciously introduced tasks through which students were able to:

- use the text uncritically as a source of information
- use a metalanguage to talk about how words and pictures worked together to present this information
- construct an alternate text and thus challenge an assumption that this text was arbiter of what could be said about Uluru and how it could be said

I hinted earlier that playing in this way with a text is problematic. It raises for both teacher and students questions about the limits of challenge to authority, about where critical inquiry stops, about who decides which texts will be challenged, and about who initiates challenge. These are questions that need debate—and to which there are no simple answers.

How Do Science Texts Construct Knowledge for Children?

JACK: (aged 7, an independent reader and writer) We are writing about books that make us seem stupid because George read us this book called *How Machines Help* which John Sheridan wrote and it said Can you chop down trees with your hand and Can you cut paper with your fingers and Can you pick up a car and we did writing about what they were like.

TEACHER: . . . Anyone like to add to that?

ALEX: (aged 7, a fairly independent reader and writer) John [Sheridan] made us feel stupid. He didn't really know that kids really knew that. And [he thought] that people don't know anything.

The inquiry into *Sunshine Books: Science* (1992), briefly explained by Jack and Alex in the transcripts above, began when six-year-old George was reading aloud *How Machines Help,* a text geared at Level One. As I watched George reading carefully to his intently listening classmates, I started to hear what he was reading—not *how* he was reading (the customary focus for teachers), but *what* he was reading. The writer posed a series of questions and made a series of statements in answer to the questions. Each of these was illustrated with a full colour photograph:

Can you pull out a nail with you fingers?

A hammer will help you pull out the nail.

A hammer is a machine.

Can you lift a car with your hands?

A car jack can help you to lift a car.

A car jack is a machine.

This text suggested that its five- and six-year-old readers had learnt little about how the physical world works from their lives outside school. The photographs were clear and realistic; the children and adults, shown using their hands and then the machines, were pictured with intent expressions. The photographs gave status to the questions and statements as seriously posed inquiries and pieces of information. I could detect no hint of humour or playfulness. Despite the often ludicrous questions, the text didn't invite children to enjoy a bit of a joke while they were informed about machines.

The text seemed to produce child readers who accepted without question both the text's view of what they should know about machines and the form in which this information was wrapped. Previously I had encouraged students to use this text and others in the series as though they were neutral reading material and to use them as sources of easily accessible information. Yet the story of my relationship with this series was not quite this simple. During the previous year, as teacher-librarian at another, comparatively lavishly resourced school, I had advised against buying these books. While not all titles were as dismissive of young readers as knowers as *How Machines Help*, many exemplified a number of the problems with science books written for classroom use described by Unsworth (1993). They were marked by simplistic and misleading text and by inappropriate use of discovery learning (Unsworth, 1993).

When I found that my new school had bought the series, I included several of the books in the classroom bulk loan of library books. The decision I had made the year before did not now seem so clear cut. I now treated these books as attractively photographed, easy-to-read informational texts for young readers. They were part of a widely marketed science course developed by a respected multinational publisher. Uneasy though I was at the uncritical position I was taking toward them, in effect I accepted their claims to be suitable books for young students to read.

What made me decide to take action was the realization that I was helping to validate the text producers' decision about what and how young children should know about the physical world. I needed to introduce talk, questions, and activities that would encourage students to inquire into how texts in this series constructed them as knowers.

Producing Different Kinds of Knowers

Sunshine Books: Science looked like the other books I encouraged students to read freely and frequently at home and at school, by themselves and in groups, silently or out loud. The print was large and clear, vocabulary was controlled, and higher-level texts in the series took up more complex concepts. Generally, my focus was on the students as consumers of the text's meaning, not as challengers of the text's meaning. Now I faced a challenge of my own: How could I draw students' attention to the assumptions that "How machines help" seemed to be making about students as knowers about the physical world? And how could I encourage them to make other books in the series the object of critical inquiry?

The investigation took place in two moves:

1. I shared my critical interpretation of *How Machines Help* with students.
2. I encouraged students to investigate other titles in the series.

I explained to students that when children are learning to read, adults expect them to read books in a variety of ways. Often, adults expect them to read the words just to get practice in reading; they may not expect children to take much notice of what the book is telling them. At other times, adults might want children to read to find out things that they didn't know.

The questions in *How Machines Help* seemed to pose no challenge to most five- or six-year-olds; the information was largely everyday commonsense knowledge, so I commented: "While George was reading aloud to you, I started listening to the questions and information John Sheridan, the writer, had included in the book. I began to think about the sort of child he was writing for. I realised that the child he seemed to be writing for in some ways wasn't much like you."

I then suggested that readers can get ideas about what writers, illustrators, and publishers think about them from asking some questions about the books they read. I went on to frame some questions designed to help students inquire into the sort of child reader produced by *How Machines Help:*

> Who are the questions in *How Machines Help* for? Do you know the answers to the questions John Sheridan asks? Do you think that most children your age would know the answers to these questions? I wonder why he has put questions into the book that most people your age already know the answers to?
>
> Listen to each sentence in the book that tells the reader some information. What information did you know already? What didn't you know already? What pieces of information would children your age know already? I wonder why he has put information into the book that most people your age already know the answers to?

Students agreed that although they knew the answers to the questions already, they learnt that a number of common items such as scissors and hammers are machines.

I commented: "It seems to me that John Sheridan doesn't think that you know much. It's as if he thinks that five-year-olds haven't learnt much about things in the world. It almost seems that he thinks you are stupid"; "These questions don't seem like real questions to me. John Sheridan asks questions that most five-year-olds already know the answers to."

Students then worked with me to produce the following chart summarizing our discussion about how this book positioned them as knowers:

> **How Machines Help**
> The writer of this book writes for children as though they're stupid, know nothing.
> What John Sheridan tells us that we already know:
> You can't pull out a nail with your fingers . . . unless the wood is soft or you have a hammer.

I have emphasized in this account that my reading of how students were positioned as knowers (that is, that they didn't know much about the everyday physical world) was the focus of this discussion. My intention was to share with students my interpretation of the text. In effect, I gave them permission to talk about *How Machines Help* quite differently from the usual ways. They responded enthusiastically to the chance to investigate and to reject the picture of them created by the text.

This is not the place to speculate about their reasons for taking up my way of reading the text. (See O'Brien, 1994, for a detailed analysis of the classroom discourses associated with critical text analysis.) I want to emphasise that I thought it important to ask some questions and to make some clear statements (in my position as teacher, as authority figure) so that students could think about how they used texts and how texts used them, instead of students taking texts for granted.

Having shared my reading of the text, I then set up an investigation across the reading series focusing on how students were constructed as knowers. My approach was to encourage students to read with two things in mind: (1) what they already knew, and (2) what was new to them. In this way, I made it possible for them to think about themselves as knowers—as readers who had knowledge about the topics taken up by the books. My aim was to set students up not to investigate the topics covered by the texts, but to investigate the texts themselves.

I framed the task in this way:

> Thinking about science books:
> 1. Some writers seem to think that children know nothing.
> 2. Here are some of the things that we know already.

Students spent about twenty minutes in mixed age and ability level groups of two or three, reading, talking about, and writing about one or two books they had chosen from the first and second levels of the series.

Students' writing illustrates that this task made a range of approaches available to them. Nannette (age five) and Chloe (age eight) took the investigation no further than repeating my original reading of how John Sheridan treated his readers:

> John Sheridan makes us feel stupid because he makes stupid questions. He makes us feel stupid. Question: Can you lift a car with our hand?

Travis (age seven) went for the grand statement:

> Everyone knows that we need light to see in the dark [with "everyone" highlighted and circled].

Kath (age five) and Allie (age eight) produced a detailed analysis of what they read, organized around what they already knew and didn't already know:

> We already know the sun makes light
> We already know lasers make light . . .
> We didn't know fish can make light.

Martha (age 8) used the heading "Stuff that some people don't know" and then made a list:

> Some spiders live in the ground
>
> Some spiders live in the water
>
> They catch insects in the webs. . .

George (age six) had been reading *How Machines Help* when I began the investigation. He and Mandy (age six) used the task to answer the questions in that book, treating them as real questions:

> No you can't pull
>
> No you can't lift
>
> No you can't chop. . .

Paul (age five) and Ray (age seven) turned their scorn on "Does it float?":

> Everybody knows that the ball is floating in this book
>
> Everybody knows that the leaf is floating on the water
>
> Of course a fish swims under water

Students spent some time sharing what they had found out about these books. Many discovered that the books they read were full of things they didn't know about; others found that their books were a mixture of known and unknown material. They also found that they and their peers knew a range of things about the topics covered by the books. Others found that they already knew just about everything they read. They didn't find any other books that seemed to ask the sorts of questions we had come across in *How Machines Help*.

This investigation was clearly limited, informal, and largely unstructured; it was my response to a series of books that I judged demanded immediate attention. It provided a way to help students treat with some degree of suspicion books that looked as if they were just right for kids. I don't claim that this series is never of use. What I do claim is that teachers need to show student readers how to stand back from informational texts and ask not just, What does this book say and how does it say it?, but also, What does it say about me and how does it say this?

A short anecdote sums up many of the issues associated with a critical approach to classroom texts. I established these investigations into science books in order to offer students some opportunities to challenge what texts were saying to them and about them as readers and as knowers, and so that they could stand in new positions in relation to texts written specifically with them in mind. But when I gave an account of the talk and tasks around the Sunshine Science series in my classroom to a group of elementary school teachers, I found that many didn't view my approach as a valid way to approach these texts. In fact, many of their responses were hostile. They suggested that I had ignored the intentions of the writers to produce simple texts suitable for children to read; that the texts should be used only as suggested in the accompanying teacher's handbook; that I was manipulating students to see things that weren't there; that I was looking for things to criticize and of course I had found them; that students need to start off reading about things they are familiar with; and that I was destroying children's innocent enjoyment of simple, colourful texts. At the time, I was somewhat surprised by the vehemence of this attack. Quite clearly I had tapped into some strongly held beliefs about children and their relationships with texts, particularly science books.

I have since come to the conclusion that some of these teachers saw as inappropriate my challenge to the authority claimed by producers of texts (and accepted by teachers) to define and package versions of knowledge for young students. Texts, however, are not innocent. These spare, appealing science books, for example, do more than supply information or provide entertainment and reading practice. They produce a version of the social world deemed suitable for children to access, and they produce particular kinds of authority relationships with their readers. In other words, these texts have the potential to define what students need to know, and through these texts, limits can be placed on the sorts of reading and inquiry students are able to undertake. The critical inquiry I have described aims to pose questions and set tasks that show students how it is possible to challenge textual claims of authority. At the same time, I am aware that challenge to authority is in many situations a problematic response. Critical inquiries don't close down debates; they open up entire new areas for consideration.

Conclusion

Student inquirers learn to take up a range of positions in relation to texts. I have demonstrated how classroom talk about and activities in conjunction with particular texts make it possible for students to:

- learn to use a metalanguage in order to gain access to information about the content of a text; learn to challenge the potential of the text to impose limits on an inquiry
- browse through a factual text, access the information it provides, and compare methods of presenting factual material; also, change their relationship to this text and approach it as a source of innovation and speculation
- read a number of the titles in series books with a partner and consider the information in light of what they already know about the topics

The sort of inquiry I have described raises many questions. Many teachers worry that I am merely "putting words in students' mouths," or that students "say what the teacher wants to hear." I am; and they do, of course. But these objections miss the point. They are based on a misleading notion that a teacher who does not challenge the authority relationship constructed between texts and their readers is in some way remaining neutral, or that texts themselves are neutral unless a teacher intervenes. All texts (and all teachers) have political positions, acknowledged or unacknowledged. My position is that teachers need to adopt a pedagogy that makes it possible for them and their students to investigate the positions taken up by texts as well as the sorts of readers and inquirers they produce in the process.

References

Badger L. (1990). Non-fiction writing: What children learn from nonfiction reading. *Australian Journal of Reading, 13*(3), 215.

Baker, C., & Freebody, P. (1989). *Children's first school books: Introductions to the culture of literacy.* Oxford: Basil Blackwell.

Brian, J. (1992). *Amazing landforms.* Flinders Park, South Australia: Era Publications.

Freebody, P. (1993). Social class and reading. In A. Luke & P. Gilbert (Eds.), *Literacy in contexts: Australian perspectives and issues.* St. Leonards, New South Wales, Australia: Allen & Unwin.

Gilbert, P. (with Rowe, K.). (1989). *Gender, literacy and the classroom.* Carlton South, Victoria: Australian Reading Association.

Luke, A. (1993). The social construction of literacy in the primary school. In L. Unsworth (Ed.), *Literacy learning and teaching: Language as social practice in the primary school.* South Melbourne, Australia: Macmillan Education.

O'Brien, J. (1994). *It's written in our head: The possibilities and contradictions of a feminist poststructuralist discourse in a junior primary classroom.* Unpublished master's thesis, University of South Australia, Adelaide.

Petty, K. (1990). *My first book of knowledge*. London: Conran Octopus.

Sheridan, J. (1992). *How machines help*. Melbourne, Australia: Rigby Education.

Sunshine books: Science. (1992). Melbourne, Australia: Rigby Education.

Unsworth, L. (1993). Choosing and using information books in junior primary science. In L. Unsworth (Ed.), *Literacy learning and teaching: Language as social practice in the primary school*. South Melbourne, Australia: Macmillan Education.

CHAPTER NINE

Examining Poverty and Literacy in Our Schools: Janice's Story

CONNIE L. WHITE
Annapolis Valley Regional School Board, Nova Scotia

Janice's story is about inquiry into poverty, literacy, and schooling. In this chapter, I explore the discourses and practices of Janice's classroom and school in an effort to understand how a culture of poverty is constituted both at school and in our society. Janice was a six-year-old child, and I was her teacher since she first arrived at school. Janice, like many other white children of working-class and welfare families in my whole language classroom, was invited to participate in naming her world through a multitude of invitations to read, write, and talk. But Janice's world of poverty is not easily accessible through these invitations, and therefore her world remains out of reach and unchanged, and the practices of her school and classroom remain unchallenged. By pushing my own beliefs about whole language learning and by taking up the provocative challenges of a number of critical literacy theorists, I examine how Janice, her classmates, and their siblings are positioned at an educational disadvantage through present and past practices at their school. Through Janice's research and learning, I raise new questions about and possibilities for a more "just" practice for all of the students in her classroom.

The story the class is listening to is Eve Bunting's *Fly Away Home* (1991), the story of a little boy and his father who do not have a "real home" and must live in an airport because they are too poor to afford the rent for an apartment. This reading of the story actually elicits more conversation from the class about airports and planes than it does about being homeless or poor, in spite of the fact that far more of the students in this classroom live in poverty than have experienced a plane trip or a visit to an airport. The few students who can describe an airport, plane, or trip they or someone in their family has taken command a quiet respect from the other students. They listen with obvious interest and direct occasional questions toward the students who are talking about their experiences with airports or planes. Janice's loud, shrill voice joins the voices of expert speakers as she begins to relate "fun trips" she has taken on planes.

Janice's voice breaks the quiet, respectful listening and ends the questions. The students' eyes turn toward their teacher, not toward Janice. Many of them realize, with what appears to be an uncomfortable confidence, that Janice is making up her stories of fun trips on the plane, and they look to their teacher to get them over the uneasy hump of not knowing what they should or can say to Janice, or how to get beyond her story and into a conversation again.

This classroom discussion took place in the fall of 1994. As a teacher, I was anxious to find out whether the students would talk about poverty and raise questions about it. Would these often silent children from poor families find their voices, make connections, and raise issues about their own lives if I provided books on poverty? I had hoped the students would raise questions that would in turn create empowering opportunities for them. I have been interested in such questions ever since my exploration of critical literacy in course work with Andy Manning, Jerome Harste, and Barbara Comber. Also, through conversations with a graduate student doing research on critical literacy in my classroom the previous year, I had started thinking more consciously about the conversations and questions the students were engaging in or avoiding (Mackay, 1994).

It is important to note that because of classroom research I had been involved in (White, 1990), I had made dramatic changes in my approach to literacy and learning in my classroom. Through more than a year of data collection involving observations, journal keeping, videotaping and audiotaping, and reflective writing, I had discovered how important it is for students' understandings, questions, and interpretations to be heard and discussed in the classroom. One of the striking discoveries I had begun to make was that although the majority of students in my class lived in poverty, no one ever seemed to talk about it or question it. I was surprised that day when Janice used the story *Fly Away Home* to fabricate stories about her experiences.

When I eventually led the conversation into a discussion about poverty and the plight of the little boy in the story, Janice joined the other students in expressing pity for the young main character, but she fell silent as we talked about the circumstances that appeared to have led this little boy and his father to live in the airport. O'Neill (1990) writes:

> Readers whose primary response diverges from the dominant reading will gradually have their response modified, undermining rather than strengthening their perceptions of themselves as competent readers. At the same time, the discourse is likely to marginalize the relevance of their life experiences to literary readings. They will always get it wrong unless they subordinate their experience to the dominant cultural reading. (p. 89)

The discussion in our classroom of poverty seemed to be dominated by those students whose life experiences were more privileged.

Whose stories do we encourage to be told in our classrooms? Whose stories *should* we encourage to be told in our classrooms? Who is kept safe when stories are silenced? And how does the silencing of stories happen? (See Timothy Lensmire's essay in Chapter 6 of this volume for similar experiences regarding voice.)

Janice is poor, yet in a classroom that has been structured to invite readers to bring their own responses and questions to the texts we read and invites writers to tell their own stories, Janice has not often talked of being poor. Instead, she frequently tells her fantasy stories of airplane rides, strawberry trees growing in her yard, expensive toys she has at home, and family outings she has been on.

Many of Janice's classmates' families live well below the average Canadian family income. But poverty is not something we've discussed much in our classroom. I am not comfortable with this avoidance, but I've not known how to talk about it with the students either. Nothing in my own experiences growing up in school or at home prepared me to talk about poverty through any discourse other than one of pity, shame, or blame. The creation and maintenance of poverty through our society's institutions wasn't something I was able to see by myself, and it certainly wasn't something I studied in any of my early university courses. Without a better understanding for myself, I feared leading the students into conversations that would leave those most vulnerable feeling exposed, blamed, or ashamed. By not talking about poverty, however, I am very much afraid that I may keep Janice and many of her classmates on the outside looking into a world created by others' stories.

I am concerned about Janice and her classmates. I am concerned about their older siblings and those who have not yet begun school. I am concerned because they will spend nine, ten, or more years of their lives in an institution that claims to educate them and give them hope for a different future. Yet many of them, if not most, lose the promise of that future in the early years of their school lives. I am concerned that children of poverty grow into adolescents in poverty, who grow up to become adults in poverty, who give birth to a new generation of poverty. I don't have to look into a crystal ball to see that this cycle is real. The school where I teach has already taught a generation of poverty, and it opens its doors each September to the children of that first generation. Janice's mother sat in her daughter's classroom twenty-six years ago. While Janice's mother had another teacher and experienced teaching approaches different from those Janice is experiencing today, I've begun to seriously wonder whether anything has changed much in those twenty-six years. I've wondered whether Janice and her siblings are doing anything more than marking time to the slightly more modern beat of an old song—a song that has no room for their voices in its chorus.

For Janice and the hundreds of students like her who have begun their school years in my classroom, the hope dims too quickly. There is a business world and an economic world outside our classroom that blames schools like Janice's for the poor prosperity of Janice's country. They frown on dropouts like Janice's mother, pointing the finger of blame at her and individuals like her who make the so-called unwise choice to leave school early. These economic and business worlds are joined by our provincial governments, who blame many of the country's financial problems on the high cost of supporting Janice, her family, and many others like them. They blame Janice, her parents, and her school for the lack of a proper education and marketable job skills. These same bureaucrats who spend thousands of dollars on stay-in-school coordinators, projects, advertising, slogan awards, and initiatives have never asked Janice's mother why she left school. From their positions of power, the worlds of business, economics, and government have a public voice through the media, through which they keep the finger of blame for poverty pointed firmly at those who have been denied a voice.

Poverty is primarily visible through a discourse of blame, and while I am only beginning to grapple with the larger forces of politics in the "making of the poor," I am growing more and more concerned about the role that I, as Janice's teacher, and her school play in that creation. Nine, ten, eleven years or more in an institution of learning should offer one of the most enthusiastic youngsters I've met in my teaching career some hope that she can access the same resources and privileges as Gwen, Tom, or Bobby, who come from lower-middle-class families. But already I see that possibility slipping away for six-year-old Janice, while it is taken for granted by her more privileged classmates, who are in a minority in her classroom.

This chapter is a search to understand poverty as it intersects with Janice's education and is maintained by the process of schooling. In many ways, it is an exploration of the discourses and practices of my own classroom, but it attempts to go beyond that to look at how school creates a culture of poverty for children such as Janice. It is not a chapter with methods or answers, as much as I would like to have access to both if they could help Janice before she leaves my classroom in June. Arriving at new understandings can be a painfully slow process when children and caring relationships are at stake.

Exploring Assumptions of Inclusion in Classroom Discourse

Much of what I've been doing in my own classroom in the last five or six years has been guided and informed by my own reading and classroom research (White, 1990). Based on what I have believed and discovered about learning, I have set up my classroom as a safe environment in which to take risks. I've issued many invitations to my students to actively participate as readers and writers, as the learners I believe they all are. I've encouraged them to ask their own questions and to take ownership of their own learning. I've tried to make it clear to them that they have a voice in their classroom and that together we can negotiate their days in ways that will be meaningful for them as learners. I've urged them to name their world, to seek connections, to make new meanings, and to arrive at new understandings. While I've made an effort to support learning in all areas and all parts of our school day together, the place I have most passionately watched, pushed, and listened for these things to happen has been in the story corner, where the students spend much of their time.

In *Curriculum as Conversation*, a keynote address given by Andy Manning at the Western Australian Reading Conference in 1993, Manning states:

> Learning involves making sense of new experience and making sense of new experiences involves making connections between the new experiences and what we already know. It is therefore, less a matter of accumulating information, adding bits of knowledge, than a process of continually adjusting and reconstructing our understandings. (p. 5)

I have thought of my classroom as a place that supports learning through its many invitations to question, make connections, and seek new understandings. I've watched the students question, talk, and argue about many things they have encountered in the books and discussions in the story corner. I've watched understandings grow and change through dynamic and energetic conversations, but until recently I hadn't realized it was highly unlikely that the students would question, argue, or talk about things they could not see or hear. Except for the fairy tale version of poverty found in stories such as "Hansel and Gretel," "The Elves and the Shoemaker," and "Cinderella," poverty as a theme has been virtually absent from the large selection of books in our story corner. *Fly Away Home* was purchased and placed there only a year ago.

More than half of the students in my classroom this year come from homes whose only source of income is unemployment insurance or welfare. Many others have single parents working for minimum wages. Yet in our many discussions and conversations, poverty is not an issue we have explicitly raised or questioned.

I felt I needed to explore further whether making texts and conversations about poverty an explicit part of literacy in my class would help students like Janice to risk sharing their own life stories about poverty. Would such regular practice create an environment Janice would perceive as safe?

According to Allan Luke (1991), "There are no exemptions to offer. Teaching the word, we selectively socialize students into versions of the world, into possible worlds and into a vision of the horizons and limits of literate competencies" (p. 139). When the many books and conversations in our classroom do not speak (or speak well) from a position of poverty, Janice is being selectively socialized into particular versions of the world. When Janice does not hear about her world in the many conversations in the classroom, except perhaps through murmurs of pity, her vision of possible worlds is limited and new horizons obscured. In an environment that claims to invite her to talk about her world and explore new worlds, Janice may well be learning that she and her world are invisible.

> Hey! Mrs. White! Connie! I gots a cat too! Her gots a really funny place on hers head where we thinks Jason's dog bits her. There's a great big chunk outta it. Look hers scratched me too! Right here under my eye. It hurt real bad but Mom put water on it an' it's gettin' better now.

Here Janice did what many of the students automatically do while I'm reading. She invited herself into a conversation that began while I was reading an information book about cats. The student who chose the book for me to read had a story he wanted to share about his cat having kittens, so he stopped my reading of the text early to share the news, using the pictures in the book to show us what his new kittens looked like. As a number of other students joined in with recent updates of stories about their cats,

Janice eagerly spoke up, anxious to share her story too. Unlike her contribution to the story *Fly Away Home*, when Janice raised her voice to join this conversation, she had her own experiences to tell and they seemed to "fit right in." This time the other students indicated belief and interest in Janice's story. They looked more closely at the swollen red mark under her eye and asked questions about the size and kind of injury her cat had received. Bobby wanted to know if Janice's mother had taken the cat to the vet. With a glance toward me, Janice shook her head saying, "Nah! Hers head just gots better by itself." Bobby crunched up his brow and gave Janice a puzzled look, before Gwen picked up the conversation by telling the class that her cat had to go to the vet last summer for stitches when she got caught in a thorn bush. Several other students joined in with their stories of cats or other pets who had had injuries requiring a vet's attention before we continued with the reading of the text.

Conversations like this one are common in our story corner. Often, though not always, the student who selects the book for me to read opens the conversation or raises the first question, with others usually choosing to join in when they have a story to share or their own questions to ask of the text, of me, or of the other students. Anyone listening to these conversations might find it difficult to understand my concerns about Janice's voice being silenced in our classroom:

> Janice's voice, in fact, is very loud and often heard, but it's not what Janice is saying, rather it is what she is not saying and the questions she is not asking or causing the others to ask that has really begun to concern me. In spite of all her efforts to be heard, I think our classroom discourse has already begun to silence Janice. (My journal reflections, 1994)

Many conversations similar to the one about cats have caused me to wonder what invitations are really issued through the books we share and the conversations that grow from them. Are the invitations really there for all students to make sense of their "lived" experiences and participate in the creation of a conversation, or do these invitations carry messages of exclusive right to particular kinds of conversations? Comber (1992) writes, "While Whole Language teachers value the student there is not necessarily an awareness of students as gendered, cultured, politically situated people" (p. 3). Janice didn't enter the conversation to talk about poverty; she entered the conversation because she, like the other students, had a story to share about cats. But embedded in her story was the much more encompassing, almost invisible, story of poverty.

Information books and pictures of cats like Janice's or those of many of the other students in our classroom are missing from our story corner. There is no information about cats that must fend for themselves because the families who own them don't have enough money for food for themselves, let alone food for their animals. There is no information about cats that are owned for the sole purpose of keeping mice and rodents under control in their owners' homes. There are no pictures of cats whose heads have bites out of them which must heal on their own because there is no money for the family to go to their own doctor for the medicine they need, let alone to get their pets medical attention. If there were books like this in our story corner, I expect the conversations and questions would be quite different.

I have used the story about Janice and her cat to talk about what books in our classroom assume and what is missing from books and conversations in our classroom. I have the recorded data notes from this event, but the issues were really not much different when the students talked about shopping trips with their parents as we read Robert Munsch's book *Something Good* (1990), or when we read the traditional story *The Night Before Christmas,* or when we read countless other books in our classroom. The experiences these books offer appear to invite connections from particular students, but not many of those students reside in my classroom. Janice's parents shop for groceries once a month when their welfare checks come in the mail. Janice and her siblings are in school when their parents do the grocery shopping so that the children won't pressure their parents for the treats that Munsch's storybook character works so hard and hilariously to get. Janice is still waiting for a piece to the toy Santa left her at Christmas. The toy was secondhand and no one noticed it was missing a necessary piece before delivering it to Janice's family on Christmas Eve. The pictures of the stockings "hung by the chimney with care" in several of our Christmas books offer pretty, fanciful images and dreams that many of the students in my classroom do not have the luxury of experiencing. So what do these books offer these students?

Luke (1991) suggests that when teachers "teach children to love books," they operate from an assumption that books and reading, regardless of the text, are both good and educationally sound for *all* children in their classrooms (p. 142):

> Through my own sharing and demonstration of reading I have nurtured a "love of books" in my classroom. It is troubling to consider that we have been busy loving books that have left many of the children in our classroom and their lives invisible. (My journal reflections, 1994)

It is troubling to realize that we have been encouraging conversations and discussions about books that have assumed all children share middle-class experiences. It is troubling to realize that as an adult woman and teacher, I have not paid attention to the lies and the convincing illusions of many of the books I have placed in our classroom. It is troubling to realize that in a classroom intended to encourage all students' voices, the invitations issued there have caused some students like Janice to struggle to find different voices through others' stories in their efforts to be heard.

Naming Whose World in the Classroom?

We learn by making sense of new experiences and making connections between those new experiences and what we already know (Manning, 1993), so what happens when children come to school unable to make connections because of what the classroom environment and practice offers them—or doesn't offer them? Or what happens when the seemingly innocent connections they make are unthinkingly accepted or celebrated rather than examined or scrutinized for the ways in which they are knitting those children into the fabric of a society that is already oppressing them? What happens when children are asked or expected to leave both their experiences and any hope of asking honest questions outside the classroom door so that they can begin the "real business" of school learning? What happens when the discourse of school, the literacy of school, and the culture of school hold some children hostage while at the same time excluding them? Can children ever question the discourse and culture of a dominant group from a subordinate position created by the culture and discourse of that dominant group?

According to Manning (1993):

> Language plays an important part in learning. First it allows us to name our world. It allows us to take our experience, name it and in the process distance ourselves from it, that is, look at it, turn it over, reflect on it, decide how we feel about it. Language does a second thing. Just by virtue of the fact we have named our experience, we give others access to our experience. Others too can look at it, turn it over, study it, reflect upon it and decide how they feel about it. A third thing can happen. We can learn from it. The process of languaging supports reflection and learning. (p. 11)

Janice has been trying to name her world at school. She named it when she shared her story about her cat. She named it during writing time one day when she told me that her bedroom ceiling is full of holes so she gets wet when it rains and that she is afraid of the rats looking for food under her bed at night. She named it when she told us that the information book she brought so eagerly to share with the class had been found at the dump during a family search for clothing and articles for the house. Janice names her world every time she has to ask her parents for money for a class trip, party, or function: "Mommy don't gots no money today. Maybe on Friday," she tells us hopefully.

If by naming our experiences we give others access to it, what happens to children like Janice when they openly accept the invitation to name their world? What do we do with and to Janice's world when she trusts the supposedly risk-free environment we establish for her? O'Neill (1990) states:

> If classroom discourse does not make explicit assumptions about the constructedness of texts and the cultural values that texts might endorse, then the personal growth model will validate the

> primary spontaneous response which has the greatest degree of fit with the dominant culture. (p. 88)

When Janice volunteered information about her cat, she quickly realized she had fallen short of an expectation for her story when she had to reply to Bobby's question about why her mother had not taken the injured cat to the vet.

When Janice described her bedroom ceiling, the rats under her bed, and her fear, she was met with surprised looks and silence from the two other girls at her table. She was also met with a most inadequate response from me, her teacher. Feeling totally lost about how to handle this unexpected, shared experience, but not wanting to ignore it, I asked all three children at the table if they had any thoughts about why our homes could be so different. Because the two little girls who definitely don't have holes in their ceilings or rats under their beds shrugged at my question, the onus for response fell to Janice, who responded sadly, "Just 'cause, I guess."

When Janice shared her story of finding her information book at a family outing to the dump, she made obvious efforts to ignore the shocked responses of "at the dump!" made by three of her classmates, and noticeably warmed to my comment that I was always surprised to learn what valuable things people threw away and that I was really glad she had found this book because we could certainly use it in preparation for our class trip.

Rather than tell me in the classroom that she doesn't have the money needed for class trips and parties, Janice now waits for me in the hall so she can tell me privately that she will probably have it tomorrow or the next day: "Will that still be okay, Connie?" she whispers.

Manning (1993) says, "It's the reflexivity that's important here, that helps us get beyond navel gazing. . . . Action involves doing, reflection a making of connections and reflexivity, a repositioning of oneself in the world as a result of the learning" (p. 7). How can Janice or any of us reposition ourselves through the naming of any of Janice's experiences? We didn't take the time to talk about them or study them. We've barely offered Janice a place to make connections and reflect, let alone a place to take action through learning.

If we really want children to name their worlds, why do we struggle with Janice's named experiences? Do we really want to hear them? As we have made efforts as whole language teachers to celebrate each and every individual child, we have also opened the door to a much bigger issue. Individual children's lives are constructed by their culture. When we say we want to hear from children, are we really prepared to hear about their culture? Are we ready to bring that culture into the classroom and talk about how it is constructed and maintained by society and by our schools? Are we ready to include the children by asking Shannon's question, "Why are things the way they are?" (Comber, 1992)?

The invitation to children to name their world should not leave some of them standing in the shadows of others' worlds feeling exposed and vulnerable. It should not bring their experiences to the forefront and then dismiss them. Nor should the invitation to name the world and celebrate that naming carry exclusive rights for particular children only.

Silencing the Poor at School

Janice's mother brought Janice to school to register her in May two years ago, just a few days after Janice's fifth birthday. Although we hold registration for the new five-year-olds in May, they do not officially begin school until the following September. We first met Janice on a balmy May morning when she burst through the door of our gym and squealed in delight, "Me's startin' school a'day." As Janice dashed off to look at the toys we had placed in the middle of the room for the children to play with, I greeted her mother who, looking tired and nervous, had followed Janice into the gym.

The storybooks and conversations in Janice's classroom are not the only texts that exclude her. Janice is positioned in poverty, silence, and "otherness" in most contexts at school. Although I am just beginning to become aware of my role in this, I now see that it began to happen for Janice even before her first official day at school.

In spite of the fact that our school serves many families who have much less income than those in our more affluent neighboring communities, there is no special funding for the low-income students who attend. Although there is a formula that determines each school's budget, including each school's spending quota for a government-regulated Book Bureau, this formula is calculated on the number of students in the school, not on the economic status of those students.

While some of the basic supplies such as paper and textbooks are taken care of through this budget, items such as pencils, markers, crayons, scissors, glue, art supplies, notebooks, etc., are the responsibility of each individual student. Because many of the students in our school don't have books or crayons at home or haven't worked with scissors, glue, play dough, or other art supplies before coming to school, we teachers are often caught in a double bind of not wanting to ask students for money for supplies they can't afford, but at the same time wanting to offer them the opportunities to work with the same resources and materials that other students are working with. When Janice came to school to register, we asked her and all the other children registering for $30 to buy their school supplies for the year. Janice has six siblings, five of whom are already in school.

When Janice and her mother came to register her, they entered a room filled with toys for the children and tables designated as places for parents to fill out forms or to meet with teachers. As Janice scooted around the room, from child to child, and from play area to play area, her mother took her place beside other parents at the long table and slowly opened the file folder in front of her. It took Janice's mother a long time to fill out the three pages in the registration folder. She glanced up at Janice a few times, looked over at the teachers' area, and stared out the window. Eventually she stood up, and after stopping to tell Janice to remember she was in school now and had to be a good little girl, she walked toward my table.

How were Janice and her mother positioned at school on registration day? The registration forms that asked Janice's mother to name her occupation and that of Janice's father; the large empty space on a page asking for Janice's nursery school, Sunday school, or other early learning experiences; the open receipt book at the "interview" table poised and ready for the parent's name to be inscribed beside the $30 amount we'd designated as needed for school supplies; and the dressed up clothes we teachers wore that day were only a few of many aspects of school encounters that placed Janice and her family in inferior and threatening positions.

Janice's mother did not write "welfare" beside her occupation or that of her partner's. Fidgeting with the unopened purse on her lap, eyes looking away from me, Janice's mother said she'd forgotten her checkbook and she hoped she could pay Janice's $30 school supply money another day. On the page that asked for Janice's early learning experiences, she did not write that weekend family dances, which included all members of Janice's immediate and extended family, offered Janice lots of conversation and storytelling opportunities. Janice spent her dance nights listening to her grandmother's stories of the past. She did not write that Janice was learning to find her way through the dump to salvage things they needed for their home. In the "welcoming space" provided on one of the registration sheets, where parents were invited to write freely about the things the children enjoyed doing at home with their family, Janice's mother did not write that Janice spent a lot of time watching television and movie videos with her family. As she sat down at my table, Janice's mother was visibly uncomfortable when she handed me her papers with the blank spaces.

The interview with Janice's mother was difficult for both of us. I felt there were different questions I should ask of Janice's mother, but I didn't know what they were. I felt there were questions Janice's mother wanted to ask of me, but she sat quietly, waiting to be asked questions or to be told what to do next. While I referred to the blank spaces on the forms she'd handed me and asked if there was anything she had thought of that she would like me to write in those spaces, Janice's mother shook her head and looked anxious for our time together to end. After she left my table, Janice's mother picked up Janice and moved on to be seen by the public health nurse and the speech and language consultant for our area, and then the hour-and-a-half registration process was completed. As Janice's mother took her daughter firmly by the hand, indicating it was time to leave, she glanced back toward the tables where we teachers were sitting. Watching them turn to leave, I imagined Janice's mother knew she had exposed her world to us. In spite of the blanks she had left on her papers and the noncommittal shake of her head she'd given in response to many of our questions, Janice's mother must have known the judgmental eye of the institution could see her.

When Janice and her mother left after registration, we teachers talked about the torn and faded blue dress Janice's mother wore and said how nice it was that Janice's mother had tried to dress up for her daughter on this special day. Silently, I wondered how Janice's mother felt about the clothes we teachers had worn for Janice's special day. We lamented that it was not likely we would ever see the money for Janice's school supplies and wondered how we would buy what she needed for school. We talked about the unlikelihood that Janice's mother would follow our advice and read to Janice over the summer, and we wondered whether Janice's mother had taken so long filling out her form because she was having difficulty reading. We shook our heads and wondered why her mother would buy a TV, VCR, and movies but not spend time reading to Janice or her siblings, and when she could not pay for their school supplies.

How do we know that school has the right perspective? Who determines how we should dress to come to school? Who does that decision privilege? Who does it discriminate against? Who decides what kinds of questions we should ask about children's lives when they come to school? Whose values does this privilege? Whose values does it call into question? Who decides what we should read and how we should speak? Who does this practice give voice to? Who does it silence? Who creates and maintains our schools? Who do they benefit? Who do they marginalize?

Bronwyn Davies (1993) writes:

> What children encounter in schools is a "regulated and polymorphous incitement to discourse" (Foucault 1978, 34). In classrooms [where] formal ownership of knowledge is assumed by teachers—[who] have the authoritative codes for interpreting meaning—children do not have the freedom to innovate with or to reject adult interpretations. What they have formerly learned in the process of learning to engage in discursive practices is now subjected to authoritative teaching. The categories to which they have been assigned are now potentially subsumed under educational categories of success and failure. Getting it right is not just a matter of being able to converse competently, but a matter of

> becoming competent in the terms that the teacher designates as competent. (p. 153)

Janice's mother wants her daughter to "get it right." Beginning with registration day, she makes it clear she wants Janice to remember that being in school means being a good girl. In spite of the fact that she is obviously uncomfortable with them, Janice's mother doesn't question the rituals of registration day. Although she was failed by her own schooling, Janice's mother takes the blame on herself and believes that because she herself failed, Janice should not question the rituals of classroom or school life. In the year and a half since I've known Janice's mother, she has never questioned me or any school authority. Her only defenses against school's authoritarian intrusion on her life have been her silence and her absence.

In spite of her desire to see her daughter do well at school, I have seen Janice's mother on only one occasion other than registration day. Each year our school holds three regularly scheduled parent-teacher meetings. So far neither Janice's mother nor her father has attended any of these, nor any of the meetings for their other children. In addition to the school-scheduled meetings, I hold monthly meetings for the parents of the children in my classroom. These meetings have been my attempt to remove some of the institutional barriers that I feel have restricted parent-teacher relationships and limited conversations and communication. I have felt over the years that these meetings have helped parents have a voice in what happens in the classroom. We've talked extensively about curriculum and ways of teaching and learning; we've talked about classroom needs; we've shopped together to place books and supplies in the classroom; we've planned class trips; and we've decided on fundraisers together.

Our classroom is no longer shaped just by me; it is also shaped by the parents of more privileged children such as Bobby, Gwen, Ellen, and Linda. Over the past couple of years, I've become aware that while parents have been sincerely invited to participate in their child's classroom, it has usually only been the parents of particular children who have accepted the invitation. I have begun to wonder if my gestures of opening the doors wider to parents may, in fact, be more oppressive than ever to Janice's parents.

For Janice's mother, who really does care about her but who finds the school such a silencing place to be, no doubt it was easier to find excuses for not attending three parent-teacher evenings than it was to find excuses for the extra ten meetings for my class. Janice's mother has not come to any of those monthly meetings.

If Janice's mother had come to the monthly meetings, what could she have said? Have those meetings been invitations to inclusion or to further silence and exclusion? Has there been a way for Janice's mother to tell us that she finds it difficult to attend the meetings or special events because often her car does not work and when it does there is not enough gas to take an unscheduled trip to the school to pick up a sick child, let alone to attend the extra meetings? Could Janice's mother have told us that she does not have the money or the supplies to bake for our fundraising cookie sales or to buy raffle tickets for our baskets? Could Janice's mother have told us she wished we didn't hold Christmas concerts, because Janice begged to have pretty dresses like other girls in her class or school and because she didn't know what to say to Janice when she begged her to go to the concert to watch her on stage? Could Janice's mother have told us that buying inexpensive valentines for five of her children to give out to their classmates made a big difference in what she was able to buy the family for supper? Could Janice's mother have told us she would rather we didn't take her daughter on class trips the rest of us were so excited about? Could she have told us she didn't know where she would find the extra lunch money or money for a ticket to a play? Could Janice's mother have found a way to respond to judgmental frowns and raised eyebrows when other parents realized she owned a middle-class luxury item—that is, a VCR? Would it have been more acceptable to these lower-middle-class parents to know that Janice watched a TV and a VCR that were found at the dump, or one that Janice's mother had purchased from a real store like they did? Was there really a way she could say what she needed to say? How often should I expect Janice's mother to dress up to come to school?

Exclusion and silencing don't just happen. They are not the consequence of one event. They are constructed through continual acts of oppression that sometimes occur through knowingly deliberate actions and sometimes through actions of less conscious intent. Oppression can happen through the almost invisible layering of repeatedly positioning subjects in subordinate positions through events that are introduced, controlled, and maintained by those in more powerful positions.

The Myth of Equal Education

"I so proud of Janice. She do hard work and is good girl." This is the comment Janice's mother wrote on the back of Janice's report card before sending it back to me last term. As I looked at the large bold handwriting on the report card, an overwhelming sense of helplessness hit me. Her comments made me doubt whether Janice's mother had actually read much of the two-page anecdotal report I had sent, and I wondered what she had understood from what she had read. I wasn't even sure what Janice's report card said to me. I was not certain I had written the report for Janice's mother. Somehow the file that would hold the carbon copy to be read by Janice's teachers after me was a major factor in my mind as I tried to write clearly and convincingly about Janice's many strengths and eager attitude. Looking at Janice's mother's writing again, I worried about where school would take this wonderful little girl whose mother was so proud of her.

Janice is indeed doing good work. She is independently reading the text of many of the books in our story corner. It is difficult to keep markers, paper, and pencils out of her hands as she writes storybooks, messages, letters, and cards in easily readable spelling approximations. Her determination to push herself into every challenge offered in the classroom has ensured that she is working beside the strongest math students in the class. Janice is happy and extremely helpful to everyone in our class and in our school. Janice does not question what is asked of her, why it is asked of her, or where it is taking her. Right now, Janice is the good girl her mother wants her to be.

Connell (1993) writes:

> Researchers in France, the United States, Britain, Canada and Australia, all found the relationship between school knowledge and the production of social inequality to be a key issue.
>
> A crucial policy conclusion follows. Justice cannot be achieved by distributing the same amount of a standard good to children of all social classes. Education is a process operating through relationships which cannot be neutralized or obliterated to allow equal distribution of the social good at their core. That good means different things to ruling class and working-class children, and will do different things for them (or to them). (p. 19)

Although Janice is doing well in school right now, her older siblings, some of whom have already moved into the junior high school, are not meeting with the same success. Homework assignments not done, tests not studied for, public speeches and projects on the rain forest brought in late or not done at all, science fair entries carelessly constructed, irresponsible attitudes toward schoolwork—all have been cited on report cards and by teachers as problems for Janice's brothers and sister.

While I would like to call into question the assumptions that lead teachers to assign homework on a regular basis, give marks for creative writing with deductions for spelling errors, or designate a portion of a term science mark to the individual results of efforts and scores on a countywide science fair, right now these are the practices giving life and measurement to the curricula of Janice's siblings and their classmates. These are the things that determine whether they are experiencing success or failure at school. The "standard good" being delivered to all is doing different things for different students. Not much has changed since Janice's mother went to school; the scene is an all too familiar one. The curricula, the assessments, and the standard good that failed her have already begun to fail her children.

According to Connell (1993):

> Though the school is a distinct institution, with doors of its own, education is never a closed system. Schools are interwoven with their milieu. Their design and functioning presuppose relationships with families, workplaces, labor markets and neighborhoods; and the way schools are designed, as Dorothy Smith notes, presupposes that an adult is in the home during normal adult

> working hours, i.e., it assumes a non-employed mother. The custom of setting homework presupposes a home where schoolwork can easily be done; and so forth. (p. 28)

Janice's mother did not complete school and she has sole charge of the children's schooling. Do we really believe Janice's mother can buy Janice's fourteen-year-old sister the supplies she needs and help her create a science fair entry that can do well when it has been assigned for marks and competition? When Janice's thirteen-year-old brother fails his math exam and is told to get extra help, do we really expect Janice's mother to get him a tutor as Gwen's mother and father did for her older brother? Janice's family spends a lot of time together with extended family, sharing the present and past through verbal storytelling. When Janice's eleven-year-old brother is given a writing assignment to describe his Thanksgiving weekend, do we expect him to write his family's story, complete with dialogue, in school language or in the language he shares with his family? Who in his family can help ensure he will not lose marks for misspellings and incorrect grammar? When Janice's siblings carry their homework to the crowded kitchen table after supper, do we expect Janice's mother to know how to help her children study for the same tests that failed her? And when I, Janice's teacher, advise Janice's mother to read to her at home over the summer, do I realize that reading for the sake of reading will not necessarily be helpful to Janice? Do I realize that I have suggested that her mother read to her from the very books that make Janice's life and that of her family invisible?

Learning to Read the World

Janice is so full of energy, hope, and determination that it's difficult not to see her as the biggest question of my teaching career. But this chapter is not just about Janice; it is about her siblings, her friends, and her many classmates whose lives, just like hers, are caught in the cycle of poverty. Where is school taking them? Twenty-six years from now, will their children come to our school and perhaps sit in our classrooms to receive the same "standard good" that Janice and her classmates are receiving now? What good has it done? What good is it doing? What good will it ever do? How can our classrooms and our schools come to mean something different for these children? Connell (1993) says:

> If the school system is dealing unjustly with some of its pupils, they are not the only ones to suffer. The quality of education for all the others is degraded.
>
> I would like to shout this from the rooftops every time I hear another argument for the "gifted and talented programs," for tougher "standards" and stricter selection, for streaming or tracking, for merit awards and opportunity schools and honors programs. In short, for any of the hundred and one affronts to equal provision of education. All education that privileges one child over another is giving the privileged child a corrupted education, even as it gives him or her a social or economic advantage.
>
> The issue of social justice is not an add-on. It is fundamental to what good education is about. (p. 15)

I believe that children, in fact all of us, have to be able to name our worlds in order to learn. I believe that before we can understand how to take action to outgrow ourselves, we have to name our experiences and reflect on and study them, and I believe this has to happen among others who are investing in their own learning as well. We don't learn alone; learning is a social process. The beliefs I hold and operate from have grown and developed because of my own learning. Children like Janice have been teaching me about learning for a long time now.

But Janice has also shown me that naming the world is not easy, not even desirable for many children and adults. When texts present children and their families' lives as invisible or undesirable, where do they learn the language with which to name their world and who is going to understand that language when they try to speak? Is it safe for them to speak? Is there anyone who wants to hear it? If Janice and her mother were to name their world in a way that required all of us to listen, to study, and to reflect on those experiences, the conversations at school and in Janice's classroom might have to change forever. Are Janice's school, teachers, and classmates ready for that to happen?

The students in my classroom are trying to make connections all the time. They are intrigued when we read books and talk about the rain forest. They can find the rain forests on maps and globes, and they can tell me which animals are in danger because their homes in these forests are being destroyed. They want to understand how this relates to my constant reminders that "Yes! Although we love to write and draw, we have to be careful not to waste paper." They connect my worries to their questions. They tell me that their own homes are surrounded by trees, so perhaps the world is not running out of trees and we don't have to be as careful as I have suggested. We talk and read about the animals whose lives will be endangered as their homes are cut down. These students want to talk about the animals they have at home. They care about their animals, even if they are only with them for a winter before they are slaughtered for food. They need to talk about how killing animals for food is not the same as pushing a species to extinction. Then we find the golden toad and learn it is endangered partly because it has been used as a delicacy for food in some countries. They become angry at the notion that animals are killed for food that is a treat, not a necessity. We stop for a brief conversation about the treats we eat to wonder what we might be endangering. They ask to learn more about the animals of the rain forest, and they are anxious to contribute their thoughts about how the destruction might be stopped. Understanding the rain forests' role in the life cycle of our planet is a complex concept for them, but the rain forest books and the atlases in our classroom are well worn, the conversations endless, and the search to understand more never ending. Connections make new understandings that become a part of us and create a craving to know more.

In order to make sense of our world, we need those connections; we need to understand so that we don't operate blindly in our efforts to change the way things are. As a child, I was not invited or expected to make connections when I went to school. My learning was supposed to be the "adding bits of knowledge" kind (Manning, 1993), or as Freire called it, "the banking method" (qtd. in Bigelow, 1991), in which students were receptacles for deposits of knowledge from their teachers and texts. The only questions we were invited to ask were those that added more information to the supposedly growing bank of knowledge. I didn't have the opportunity through my learning to locate my experiences socially, to understand how I was being constructed as a white lower-middle-class female. I did not see that my family, my teachers, my school, my church, my neighbors, and all the other players in my life participated in creating who I would become.

Only in the past few years, through my own studies, have I begun to articulate my questions and try to locate experiences socially, probing the social factors that made and limited who I am as a woman. The journey was incredibly painful and not without anger (White, 1994). Part of what frightened me about taking this journey was that I might see more, know more, and still be trapped in the same place I'd been when I began the journey. I believed there was more safety in not knowing about things I could not change. I was also afraid that in leaving behind the old understandings, I would move to a place where I would be alone with my new understandings, anger, and pain. Would I still know how to talk to those who shared my life before I began to probe and search? Would I still want to? Would they?

Two years ago I made the choice to take that journey. Although I made that choice in part as a response to a commitment to a master's program, the decision to probe and search was really mine to make. Although it would not have been easy, I could have walked away from the master's program. I did not need the degree for my job. I had enrolled in the program for myself.

Janice and her friends cannot walk away from school. They've just begun their journey, and they don't have a choice about whether to stay, at least not for a few years yet. If Janice and her classmates begin to probe and search, the possibility of encountering pain and anger are very real. Having to cope with alienation or misunderstandings from those who share their world becomes a strong possibility. Learning about poverty cannot be an "add on" piece of knowledge for any of us. Connections will be sought, experiences will be named, new understandings will begin to take shape, and Janice's eager, cheerful smile might well disappear. That is a risk, and a big one. But the risk of allowing an unquestioned future to lead Janice, as it has her mother, back to an unchanged classroom practice twenty-six years from now seems by far the bigger risk.

Edelsky (1994) writes, "Progressive language educators' theories-in-practice, therefore, could just as well be a kinder, gentler way to maintain those systems of dominance—a kinder, gentler way of keeping us as far from a democracy as ever" (p. 255). Janice's story is not just about Janice; it is about a culture of poverty. My teacher story is not about one teacher's experiences in a classroom; it is about an institution that maintains a status quo that gives power to the privileged. This chapter is not about one individual child; it is about the society we live in and maintain through our institutions and practices.

We can't talk about poverty in our classrooms and ignore Janice's life and those of many other students. This will make these students' positions vulnerable and not necessarily by their choice. It will make us all vulnerable, whether we like it or not. Bobby really wanted to understand why Janice's mother had not taken her cat to the vet. The three little boys who exclaimed "At the dump!" at Janice's revelation that she got her book there wanted to know more about how that came to be. Children won't learn about poverty in the abstract—they need to feel it deeply. It's time we all felt it deeply.

It's not okay that we didn't talk about Janice's cat from the point of view of the disadvantaged and that we didn't take a closer look at how she and her pet were positioned, both in the book we were reading and the conversation that followed the reading. It's not okay that Janice felt it was safe to name her world and so told me and two of her classmates that she had rats under her bed and holes in her ceiling and that she was afraid, and that we let the conversation wither and die without talking about what we assume when we talk about our homes at school and why those assumptions thrive.

It's not okay that Janice feels she has to meet me in the hall to tell me that she doesn't have the money for a class party, trip, or treat that a particular group of parents, teachers, or I have decided on. It's not okay that we've already shown Janice that poverty is her shame, not ours. We need to talk about who makes the decisions about what we do in the classroom and where those decisions place all students.

It's not okay that Janice must find her books at the dump while other children buy their books at bookstores and school book fairs or order them from the book club each month. It's not okay that we heard her story about searching for things her family needed at the dump without considering how difficult it was for Janice to say it and then asking ourselves why. It's not okay that we just made a place for her story and accepted it without a further look.

It's not okay that Janice feels she must adopt others' story lines in order to participate in a conversation with her classmates. It's not okay for me to assume that because I place a book in our story corner which I think foregrounds poverty, race, or gender issues that those books will necessarily make poverty, race, or gender any more visible or understandable than they were before those books existed in our classroom.

It's not okay that I dress up to meet Janice's mother. Clothes are symbols of power. It's not okay to not recognize this and change the practice.

It's not okay that Janice's mother has to look away and adopt others' story lines when she says she forgot her checkbook and cannot pay for her daughter's school supplies on registration day. It's not okay not to recognize how this positions Janice and her mother and to leave the issue invisible and unchanged.

It's not okay that I simply advise Janice's mother to read to her at home over the summer, promoting the false notion that reading good books—that is, middle-class books—will make a difference in Janice's life.

It's not okay that we assume the "standard good" offers the same thing to Janice and her siblings that it does to privileged children. It hasn't, it doesn't, and it never will. It's not okay that we promote the notion that it is the fault of Janice's mother, the children themselves, or the way they live that they are not succeeding in school. It's not okay that we don't talk about this at school.

It's not okay that Janice and her mother cannot name their world at school because it would be misunderstood or too difficult for the rest of us to look at.

There are multitudes of things that are not okay at school for those who live in poverty. But perhaps the main thing that is not okay is that we have been able to make poverty invisible and consequently never had to confront our complicity in maintaining it.

Edelsky (1994) writes:

> Those systems—of class, race, gender, whose impact is heightened by their relation to profit and the bottom line—seep into all aspects of life: public and private, in school and out. Growing up within them, we've breathed them in so they're part of our thinking, our values and our opinions. In other words, we'd have no trouble finding things to examine that would lead to exposing some system of domination. These systems show up everywhere, if we just look. (p. 254)

Where do we start looking? We can start with what we're doing, with what we've been doing, with what is happening all around us, and we can start with Janice. We can start with what it is we think we know and ask ourselves how we know it. We can ask ourselves why we are reading this book right now. Who chose it? What does it say to you, to me, to everyone? We can ask why it says different things to different people. We can ask who started this conversation. What is it really about? Who have we left out of the conversation? We can ask why that is.

We start by asking questions—of ourselves, of each other, of the students—not questions we think we know the answers to, but questions we're truly ready to research together. As teachers we can ask ourselves why it's been so hard to see some of these things ourselves. Then we can ask ourselves why it gets scary for us as teachers when we do begin to see these things and want to take action.

We need to do all of these things and more, and somehow we have to do them without trading one kind of oppression for another or, as Edelsky (1994) puts it, "*without bashing students over the head with it*" (p. 256; Edelsky's emphasis). Last fall, Jerrod spoke up during one of our many talks about how gender was constructed in the books we were reading. Sighing a bit impatiently, he asked, "Can't we just go back to interrupting you to talk when we need to, the way we used to do it?" Jerrod was in his second year with me, but throughout his first year he had always enjoyed raising questions to argue or open up discussion.

His voice was heard frequently in our story corner. During his second year with me, as I explored a critical literacy curriculum with the students, he grew restless, bored, and unhappy if I intervened and directed the discussion for any length of time.

Finding a balance may not be easy. Certain groups of students have been oppressed for a long time. Jerrod doesn't belong to any of those groups I'm most concerned about right now, but he's a bright and sensitive boy and we're going to need him to listen and to care. We have to be careful not to turn some students off while trying to turn others on.

Our classroom is a place where we read and write and talk a lot. It's a place for naming our worlds and making connections. This has been the case for some more than others, and now it has to become a place where we can *all* name our worlds, so that *all* of our worlds can be studied, thought about, and acted on. We have to put aside blame and not get lost in pity. And we have to look at what we haven't wanted to see. Our classroom has to become a place where we talk about how all our worlds have been created. It has to become a place where we ask ourselves whether we want to participate in renaming the world in the same way or in changing it. And then we have to understand that renaming begins with Janice, with Ellen, with Bobby, with me, and with all of us. It's going to mean caring for and about one another in ways that may feel confrontational and uncomfortable. It's going to mean accepting resistance from students, something schools and teachers are not good at doing. It's going to mean Janice might not be a good girl at school all the time, but hopefully she'll begin to learn how to talk about her world in a way that can put the school's behavior in question as much as, or more than, hers.

Janice will not be able to do this on her own.

Gilbert and Taylor (1991) write, "The key to empowerment for young women seems to lie in the development of a sense of social or collective identity as girls or young women, rather than merely in the development of a sense of identity as an individual" (p. 139). I think the need for a collective holds true for those oppressed by poverty as well. As Edelsky (1994) notes, "You can't have class action if there's no class" (p. 255).

Last year, three weeks after we'd read and discussed the book *The Girl Who Hated Dinner* (Siamon, 1979), a visiting teacher came to our classroom. She was reading the students a story before we all headed outdoors to play on the new equipment the students had been anxiously waiting to try out. Believing reading should be a time for the teacher to read and the students to be silent, this visitor was alarmed at how often the students tried to interrupt the story to talk. Finally, she said she would only allow the students who listened quietly to the story to go out to play on the equipment; those who continued to interrupt would have to stay indoors. She read on for about two more lines before Bobby spoke up: "That's not fair. We always talk about our books. It helps us to understand. And the reason you can keep us from the playground is because you're the boss and bigger than us and we're just kids." Taking the book *The Girl Who Hated Dinner* out of the book bucket beside him, Bobby showed the surprised guest how the little girl in that book had been tricked into eating her dinner by the adults in her life, and then he proceeded to talk about how many books we'd found in our story corner that thoughtlessly placed children in inferior positions beside the "all-knowing adults." The other students scrambled to find some of those books to show the visiting teacher, who quietly closed the book she'd chosen to read and began to listen instead. Then everybody got ready and headed to the new playground equipment together.

Bobby was lucky. Not all people in positions of power will accept that kind of resistance. But he felt confident in the company he kept, the conversations we'd had, and the books he had available to make a case for an injustice he felt. He experienced the strength of belonging to a collective and risked action, which successfully changed the course of events that he felt were oppressive.

This is new ground for all of us. But just as Bobby knew he should not have to accept how the students were being positioned that day, so we have to find ways to help Janice and the many other children living in poverty know that they should not have to accept how the poor have been positioned in our schools either. And we can't leave them alone with those in power to resist on their own. Together we have to find out how they are positioned in the classroom, as well as in our classroom texts and in the school's discourses and practices. They need to feel the security of the company they are in, the conversations they have participated in, and the texts they can use in order to make a case for the injustices they have suffered for too long.

I began this chapter by asking whose stories should be told in our classrooms. And whom we keep safe when stories are silenced. I believe our classrooms must become places where all students, not just the privileged, can name their world. But I also believe it's up to all of us to put those stories in motion, to help the students see the connections my schooling didn't allow or want me to see. We all need to see that it wasn't just one book, or one TV program, or one commercial, or one discussion, or one test, or one meeting, or one of anything that excluded Janice's experiences from the world. We need to see that we've all played a role in her oppression. If we silence Janice's story, we do it to benefit ourselves, the privileged and the powerful, because we don't have to work to change what we can't see. We have to look hard and see. We should not participate in giving students a corrupted education (Connell, 1993).

As Luke (1991) says:

> For our students reading the word can entail critical readings of the world, learning to be curious, skeptical, engaged and noncomplacent. But there is a preliminary step that we as teachers must make—teaching literacies requires first that we undertake readings of the world. (p. 143)

What is most difficult is that I have to expect a happy, eager, trusting six-year-old girl, who told me her world is the way it is "just because," to have patience while I learn.

References

Bigelow, B. (1991). Rethinking Columbus: Teaching about the 500th anniversary of Columbus's arrival in America [Special issue]. *Rethinking Schools.*

Bunting, E. (1991). *Fly away home*. New York: Clarion Books.

Comber, B. (1992). Critical literacy: A selective review and discussion of recent literature. *South Australian Educational Leader, 3*(1), 1–10.

Connell, R. W. (1993). *Schools and social justice*. Toronto: Our Schools/ Our Selves Education Foundation.

Davies, B. (1993). Beyond dualism and towards multiple subjectivities. In L. Christian-Smith (Ed.), *Texts of desire: Essays on fiction, femininity and schooling*. London: Falmer Press.

Edelsky, C. (1994). Education for democracy. *Language Arts, 71*(4), 252–57.

Gilbert, P., & Taylor, S. (1991). *Fashioning the feminine: Girls, popular culture, and schooling*. North Sydney, Australia: Allen & Unwin.

Littledale, F. (1992). *The elves and the shoemaker*. New York: Scholastic.

Luke, A. (1991). Literacies as social practices. *English Education, 23*(3), 131–47.

Mackay, K. (1994). *Journey into critical literacy: Towards interrogating text and teaching*. Halifax, Novia Scotia: Mount St. Vincent University.

Manning, A. (1993). Curriculum as conversation. Keynote address given at Western Australian Reading Conference. May, Perth, West Australia.

Munsch, R. (1990). *Something good*. Toronto: Annick Press.

O'Neill, M. (1990). Molesting the text: Promoting resistant readings. In M. Hayhoe & S. Parker (Eds.), *Reading & response* (pp. 84–93). Milton Keynes, UK: Open University Press.

Siamon, S. (1979). *The girl who hated dinner*. Toronto: Gage.

White, C. (1990). *Jevon doesn't sit at the back anymore*. Toronto: Scholastic.

White, C. (1994). *Beyond endings: A feminist poststructuralist analysis of identities*. Unpublished master's thesis, Mount St. Vincent University, Halifax, Nova Scotia.

Chapter Ten

Classroom Inquiry into the Incidental Unfolding of Social Justice Issues: Seeking Out Possibilities in the Lives of Learners

Vivian Vasquez
American University

This chapter focuses on my inquiries into critical literacy in practice. Children's artifacts are used as a springboard into exploring possibilities for critical classroom inquiry of social justice issues using whole language as a functional context.

> Next year I don't want to go in a portable because when it hot it very hot and when it cold it very cold so I don't want to
>
> Marianne

This message was written by Marianne, a seven-year-old with whom I worked over two years ago. Through this message, Marianne implicitly asks the question, "Why are things the way they are?" I found myself taken aback by Marianne's letter.

I cannot remember as a child of seven being comfortable making anything connected to the world of school problematic. I don't remember asking questions, expressing feelings, or expecting responses. As a young learner at school, such assertiveness was foreign to me. I was used to rows of desks, little islands of silence, the sacrifice of individuality for the sake of conformity and control. Conforming to the silence expected at school did not mean that I was in agreement. Nevertheless, as a young girl raised in the traditions of Filipino culture I was always taught to respect my elders and to do so without question. Asuncion David-

Maramba (1971), a Filipina, explains what being mannerly meant: "When a person of authority comes to the school, a priest, a person of age, or importance, he [the student] should stand up from his seat and greet the visitor with "Good Morning" or "Good Afternoon" as the case may be" (p. 348). Further, "in the classroom he [the student] should not speak unless asked by the teacher, and before answering, should get up. He [the student] should do the same when with his elders."

As a person of color living in North America, I argue that whole language and inquiry pedagogies must not ignore race, culture, or ethnicity. I share the challenges produced by my reading and thinking about critical literacy and how this led me to look differently at written conversations and letters children produce. I then demonstrate that if children have opportunities for extended conversation, they will raise questions about the world, and that written conversation and letters are great avenues to engage in this kind of inquiry. My approach is to listen to, pick up on, and build curriculum around these questions rather than shut down everyday instances in which children inquire into issues of justice in their communities and society.

Personal Inquiry into Critical Literacy

I never used to look at learning as a process that could move someone, repositioning them in a different place at a given time—that is, not until I began to read about socially critical literacies (Lankshear, 1989; Luke, 1991; Comber, 1993). Prior to experiencing these texts, my definition of critical literacy "involved taking action to resist, to expose the discourse of dominant cultures" (Vasquez, 1994, p. 39). My recent engagement with these texts has led me to reread my own experiences (Comber & O'Brien, 1993), looking from a different perspective at events and artifacts such as children's letters. Shannon (1995) argues that a critical view of reality challenges the injustices and inequalities of the status quo by asking the question, Why are things the way they are? If this question is applied to texts and discourses as well as to social conditions, students begin to participate in a critical literacy curriculum.

Participating in this curriculum calls for teachers to initiate students into a socially critical approach to literacy by problematizing texts (Comber, 1993). One place to start is through disrupting social texts by asking questions such as, What does this mean? What do I do with this? What does all this do to me? (Freebody & Luke, 1990).

In a more recent article titled "Education for Democracy," Edelsky (1994) addresses political gaps in the whole language agenda. "[W]hole language as described theoretically by me, among others, . . . can as easily support *avoiding* looking at [issues like] white privilege . . . as they support looking *at* it" (p. 254). Edelsky argues that progressive theories such as whole language don't go far enough because they don't tie language to power, tie text interpretation to societal structures, or tie reading and writing to perpetuating or resisting social attitudes and institutions.

Revisiting children's letters and written conversation, I have realized how much of what I have been doing in the name of hearing students' voices that challenge taken-for-granted social structures has only scratched the surface. My intent here is to explore where critical literacy experiences could have unfolded. For me, this exploration constitutes a starting point for understanding how I can help children become critical readers of text and how children's inquiries can help me support the possibilities for critical literacy in the classroom.

The possibility of exploring critical literacy is rooted in my experience with whole language philosophy both in theory and in practice and as a person of color going to school in Canada. I briefly explain how my history as a student locates me in a critical project.

A Personal Aside: A Voice from the Past

When I was ten years old, my family and I packed a life's worth of belongings into fourteen suitcases and immigrated to Canada from the Philippines. A year later I met Mrs. Anderson, my grade 6 teacher. While I was in grade 6, I thought she was a good teacher because she always had many things for us to do. Looking back,

I remember noticing that in Mrs. Anderson's classroom there wasn't time to think because we were always so busy. We had time only for the things that grade 6 students were supposed to do. "Don't stand there thinking about it, just get it done!" she often said.

One of the grade 6 projects was individual research on a topic dealing with mammals or insects. This thing called research was foreign to me. I had not run across this activity in previous years of schooling. School rules in the Philippines were different from the rules in the Canadian school. In the Philippines, the only time I was allowed to talk inside the classroom was after having figured out an answer to a question, raising my hand, and then being chosen to answer. In other words, students were expected to listen, not to ask questions.

When Mrs. Anderson assigned the research project, I had no idea where to begin. I wasn't accustomed to asking questions of the teacher, so I remained silent in my confusion. She did mention that the encyclopedia was a great source of information and that we could "find our research in there." So off I went to find the encyclopedia with the research in it. I found the "I" volume first, which was how I decided to do my research on insects. I began to read, write, and copy the information.

When Mrs. Anderson decided it was time to share our research, we brought our chairs to the front of the classroom. I remember feeling a bit silly sitting up at the front of the room, as though we were members of an orchestra. Mrs. Anderson looked like a conductor with her pointer stick in hand. As she stood in front of us, I realized that Mrs. Anderson didn't just look like a conductor—she was the conductor.

The symphony began as the last chair was set in place, forming a semicircle in front of Mrs. Anderson. One by one, with a wave of her stick and a nod of her head, we were called up to the front to perform individually. Most of the presentations went on with limited interruption from Mrs. Anderson. She liked what the students had written. I thought she might like what I had written. I had used my very best Assumption Convent handwriting. (In the Philippines, many of the private schools, one of which was Assumption Convent, my school, had a signature way of forming letters, or handwriting. It was easy to tell which school a student attended by the way he or she formed letters. Further, certain schools were labeled *the* schools to attend. Assumption was one of *the* schools.)

My turn arrived. I was nervous. I could feel my voice shaking through my arms into my hands and onto the paper I held tightly. After I had read a few lines, Mrs. Anderson asked me to stop. "Just wait," she said. With this command, she walked to the back of the room, picked out an encyclopedia from the bookshelf, turned to the page where I had found my research, and then asked me to continue reading. I was no longer reading alone. I read from my research and Mrs. Anderson read from the encyclopedia. I kept trying to stop reading but every time I did she would demand that I continue. I was sure hours had passed before she finally stopped reading, but when I glanced down at my research I had not even gotten past the first page.

"There's no sense in you being here!" she shouted, and I wondered what she meant. Why was she so angry? What had I done wrong? In a way, I felt as though I was no longer there. I was numb. The next thing I heard her say was, "You might as well put the encyclopedia down on your chair and leave." I did what she asked. I had been taught not to question. Before I could take more than a couple of steps, her voice rang in my ears once more: "Where do you think you—are—going?"

The rest was a blur both mentally and physically as I fought hard to keep the tears from flowing. I didn't know if crying was allowed.

I hated reading after that. I hated writing even more. For a long time, school was not about learning, reading, or writing but about games. To play the classroom game, you had to know the rules. I learned them the hard way, but I learned them. Mrs. Anderson didn't know that: she thought she had taught me a lesson on research.

In thinking about my experiences, I realize how much of who I want to be as a teacher today is rooted in how I saw myself positioned as a learner. This chapter analyzes my attempts to get student agendas out on the table in the hopes of finding ways to support student inquiry. More specifically, I explore how children are positioned as students and how they might take action about their concerns.

A First Reading

In the classroom, I have tried to provide the students with opportunities to express their thinking in a way they find comfortable. I try to provide conversational space and tools with which to explore the complexity of text and talk. Some of the students I worked with use writing as a vehicle for discussing what is on their minds.

I collected the written conversation and letters that follow while working with six-, seven-, and eight-year-old children in an urban multiracial community. These artifacts are presented in their original form with the exception of the children's names, which are pseudonyms. After presenting each letter, I describe the context in which it was written and summarize my thoughts about the written conversation and letters at the time they were written.

A Written Conversation with Alan Jason

As report card time drew near, several students became worried about receiving their report cards. One of these students was Alan Jason. Regardless of what I said, he worried. In a written conversation, he attempted to talk himself out of worry, claiming that "report cards can't hurt" anyone (see Figure 10.1).

Before receiving the written conversation from Alan Jason, I had several talks with him regarding what reports were for, explaining that I see them as tools to help parents and teachers work through how to help children learn better. I agreed that he was right that report cards really do just tell you and your parents about what you are doing in school and that they can't hurt anyone.

Eric's Letter

Our classroom included students who come from nine different cultural backgrounds, none of which was French. Out of the nineteen students in the class, only three did not speak the language of their heritage at home. There were also two children who joined our community without previously having spoken English at all.

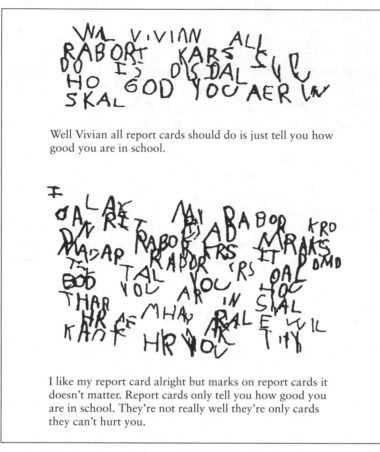

Well Vivian all report cards should do is just tell you how good you are in school.

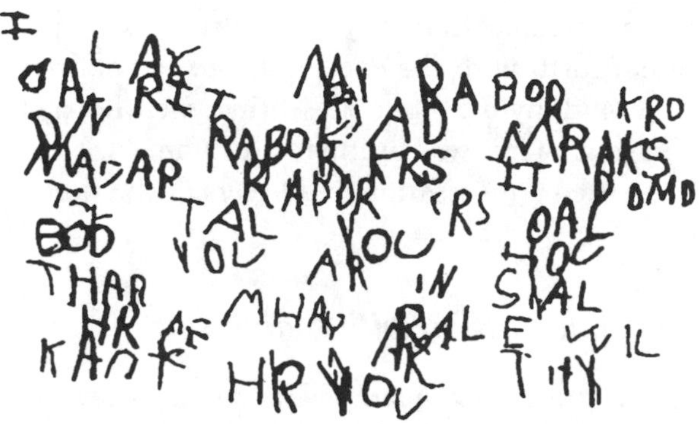

I like my report card alright but marks on report cards it doesn't matter. Report cards only tell you how good you are in school. They're not really well they're only cards they can't hurt you.

FIGURE 10.1. *A written conversation with Alan Jason.*

This raised a lot of interest in other languages, leading to the questioning of the French lesson that was held for twenty minutes each day. In conversation the students expressed displeasure with being forced to learn French when the languages they wanted to learn were those of their friends in the classroom. This, they felt, would make more sense than learning French just because "the principal and the people in the big building said we have to." One student decided to write a letter to the school board (see Figure 10.2).

Eric wrote his letter after a written conversation between us about learning other languages. He wrote:

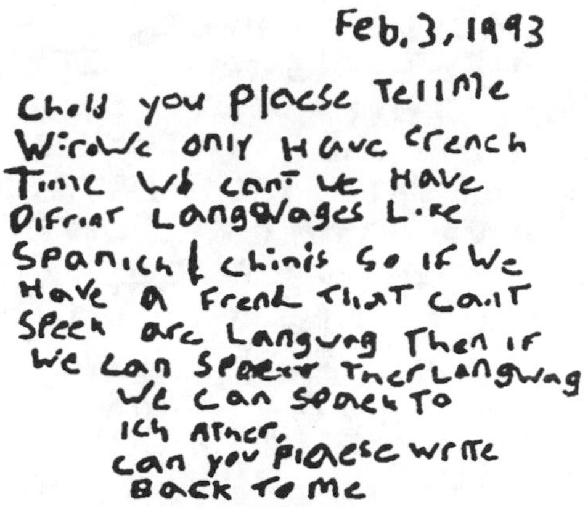

Feb. 3, 1993

Chold you plase Tell me
Wirowe only Have French
Time Wi cant we Have
Difrint Langwages Like
Spanich & chinis so if We
Have a frend that can't
Speek are Langwag Then if
We can Speak Ther Langwag
We can speak To
ich Ather.
can you plaese write
Back To me

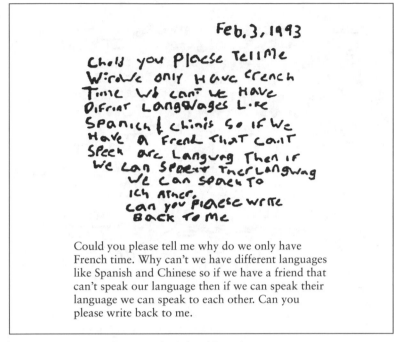

Could you please tell me why do we only have French time. Why can't we have different languages like Spanish and Chinese so if we have a friend that can't speak our language then if we can speak their language we can speak to each other. Can you please write back to me.

FIGURE 10.2. *Eric's letter to the school board.*

> Why can't we have different languages every week so if you have a friend that can't speak your language you could talk to them

I wrote back: "That's a wonderful suggestion, Eric. You could ask Cathy Reyes, she is someone who helps make some of these decisions." Shortly after his letter was sent, Eric received a reply stating that if he wanted to learn another language he could attend heritage language classes that are held on Saturday mornings. Together Eric and I read the response he received, after which nothing more was said.

Lyndsey's Letter

Lyndsey handed me a letter (Figure 10.3) when I returned to school after a day of absence. She was not alone in her discontent with the way the supply teacher had treated the students, and so on this particular day we started the morning with a class meeting

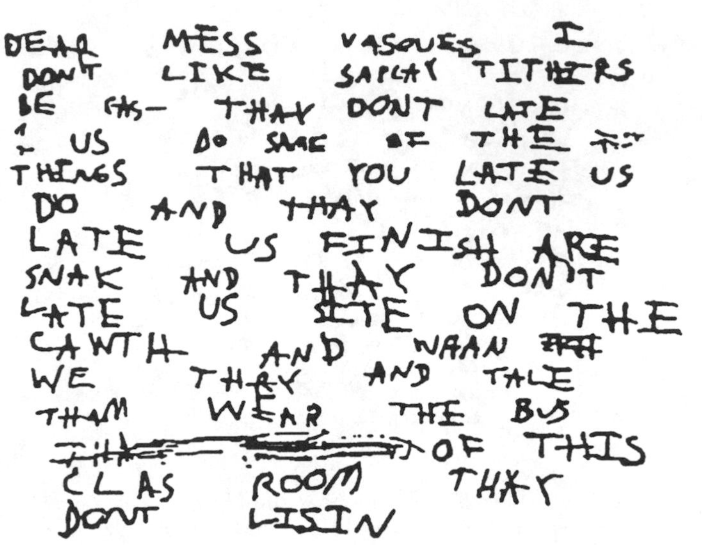
DEAR MESS VASQUES I
DONT LIKE SAPLAY TITHERS
BE CAS- THAY DONT LATE
US DO SAME OF THE
THINGS THAT YOU LATE US
DO AND THAY DONT
LATE US FINISH ARE
SNAK AND THAY DONT
LATE US SETE ON THE
CAWTH AND WAAN
WE THAY AND TALE
THAM WEAR THE BUS
OF THIS
CLAS ROOM THAY
DONT LISIN

Dear Miss Vasquez, I don't like supply teachers because they don't let us do some of the things that you let us do and they don't let us finish our snack and they don't let us sit on the couch and when we try and tell them we are the boss of this classroom they don't listen.

FIGURE 10.3. *Lindsey's letter.*

called by Lyndsey. At the meeting, students raised the issue of why supply teachers felt the need to take over a classroom that "isn't theirs to begin with."

The students expressed concern about what would happen the next time I had to be away, and they made a number of suggestions:

> Well, Miss Vasquez, just don't be away any more then we won't need supply teachers.
>
> If you have to be away again can you ask for Mrs. Williams cause she doesn't tell us what to do all the time.
>
> Oh and don't send Mrs. Cole. She yells too much.
>
> Maybe you should leave a note to tell the supply teacher that we made decisions here about what to do in the day.

I responded to their concerns about supply teachers by acknowledging their requests. Aside from this discussion, nothing more was done about the issue other than making sure the next time I was away to ask for Mrs. Williams and to remind the supply teacher dispatcher not to send Mrs. Cole. I also wrote a letter addressed to future supply teachers outlining what a day in our classroom might be like and explaining the atmosphere we had attempted to create as a class.

Laura's Letter

Our school is a Roman Catholic school. As such, as long as they have their baptismal certificate, all students receive the sacrament of Holy Eucharist, or first Holy Communion, when they are in grade 2. Laura has older siblings who together with their parents receive Holy Communion every Sunday at church. Laura had always gone up to the altar with her family and watched the sacrament being given. She felt that she had been left out long enough and wanted to be able to do something about it, feeling that she was ready to receive Holy Communion when she was six years old.

As a result, when the parish priest came to visit our classroom, Laura was ready with her concern. She shared her thoughts through a letter written to the parish priest (Figure 10.4).

When Laura first came to me with her question, my response was, "What do you think?" I wanted her to consider possible reasons for the "Communion is received in grade 2" rule. I mentioned that the parish priest was due for a visit and that might give her an opportunity to voice her concern. When he arrived, the priest explained that the church feels children are ready to accept the responsibility of receiving the sacrament when they are seven. Grade 2 happens to be the year that most children turn seven.

A Critical Reading

> While we can't totally escape our culture there's just no such thing as atheoretical, unbiased experience, knowledge or practice. (Manning, 1993)

HOW CAME YOU HAVE TO HAVE HOLY
AMONEN WHAN YOUR 7 OR 8
HOW CAME YOU CANT HAVE
IT WHAN YOUR YUNGER
BECAS I WANTD TO KNOW
WHY OLDIR PIPEL CAN HAVE
AMONEN BUT YUNGER PIPEL
COLDNT. BECAS ITZ NOT RELLY
FAIR IF YUNGER PIPEL CANT
HAVE AMONEN. BECAS I
FELL LEFT OWT

How come you have to have Holy Communion when you're 7 or 8 How come you can't have it when you're younger Because I wanted to know why older people can have Communion but younger people couldn't. Because it's not really fair if younger people can't have Communion. Because I feel left out.

FIGURE 10.4. *Laura's letter to the parish priest.*

The students use writing as a way to make their voices heard. As a teacher, I have a responsibility to ensure that the agenda implicit in the issues they raise through the letters is placed on the table alongside all other students' agendas. Edelsky (1994), while speaking of critical literacy classrooms, argues that every individual's agenda ought to have space in the curriculum and that the teacher's agenda must count as another agenda and not as *the* agenda. The letters written by the students in my classroom demonstrate how I may have created a space to help them problematize situations they found unfair. As demonstrated by the letters, students do write about things of importance and urgency. Unfortunately, in the dominant school culture students continue to be viewed and treated as second-class citizens who do not need to be heard. I find myself reassured by what Harste and Manning (1992) describe as a theory of voice. Operationally, "this notion gets translated by inquiring teachers into as simple a question as 'How do I hear from Jason today?' 'What would I have to do to make Jason the center of my curriculum?'"

(n.p.). Nevertheless, I ask myself, Is the discourse of resistance available to the students I work with exposing them to self-defeat? When students are given permission to take up a critical position, a possible side effect is social rejection. Outside of our classroom, these letters were not accepted. While I didn't realize this at the time, adult response was negative; the students were seen as rude or know-it-alls. Adults may have difficulty responding because young students are not supposed to be asking these kinds of questions.

Although I provided spaces for students to ask questions, I was not able to take their learning as far as I could have. By making this statement, I don't mean to beat myself over the head or to be self-critical. I am simply revisiting my footsteps. As I revisit the letters, I filter my thinking through Edelsky's (1994) work on what a critical literacy curriculum might look like; Dyson's (1993) work on the social worlds of children as they write; Peterson's (1994) work on social justice; as well as Brodkey's (1992) notion of reading and writing in the margins, along with the questions raised by students I currently work with, and conversations with friends, colleagues, and parents. From where I stand now, I can see how I could have addressed differently the issues raised by these students through their letters. In the remaining part of this chapter, I outline what I might have done in each of these situations—responses that might have taken student inquiries into an analysis of institutional power.

In my original response, I assured Alan Jason that report cards couldn't hurt anyone, that they are only supports to help teachers and parents figure out how to help children learn better. What I didn't tell Alan Jason is that report cards often don't have anything to do with supporting learning and oftentimes they are written for everyone but the student. I didn't tell him that many times they do hurt students by shaping future teachers' thinking about what a given student might be like. I didn't tell him that the way the report card is set up does not reflect the process of learning that unfolds in the classroom, nor does it account for the learning that extends beyond it. Report cards ought to be tools with which to mediate experience and discover how to best support a student's learning. Instead, they are used to construct students in a certain bureaucratic way. As in my response to the other students' letters, I didn't tie the use of report cards to influential systems of power that demand report cards in schools.

My support of Eric's inquiry into the imposed French curriculum took the form of giving him the name of someone on the school board who helps make decisions about curriculum. My nonmention of the fact that French as a language to be taught in schools stems from a political decision that doesn't necessarily have anything to do with students, supports a decision placing French in a position as a subject to be taught in the first place. My nonmention of the fact that limiting the teaching of heritage languages to Saturday morning marginalizes minority cultures supports the existing marginalization of minority cultural groups. Nonmention supports the interests of those in positions to control children's lives at school.

While reflecting on the way I responded to Lyndsey's letter, I realize that the role I took on was that of mediator. I acted on her behalf rather than supporting her right to act for herself. Although I took heed of all the students' suggestions regarding how to best prepare for the coming of a supply teacher, the final decision about how these preparations were to unfold remained mine. Therefore, my way of preparing for the next supply teacher did not empower the students or place them in a position to demand respect.

My response to Laura's inquiry (see Figure 10.4) into the age restriction for receiving Holy Communion leaves me puzzled. What the letter did not reveal is that at the same time that Laura raised the issue about Holy Communion, she also raised an issue about Holy Confession, or Reconciliation, as it is now known. Preparing for Reconciliation usually takes place when children are eight years old (grade 3). In the case of Holy Communion, I redirected her question to another authority figure when instead we could have had a sustained discussion alongside the priest's comments. In the case of Reconciliation, however, which she was not supposed to engage in until the following year, I was able to access information and pass it on to Laura and her mother so that they could make a case for themselves. This activity took place outside of school, and as a result Laura received Reconciliation while still in grade 2.

Was it easier for me to give Laura and her mother the tools to take action outside of school than to take action in school? In doing so, did I give Laura an advantage over the other students by not giving the others access to the same opportunity if they so desired it?

In retrospect, I suspect that my avoidance of direct action may be related to my Catholic upbringing and also my institutional position. Questioning the ruling of the church would have placed me in a position of vulnerability as a teacher in a Catholic system that I was not prepared to take. Handing over the tools to someone else, however, demonstrates that I do recognize certain practices as problematic and that I do want action to be taken, but that at the time I didn't want taking action to rest on my shoulders.

Revisiting my students' written conversation and letters has confirmed my commitment to creating curriculum differently. Some of this change rests on the shoulders of what Edelsky (1994) describes as vintage whole language, the stuff that may already be taking place. This includes recognizing that curriculum ought to be grounded in the lives of students (Harste, 1993). Grounding curriculum in the lives of students means that as a teacher, my role includes listening and looking differently at the students' implicit and explicit questions in order to shape curriculum based on the underlying issues, not just surface issues. Thus, when Curtis and Richard act out Power Rangers day after day, I recognize that maybe what they are interested in isn't so much Power Rangers as what Power Rangers represent. And when Vickie makes the statement that all Mounties have to be boys because in the Royal Canadian Mounted Police poster we have up on our classroom wall there are no girls, I address the underlying theme of how girls and boys are positioned in artifacts and texts. Recognizing these underlying issues and themes ensures that the students own the questions they ask. Owning the questions makes learning more purposeful in their lives and the lives of others in the community. This leads to another whole language principle: building a classroom community. Within this community, Edelsky (1994) points out, students need to experience firsthand learning as opposed to hands-on learning. As an example, she notes that when children use Popsicle sticks to subtract they are experiencing hands-on learning, but when they make change at a bake sale they are engaging in firsthand learning. As a teacher, I need to make sure that when I say that all members of the community should be able to put their agendas on the table, that individual ways of seeing and talking about those agendas are respected; in this way, we can revisit and interrogate those agendas and act on them firsthand.

Getting to where I am currently professionally resulted from my own questioning of systems of domination and influence, and from taking action to resist the dominant discourse and to problematize the social text. Getting here was a result of engaging in conversation with others who share this thinking, from reading, from writing, and from what Edelsky (1994) describes as watching events and media informed with the question, Why are things the way they are? I agree that this is a pro-justice and equity stance. But being pro-justice and equity is not enough. We also need to be activists (Edelsky, 1994). That is, classrooms have to become places where neither students nor teachers are apathetic.

We need to start taking action against those who tell us to think within the realm of what is dominant. In making the nondominant visible, it is time we question deeply the taken-for-granted, and in educating people we need to ask, "Educating for what?" (Edelsky, 1994). One way I have taken such action is by capturing the incidental unfolding of equity and justice issues in students' lives through critical classroom inquiry.

References

Brodkey, L. (1992). Articulating poststructural theory in research on literacy. In R. Beach, J. Green, M. Kamil, & T. Shanahan (Eds.), *Multidisciplinary perspectives on literacy research* (pp. 293–318). Urbana, IL: National Conference on Research in English/National Council of Teachers of English.

Comber, B. (1993). Classroom explorations in critical literacy. *Australian Journal of Language and Literacy, 16*(1), 73–83.

Comber, B., & O'Brien, J. (1993). Critical literacy: Classroom explorations. *Critical Pedagogy Networker, 6*(1/2), 1–11.

David-Maramba, A. (1971). *Early Philippine literature.* Manila: National Bookstore.

Dyson, A. H. (1993). *Social worlds of children learning to write in an urban primary school.* New York: Teachers College Press.

Edelsky, C. (1994). Education for democracy. *Language Arts, 71*(4), 252–57.

Freebody, P., & Luke, A. (1993). Literacies programs: Debates and demands in cultural context. *Prospect: Australian Journal of ESL, 5*(3), 7–16.

Harste, J. (1993). Curriculum for the millennium: Putting an edge on learning through inquiry. *Australian Journal of Language and Literacy, 16*(1), 7–24.

Harste, J., & Manning, A. (1992). Research as conversation. Unpublished manuscript.

Lankshear, C. (1989). Reading and writing wrongs: Literacy and the underclass. *Language and Education, 3*(3), 167–81.

Luke, A. (1991). Literacies as social practices. *English Education, 23*(3), 131–47.

Manning, A. (1993, May). Curriculum as conversation. Keynote address given at the Western Australian Reading Conference, Perth, Australia.

Peterson, B. (1994). Building social justice classrooms in an unjust society. *Talking Points, 6*, 2–6.

Shannon, P. (1995). *Text, lies, and videotape.* Portsmouth, NH: Heinemann.

Vasquez, V. (1994). A step in the dance of critical literacy. *UKRA Reading, 28*(1), 39–43.

Chapter Eleven

Our Kinds of Questions You Wouldn't Find in a Book

Robyn Jenkin
Catholic Education Office, Thebarton, South Australia

Several years ago I decided to take a closer look at what my students were doing while they were conducting their own inquiry in resource-based learning.[1] I originally set out to examine the literacy demands of the process of inquiring into a topic. I soon became aware that there were no specific literacy components in inquiry learning because the inquiry became a literacy process itself, with students engaged in reading, viewing, writing, listening, and speaking. I had assumed that the questions posed by the students were simply the first step in the information-gathering process. I found instead that the construction of research questions was not a simple, discrete part of the process. Rather, it was integral to the students' experience of learning to be researchers.

Students posed a huge range of questions. I wondered why some students posed questions that could be answered using the resources available, while others attempted to find answers to questions to which there were no easily accessible answers. This led me to look closely at the kinds of questions the students were posing. This chapter looks in detail at the questions the students set themselves and the kinds of topics into which the students were inquiring, and it explores issues that appear to have influenced the young learners while they were engaged in inquiry.

Central to the inquiry approach is the student's ability to pose effective questions and use a variety of resources to find information that helps provide answers to these questions. Dillon (1986) says that "learning is seen to follow in answer to a student's question" (p. 333). Therefore, educators assume that posing and answering questions equals learning. In their study of grade 6 students, however, Moore and St. George (1991) found that only 48 percent of the questions set by the students were answered in the final written product. My study of grade 4 students engaged in their first foray into independent inquiry indicated a similar percentage. I found that the students correctly answered 51 percent of the questions they had set themselves, across nine different topics. This low proportion of questions answered concerned me, considering the value placed on the inquiry approach to resource-based learning as practised in my school. It raised a number of issues about why questions were not answered. If students' questions are not answered, then perhaps the kinds of questions posed are ineffective for their purposes. On the other hand, it may be that even though many questions go unanswered, students are learning something else about their topic. Or perhaps we as teachers, while promoting inquiry, are not assisting our students to inquire into topics and issues that are relevant to them.

My observations revealed that many students experience difficulty in posing questions to which answers can be found. Reflecting on these observations forced me to undertake two separate yet related investigations. First, I decided to examine the topics they had chosen to investigate, in order to discover whether topic choice made a difference to the framing of appropriate questions. Second, I took a closer look at which students posed which kinds of questions. In general, my initial aim was to get a clearer picture of why so many questions remained unanswered and what the consequences of this were for students.

Which Topics Can Be Inquired Into?

The students in my study were encouraged to research a topic of their own choice within the broad subject of "traditions." Nine different topics were chosen by the students including traditions related to sports, the Olympic Games, weddings, Mother's Day and Father's Day, birthdays, other general celebrations, and particular celebrations such as Easter and Christmas. Boys mostly chose the sports topics and girls mostly chose topics related to weddings, celebrations, birthdays, Mother's Day, and Father's Day. "Christmas" was the only topic chosen by girls and boys in approximately equal numbers. It appeared that gender was a factor influencing the kinds of topics chosen. This finding concerned me, so I decided to take a closer look as these topics.

It is interesting to note that the most successfully answered questions related to the topic of weddings, while the least successfully answered questions related to sports. The boys told me that they chose sports because they were interested in sports or because they knew a lot about them. A close look at the boys' questions revealed that, while they thought they knew something about the traditions of sports, their knowledge was restricted to the sport itself and sporting heroes. This raises questions about the topic itself. My intention was for students to inquire into traditions. This is a subject that commonly appears in content guides as a way of dealing with understanding culture. In Australia the recently produced curriculum document *A Statement on Studies of Society and the Environment for Schools* (Australian Education Council, 1994) promotes student inquiry into traditions as a way of achieving outcomes in understanding culture. My students inquired into the actual sport rather than into the traditions surrounding their chosen sport. In this way, the boys sidestepped the social and cultural curriculum topic of traditions and reformulated it as "sport," where they were on safe ground as far as content was concerned.

Take, for example, the case of John, who was inquiring into the Olympic Games. Although this topic lends itself to inquiry into the traditions associated with the Games, John was more interested in facts about the Olympic Games. These facts related to the history and origins of the Olympic Games, as well as about sporting achievement. As Barbara Comber says elsewhere in this volume, teachers have a different view of "what counts as knowledge." I am not suggesting that the boys made this decision consciously—that is, that they chose sports as a "boys" topic. What is interesting is that almost all the boys made this choice. The unspoken peer pressure to "be a boy" is great, and in Australia being "sporty" is a major part of mainstream role identity, as constructed in all forms of media. I am not suggesting that the boys' choice to inquire about sports is "bad." This situation did, however, make me acutely aware of the degree to which choice in the language classroom is never neutral. The boys' choices took them away from any consideration of social and cultural formations of tradition and led them into inquiries about the rules of games and records of their heroes.

Inquiry learning, then, becomes a site for gendered choices. In this case, the consequence was that boys participated in a different curriculum from girls. I did not set out to consider gender in my investigation. I did not predict any differences. Because my focus was on the inquiry process, content was in the background. I was not initially concerned about the different topics boys and girls chose. It was somewhat later, in analyzing students' questions, that I realized that students had participated in qualitatively different inquiries and, as a consequence, engaged in different kinds of learning.

Students need to see the relevance of inquiring into a teacher-set topic (Travers, 1994). Primary teachers have the opportunity to do this by immersing their students in the topic through a thematic approach across the different areas of learning. There is an inherent tension between having students follow lines of inquiry that are important to them and at the same time ensuring that students do not avoid entire areas of curriculum that might encourage them to investigate how their society works. Both teachers and students may need to resist the temptation to limit inquiry to what is safe, the taken-for-granted hegemonic knowledge that shapes our worlds.

The Safe Topics

So let's take a look at the "safe" topics, the topics into which it is acceptable to inquire; topics for which it is easy to ask appropriate questions; topics about which information may be found in books or other resources available in the school or at home. Christmas was one such safe topic. One student who knew how to play the game was Becky, who asked:

> Why do people celebrate Christmas?
> Why do we get presents?

How did people celebrate Christmas in the olden days?
Where did they celebrate?
What did they eat?
Why did people burn Yule logs?

In coming up with these questions, Becky was demonstrating that she knew exactly what kinds of questions were valued at school. She anticipated this particular school's reading of Christmas traditions. Not surprisingly, Becky answered most of her questions satisfactorily. She was one of the first students to finish her research and to hand in a poster for display in the class. I asked Becky why she chose to research Christmas traditions, and she explained that "it seemed a very interesting subject." She claimed to know nothing about the topic before she started out! I found that interesting, since it had been a class focus the previous year. Even more surprising is that her own knowledge of Christmas through her family experiences appeared to count for nothing. This was evident in her research notes, one section of which included a space to jot down everything already known about the topic. Becky had left this space blank. Finally, Becky said that she found all the information she needed in one or two books in the school library. I was interested to see in her research notes that Becky had discovered information about an old tradition of burning the Christmas tree to ward off bad luck, and yet this wasn't included in the poster she prepared for the class display. In that poster, she simply covered five of the questions she had set herself. Becky had learned how to get the job done. Yet my aim was to have the students grapple with new learning and struggle with new concepts.

The Challenging Topics

Some students did grapple with new learning by inquiring into challenging topics. Renate, who was researching wedding traditions, wanted to find out why people marry before they have children. In the context of this student's schooling in a small Catholic parish school, this was a provocative area of inquiry. More important, it raises questions about how teachers deal with students who inquire into topics with which the teachers themselves may not be comfortable. If we are serious about students being independent, self-directed learners, however, then we must not only expect topics like this, but we should also help the students deal with them. I found this a difficult area to handle. While we were reviewing Renate's research notes, I suggested that she would be more likely to find an answer to the question about marriage and children by asking adults she knew well. She decided that she would ask her parents. As a result, she wrote in her notes: "The Pope says we have to get married to have children if you are Catholic."

Renate did not include this information in her completed poster. On reflection, it is possible that my suggestion to Renate may have given her the message that this aspect of the topic was not something to research in school. This could explain why she did not include the answer in her poster. Perhaps Renate was learning to read what counted in the official school curriculum.

At this stage, I began to realize that, although I thought I was encouraging my students to inquire into areas that interested them, I was still setting the boundaries for them. These boundaries have been constructed—by curriculum writers, teachers, school authorities, parents—to cover the areas of knowledge that these groups value. By directing my students' inquiries within these boundaries, I was denying them access to a curriculum that promoted critical inquiry. Students like Becky who played the game of asking safe questions were ultimately disadvantaged because their learning was restricted. On the other hand, Renate, who asked more critical, confrontational questions, had the opportunity to grapple with new understandings.

Gender and Topic Choice

I found that some students were clearly disadvantaged by the kinds of topics they inquired into. Some students set topics that were too broad. For example, students who chose to investigate sport in general (as opposed to one specific sport such as cricket) or celebrations in general (as opposed to one celebration such as Easter) answered a significantly lower number of questions than students who chose to investigate more specific topics. It is interesting to note that, apart from three who inquired into Christmas, the boys investigated sporting topics. On the other hand, while some girls inquired into Christmas, the others tackled celebrations such as weddings, Easter, birthdays, Mother's Day, and Father's Day.

Some research suggests that boys and girls write about different topics in free writing. Gilbert (1989) cites Poynton, who found that, within a particular genre (in this case, narrative writing), boys and girls write about different topics. Similarly, Kamler (1992), who observed a boy and a girl for at least once a week over two-and-a-half years, found that there were significant differences in the kinds of writing they chose to engage in. For example, when she quantified the different genres written by the students, Kamler found that, while the girl wrote four "Diary" entries, the boy did not engage in any writing of this type.

If boys and girls make different choices about the kinds of writing they engage in when provided with free choice situations, this has some important implications for teachers. Given the findings of researchers such as Poynton and Kamler, it is not surprising that the boys and girls in my study made different choices about the topics into which they inquired. Reflecting on these differences forced me to realize that teachers need to be aware that boys and girls do make different choices in inquiry. It is inevitable that when students have freedom of choice into the content of their inquiry, different kinds of learning will occur. Further investigations are needed concerning the social and political effects of these differences.

What Kinds of Questions Are Acceptable to Ask?

My examination of students' questions was revealing. I identified two different ways of looking at the students' questions. First, I examined them in terms of their content, and second, I looked at the ways in which the questions were asked. In addition to the gendered nature of topic choice, students must work out what can and cannot be asked in schools. In trying to work out why some questions remained unanswered, I examined the whole corpus of student questions. Here I focus mainly on what I labeled as appropriate and inappropriate questions.

Appropriate Questions

Appropriate school questions are the kind of questions about which children's books or other easily accessible resources are likely to include information, or that teachers and librarians can answer. Examples of appropriate questions include:

> What were the things that happened when Jesus was born? (Peter)
>
> How did people celebrate Christmas in the olden days? (Becky)
>
> Why do we get presents at Christmas time? (Kelly)
>
> How did the Ashes [in cricket] start? (Christian)
>
> Why do they give rings [in the wedding ceremony]? (Dianne)
>
> How come we have a matron of honor at a wedding? (Elizabeth)

Other appropriate questions were on topics of special interest to particular students, and often they were the kind of questions about which the students had some prior knowledge. Examples of this type of appropriate question are:

> What are the fielding positions [in cricket]? (Grant)
>
> Why do we throw confetti [at weddings]? (Ellen)
>
> Why do we eat turkey at Christmas? (Kelly)

Students who posed these questions clearly demonstrated that they already had some prior knowledge of their topic and understanding about what is expected in school.

Inappropriate Questions

Inappropriate questions (or so I labeled them at the time) included elements of fantasy or morality and therefore were unable to be answered using the range of school resources accessible to students. While the total number of inappropriate questions was quite low, it is important to consider them because they demonstrate that the research process is not neutral. Teachers gradually socialize students into what can and cannot be dealt with in inquiry. At the time, questions I labeled as inappropriate included:

How does someone train a rabbit to deliver Easter eggs? (Chrissie)
What does Santa do in his spare time? (Lisa)
How does Santa fit down the chimney when he is so fat? (Lisa)

While these questions raise issues of fantasy, other questions are confrontational. It is interesting to speculate about questions such as:

Why do people go to church on Sunday? (Mary)
Why does the priest marry them [the couple]? (Dianne)
How come you can't wear hot pink? (Dianne)
Why isn't there a children's day? (Annie)
Why do we go to church? (Elizabeth)
Why do they wait so long before they get married? (Carrie)

Are these questions meant to shock? Are they meant to challenge? Are they genuine inquiry? I'd say the students' questions serve all these purposes. Students who posed these questions were beginning to grapple with concepts such as belief, change, cultural similarity, cultural diversity, and identity, but they were also confronting and challenging the sanitized version of belief systems they were getting at school. These questions set the scene for critical inquiry into traditions. Not surprisingly, most of these questions remained unanswered. In hindsight, questions such as these, which I have since labeled critical questions, could have formed the basis for discussion of a range of issues.

This research made me much more aware of my own assumptions about the kinds of questions that are acceptable for students to inquire into. It also made me aware of the implicit evaluations I made of students' questions. Furthermore, it forced me to look at the influence that teachers and teacher-librarians have in the selection of learning resources. To a certain extent, these selections reflect educators' own values and those of the local school community. This often results in few resources being available to answer questions of real interest to the students themselves. I suspect that gradually the students are trained to control the kinds of questions they pose so that they remain within school expectations. Teachers can help students to resist this positioning by ensuring that they have opportunities to critically analyze the texts they are using.

Interestingly, some students recognized that some of their questions could not be answered using the resources available. For example, after completing her research, Dianne explained, "Our kind of questions you wouldn't find in a book . . . like, 'Why does a priest marry them?' and 'Why do you get married?' . . . it's not in books!"

This raises issues about the kinds of books and other resources in elementary school libraries. In Chapter 8 of this volume, Jennifer O'Brien explores how texts position child inquirers. I would argue that the absence of particular kinds of content from children's books also helps to determine a child's "view of the world." There *are* answers to Dianne's questions. These answers are not about correct information; these answers are multiple and contested; they are about the ethics and morality of contemporary Christian families and about the role of religious doctrine in people's lives. The problem for Dianne was that these answers could not be found in the resources available in the school. One way of dealing with this situation could have been for me to help Dianne ask critical questions about the resources she was using, questions such as:

> What is missing from these texts?
>
> Why is it missing?
>
> How could it have been included?

Some students knew which topics were acceptable to investigate and thus were able to pose the kinds of questions that schoolbooks help to answer. Their topics and questions were shaped by what can be answered by using school resources. Strong social values shape what actually goes on in inquiry learning. This raises questions about the sanctity of students' inquiry questions. As a result of my research, I realized that for some of the students, question posing was difficult. I became aware that there is a very real need for teachers to explicitly teach students how to pose questions that can be answered, and how to ask the critical questions that help them deal with other issues. I also became acutely aware that school pedagogies need to be adapted to include opportunities for critical inquiry.

Conclusions

The conclusions I drew from my work with this particular class of students fell into two main categories. These categories were about gendered topic choice and the kinds of questions posed.

Gendered Topic Choice

This group of students made gendered choices about the topics into which they inquired. Not only were there significant differences in the topics investigated, but also the girls stayed within the broad topic area of traditions, whereas most of the boys narrowed their topics to concentrate on a different area of investigation. It was my intention for the students to investigate the social and cultural aspects of the overall topic. In fact, because of the choices they made, most of the boys inquired into different aspects of the topic. The result was that curriculum outcomes were different for boys and for girls.

This raises questions about what counts as curriculum content in inquiry learning. If, as I found with this class, boys and girls choose different topics, what does this mean for teachers and curriculum developers? Is it simply a matter of different learning styles? Are boys or girls being advantaged or disadvantaged by the teaching practice of providing choice within broad areas of inquiry? Does it matter that boys and girls have different outcomes? These are the kinds of questions that teachers need to be mindful of when they engage their students in inquiry-based learning.

The Kinds of Questions Posed

To a great extent, the kinds of questions posed determined the kinds of learning outcomes students experienced. For this particular class, success in answering their questions depended on the type and complexity of the questions posed.

Some students asked appropriate questions, knowing how to play the inquiry game. These students knew which questions they could ask and which questions could be answered. They knew what kinds of questions the teacher valued. Other students posed questions that were confrontational and challenging. This raises the issue of what kinds of questions can be asked at school and what kinds of resources are available in schools to help students investigate their questions. This second group of students embarked on inquiry into issues that were of significance to them. These students were not as successful. One reason for their lack of success was that these kinds of questions, those I later labeled critical questions, do not have straightforward answers. Rather, these are questions that demand consideration, discussion, and analysis. This kind of learning cannot be captured in a simple written or pictorial response.

Another factor inhibiting the students from answering these critical questions relates to the nature of the resources on which the students were drawing. Children's books and other library resources often do not provide answers to the kinds of questions some of these students were asking. This has implications for the kinds of resources available in schools.

If, as Dianne discovered, books do not contain the kind of information students are interested in, then questions must be asked about who makes decisions about the content of children's books. Are publishers producing books for children or for teachers? Are teachers helping students take a critical stance when they are using the texts available to them?

Perhaps we educators do not want students to inquire into issues with which we ourselves are not comfortable. Perhaps we hope that school resources will teach them what they can ask at school. Perhaps, by not providing appropriate resources, we gradually socialize students into undertaking lines of inquiry that are acceptable to us. On the other hand, if we are aware that the kinds of issues raised in this chapter do influence our students' learning, then we have the opportunity to critique our current practices and to undertake the necessary changes to ensure equitable outcomes for all students.

Note

1. The average age of the students in my study was eight years and eight months; most of them were in their fifth year of formal schooling.

References

Australian Education Council. (1994). *A statement on studies of society and environment for Australian schools*. Carlton, Victoria, Australia: Curriculum Corporation.

Dillon, J. (1986). Student questions and individual learning. *Educational Theory, 36*(4), 333–41.

Gilbert, P. (with Rowe, K.). (1989). *Gender, literacy, and the classroom*. Carlton, South Victoria: Australian Reading Association.

Kamler, B. (1992). The social construction of free topic choice in the process writing classroom. *Australian Journal of Language and Literacy, 15*(2), 105–21.

Moore, P., & St. George, A. (1991). Children as information seekers: The cognitive demands of books and library systems. *School Library Media Quarterly, 19*(3), 161–68.

Travers, D. (Ed.). (1994). Setting students up for successful research. In Department of Education and Children Services, *Literacy and learning program: Training and development activities for junior secondary teachers*. Adelaide, South Australia: Author.

Chapter Twelve

Young Researchers in Action

David Wray
University of Exeter

Maureen Lewis
University of Exeter

with Carolyn Cox
University of Exeter

In this chapter, we present a small slice of the work of the Exeter Extending Literacy (EXEL) project, which has been exploring ways of helping children read and write nonfiction more effectively. The project is founded on a philosophy that foregrounds the importance of children developing their own inquiry questions, and here we outline how one of these inquiry questions was used to focus the work of six-year-old students. We refer to these students as "young researchers" and show how they, with the support of their teacher, were able to approach their inquiry with the actively questioning mindset which characterizes researchers.

Amy and Kelly are two six-year-olds who work in a pleasant open-plan classroom that borders on a central school courtyard. Their grade 1 class is responsible for the upkeep of the flower beds in the courtyard, and some of the students attend a weekly after-school gardening club run by parent helpers. It is June and the school has decided to spend some money on hanging baskets for the courtyard. The students are keen to discuss the contents of these baskets, and because of this keenness, their teacher, Mrs. Cox, decides to get them involved in deciding which plants should be purchased. Later they will visit the local garden center to purchase their chosen plants, but first the students, in discussion with their teacher, realize that only certain plants will be suitable, and that in order to plan successful baskets they will have to do some research.

As part of the EXEL project at the University of Exeter, we followed the research of these students as they:

- set clear purposes for their work
- drew up a framework for recording information
- located information in a range of reference materials
- collaboratively constructed their understanding of the information they located
- made their recommendations for the purchase of plants
- were empowered by the knowledge they had constructed

This chapter is an account of the work of this class of students and an illustration of the power of an inquiry approach to children's learning. We also explore the role of the teacher in an activity such as this one. How can a teacher act as support for the learning and intervene at the appropriate points to take the inquiry just that bit further?

The EXEL Project

The EXEL project is a curriculum development project that has involved us in work with teacher groups throughout the United Kingdom, looking closely at children's interactions with texts, especially nonfiction texts. (For further details of the project, see Wray and Lewis, 1994.) We were concerned that nonfiction texts had been relatively neglected as a resource for learning and felt that an effective program of extending literacy should pay adequate attention to these sources. As part of our project, we have been developing a process model to describe children's interactions with nonfiction texts and consequently have been testing a range of strategies and materials for use in the classroom. The model currently underpinning our work in fact describes a process that, in academic contexts, tends to be labeled "research." We see benefit, therefore, in referring to children engaging in this process, no matter what their age, as researchers. The process of research, after all, consists fundamentally of setting oneself a question or series of questions and engaging in inquiries in order to find answers. An inquiry-based approach to curriculum encompasses just such a process.

We began our project with the misguided assumption that we would be chiefly concerned with children who had reached a stage of sufficient fluency in their reading that they were able to use reading as a means of inquiry. But it rapidly became clear to us that the processes involved when children were researching and interacting with texts were not age specific. Levels of experience and expertise vary, of course, as does the level of support children need, but the process is essentially the same for a five-year-old as for an adult. Just as one improves as a reader by reading, one becomes more expert at researching by undertaking research. Children encounter nonfiction texts (books, lists, notices, signs, etc.) from their earliest years, both in school and at home, yet most of the work on children's use of this kind of text has concentrated on older children. For example, the most widely known British research project on the use of reading as a medium for learning (Lunzer & Gardner, 1979; Lunzer, 1984) was undertaken with children aged ten and older. Similarly, official reports from government agencies on school achievement and practice often comment on the teaching of "study skills" to children aged eight and older but rarely mention these skills with regard to younger children. Even the requirements of the British National Curriculum suggest that these are matters best left to older students. The introduction of students to the use of structural organizers such as chapter headings, for example, is not required until age ten.

The very terms used to describe such skills also often imply a chronological hierarchy. References to "higher-order reading skills" or "advanced reading skills" have certainly led many teachers to feel that the teaching of study skills is best undertaken in the later stages of the primary/elementary school, when children are competent readers. These ideas are beginning to change and more attention has been given recently to research as a feature of the curriculum experiences offered to younger children (Mallett, 1992; Neate, 1991). We would argue that students should be introduced to nonfiction texts and ways in which to learn from them from their earliest days in school. We were delighted therefore when several teachers of very young children joined our project and we were able to undertake some of our research in infant (K–2) classrooms.

Throughout our project, we have been concerned that the work we have undertaken on children's interactions with nonfiction texts should stress the need for these interactions to be firmly located in a meaningful context, rather than taking the form of decontextualized study skills lessons. This form of working is even more crucial in the early years and, thankfully, the view of learning it stems from is already more or less universally accepted by early years teachers. All of our work has taken place within the context of the ongoing work of the classroom, which has usually meant an approach to the curriculum centered on cross-curricular inquiry.

Structuring the Research

The students in Amy and Kelly's class had a clear purpose to guide their research. Their teacher, Mrs. Cox, guided them to make the focus for their research as explicit and structured as possible. Simply asking them to "find out" about plants would have been much too vague and vast a task. Because the children were relatively inexperienced researchers, Mrs. Cox suggested that a grid would help focus their research and provide a scaffold for the kind of questions they might want to ask. Through discussion she was able to draw on their prior knowledge of gardening, flowers, and hanging baskets. As they brainstormed what they already knew, she scribed their comments. Certain "themes" emerged, which they drew together into several headings: height, spread, colour, flowers and leaves, smell. Together they constructed a grid, which the students then copied into their jotters (see Table 12.1).

Notice how the teacher was able to extend the students' technical vocabulary, substituting "fragrance" for "smell" and "foliage" for "leaves." By introducing these words at this stage, she was also preparing them for the vocabulary they might encounter when they started to look in books. Because the information the students needed to find would necessarily be technical, it quickly became apparent that the reference books already available to the class were largely inadequate in terms of the level of detail they contained. Mrs. Cox was able to make available, with the help of the students themselves, several adult gardening books and pamphlets. Many students were so keen that they persuaded their parents to take them to local garden centers and stores to find reference materials, much of which they could obtain at no cost. Of course, these materials were designed for adult readers and their vocabulary, layout, and print size made few concessions to infant readers.

Each heading of the grid the students had helped design acted both as a question to be answered and a "key word" to focus the students' research; they perhaps even helped the students scan the text for that particular word. When we discuss some of the transcripts of the students' research later, we see how successfully the grid scaffolded the students' work.

Before the students began their inquiries, Mrs. Cox discussed with them where they might find the information they needed. The students suggested several sources such as books, asking

TABLE **12.1.** Research on Plants

Research on plants for our hanging baskets						
Name of flower	**Colour**	**Height**	**Fragrance**	**Trailing**	**Size of foliage**	**Comments**

"experts" (i.e., members of the gardening club), looking at other hanging baskets, asking their parents, and watching gardening programs on television. At this point, Mrs. Cox modeled for them how they might select and use information books. As she did this, she talked about what she was doing and why, thus making what is usually an internal monologue accessible to the students. The following extract from her demonstration was typical:

> Now which of these books shall I use? This book's got flowers on the cover so it might be useful, and the title . . . yes, *Garden Flowers,* that tells me it might be useful. Now what do I do? Yes, I can look in the index. Let's look up "hanging baskets" in the index. So I'm going to turn to the back of the book. Here it is. Index. Now, it's arranged alphabetically a . . . d . . . g . . . h . . . h . . . here it is. H. Lets look for h, a . . . .

Through this kind of metacognitive modeling—that is, by making explicit to the students the thought processes she was going through as she was experiencing them—the teacher was able to give the students some important lessons on what an experienced reader does. The importance of teachers not simply telling students about the problem solving, planning, and strategic decision making that characterize the reading process but actually demonstrating these cannot be overemphasized. Modeling enables teachers to make explicit the thought processes that accompany involvement in literate activities, processes which, by their very nature, are invisible. Unless these processes are made explicit, students have no way of understanding what it is like to think like an accomplished reader until they actually become one: in other words, much of their learning is directed toward trying to perform an activity the nature of which they have no clear concept. It is little wonder that, in such circumstances, many students focus on what seem to be the visible aspects of reading, such as sounding out the words and letters.

Undertaking the Research

We video-recorded several groups of students as they undertook their research. In pairs (six students at a time) they worked around a table loaded with gardening and flower books, most of them adult texts. Mrs. Cox checked on the group at intervals, but most of the time the students worked independently. The video recorder was left running throughout the morning, and after about fifteen minutes, during which they tended to whisper to each other and glance at the camera from time to time, the students seemed to become largely oblivious to its presence. Field notes and observations were also made. We were then able to view and review the video and analyze what took place. There were several striking features of the students' work that morning.

The social, interactive nature of the task (working in pairs) was important. On numerous occasions, the students prompted each other to continue working and to try another technique if they could not find what they were looking for; discussed information; worked together to try to understand difficult texts; asked each other for help and advice; and, of course, engaged in conversation with each other. Interestingly, much of this conversation originated from the task. For example, at one point one of the student's attention was caught by a picture as he was searching for a picture of marigolds:

BARRY: Oh! look at that . . . that's . . . that's . . . . It's made out of flowers. *(Points to picture of a flower bed laid out as a ship.)*

LISA: There's a Mickey Mouse one . . . other ones in other places.

BARRY: Woah! That's brilliant.

LISA: I've seen them millions of times.

BARRY: *(to Simon)* Have you seen them at Torquay? They've got them. Made out of flowers. Them.

SIMON: Where?

BARRY: Torquay. Where they make them models out of flowers. You been to Torquay?

(Simon shakes his head.)

BARRY: Been to Paignton?

LISA: I've been to Paignton.

[Torquay and Paignton are local towns the students have visited.]

A teacher arriving at this moment might be tempted to conclude that the students were not on task, but they certainly were because they were involved in making their own connections with the material. This linking of previous knowledge and experience to new material is a crucial part of the researching and learning process, and it reaffirms the importance of conversation rather than silence in young children's learning through inquiry.

Scaffolding the Task

The video evidence also demonstrated how important the grid was in scaffolding and prompting the students through a complex task of information gathering. It reminded them of what they needed to know but also allowed them space for their own interests. Several times the grid prompted students to return to the texts for further information. For example, Amy and Kelly had, after some searching, found a reference to nasturtiums in the index of a book. The following exchange took place:

AMY: Nasturtiums . . . Nasturtiums . . . *Got it* . . . 157 . . . 157 . . . 157. *(Turning pages and checking number.)* Here. Nasturtiums. Should be here somewhere. *(Scanning page.)* There it is. Height 1 foot . . . 30 cms. Well done. I found it. *(Kelly begins to write. Amy closes book.)*

AMY: I don't know the color yet, do I ? *(Color is the next column on the grid. Amy reopens book.)* 157 . . . Right. . . . What's the color? . . . What's the color? *(Reads aloud.)* Red, orange, yellow. Red, orange, yellow. We'd better get red. *(Closes book again.)*

KELLY: How do you spell . . . ? *(Both write in color column.)*

AMY: *(Looking at grid.)* Right. Fragrance. What's its fragrance? Has it got a fragrance or has it not? I don't think . . . *(Opens book and searches for page 157 again.)* Now where's it gone?

Here we see quite clearly the grid reminding Amy of what she needed to know and prompting her to continue her research. The grid was acting as a scaffold, helping the students move from the stage of joint activity alongside a teacher toward independent action.

Using Study Skills: Practice in Context

The students used a variety of study skills during their research. They used them because they needed to use them. We observed them using index pages, tables of contents, alphabetical order, skimming, scanning, and extracting key information. Of course, they did not always use these successfully and they showed varying levels of expertise, but they were receiving practice in using important skills in the best possible way.

Sometimes they had to deal with sophisticated textual features. Amy and Kelly, for example, in looking up "Busy Lizzy" in an index, found the entry: "Busy Lizzy. *See Impatiens.*" Puzzled by this, they sensibly approached their teacher for an explanation. Few teachers of six-year-olds would plan to introduce their pupils to the use of Latin plant names and yet, occurring as this instruction did within the context of a real situation, these students were fascinated by their discovery. They also learnt about cross-referencing in an index. How many study skills programs would introduce cross-referencing to six-year-olds? Yet Amy and Kelly (by no means outstanding pupils) took it in their stride.

Most of the students were also willing to try several different techniques if their first attempt to find an answer failed. Here is Amy again, starting her hunt for nasturtiums and trying a variety of strategies.

AMY: This one got anything? *(Picks up a book.)*

KELLY: I need to copy. *(Looks at the spelling of* nasturtiums *in Amy's jotter and writes.)*

AMY: Index. It should be here somewhere. Yes . . . right . . . what does it say? . . . Nasturtiums. . . . It hasn't got it there. I'll have to go to the contents. *(Turns to the front of the book.)* Ah, here it is. *(Searches contents page. Cannot find desired entry.)* It'll have to be another book. *(Scans pile of books on offer.)*

KELLY: Look in that one. *(Points to book.)*

AMY: Yeah. I'll look in this one. *(Picks up book indicated by Kelly.)*

KELLY: *(Holds front cover with Amy.)* What's it say? *(Reads* Ornamental Kitchen Garden.*)*

AMY: This is the one I had. *(Browsing through some pages of pictures, but actively searching.)* This tells us about . . . hardy petunias . . . French marigolds . . . nasturtiums? . . . Sweet Williams . . . Lizzie Busies . . . Lizzie Busies. Midsummer Plants. *(Reading page heading.)* Marigolds. I've got some of those in my backyard.

(Muttered conversation between the two. They continue browsing.)

AMY: Where's it gone? Nasturtium.

KELLY: Have a look in another book. *(Amy and Kelly each pick up another book.)*

KELLY: Have a look in the index.

AMY: Index. Right. *(Both looking in index of their book.)*

AMY: Nasturtiums . . . Nasturtiums . . . *Got it*. . . .

As well as the structured techniques of using the index and table of contents, the students also used less structured techniques such as random searching, skimming through books looking for pictures, and flicking over pages. Since these techniques can also achieve results, it is important that we not overemphasize a rigid "index/contents-only" approach to using information books. A flexible approach is more helpful, especially as many information books are not organized terribly well. These students' relative inexperience in research meant they had no fixed ideas about what they should do to locate information. They were therefore willing to try a range of strategies rather than fixating on one that, if it had not worked, might have left them unable to continue.

That these students had a flexible approach was also apparent in their willingness to use not only a variety of research strategies but also a variety of information sources. As well as consulting books, students shared their existing knowledge with each other, asked "experts," and looked at actual examples—that is, real flowers. Again, it was clear that the collaborative, social nature of the task was crucial in allowing the students to make use of these sources.

Empowerment through Information

Two of the students we observed learnt an important lesson that morning. Lorraine and Charlotte learnt that information can be empowering. The pair had begun by browsing through the gardening books, looking at pictures. From these pictures, they decided they wanted their hanging baskets to contain tomatoes, strawberries, and a bonsai tree. They wrote the names of these three plants into the first column of their grid and were about to start looking for further information when Mrs. Cox joined them. She pointed out that their suggestions were unusual and that they would need to find some good evidence to support these choices. Charlotte and Lorraine were not deflected from their ideas and started to research. In one gardening book, they discovered a variety of dwarf trailing tomatoes. In another they found a picture of strawberries in a planter, which clearly suggested that these were trailing plants. Then they turned to bonsai trees. They discovered a section in one book on the growing and training of bonsai trees. This gave them the information that bonsai trees could be trained into shape. They reasoned from this that they could train their bonsai tree to trail over their basket. They worked out that they would need wire for this task, but they did fail to realize that it might take them fifty years to grow their tree! When their teacher returned, they were ready to argue their case and defend their choice of plants.

What these students had learnt was that, armed with the appropriate information, they could argue with powerful and important people such as their teacher. Knowledge can give individuals the power to argue their case, a lesson central to democracy. Their teacher was humane and responsive enough to concede the argument, not wishing at this point to dampen the girls' enthusiasm for bonsai. It should be noted, however, that when it came to trying to convince their classmates, Lorraine and Charlotte had a much more difficult task!

Implications

We have space here to provide only brief glimpses of young children with a real purpose and a structure that guided them in the successful use of research skills. This success is still patchy, of course, and there remain some problem areas. Children as young as this naturally often find the business of making sense of complex information very difficult. Yet our work does show that with a clear purpose to motivate them and an explicit structure to scaffold their work, young children can and do become researchers. The implication can be made quite forcefully that we must not underestimate what these children are capable of. The sooner they begin to work with books in this way, the more likely they are to develop their research skills, hopefully making redundant the familiar complaint of teachers about students copying entire sections from reference books. Experience with research should definitely be part of the rich interaction with books provided in the best early years classrooms. This is true, we would argue, whatever the abilities, ages, and backgrounds of the students.

Our research also persuades us that until we have observed students in action following on through the demands of a clearly focused inquiry question, we can say little about their capabilities or limitations. Children act to their potential only when they are excited and driven by an inquiry need.

The role of the teacher seems to us to be twofold in such an inquiry-based curriculum. He or she first has to create a classroom environment in which inquiry is central. This can call for some skillful negotiations with the demands of a subject-focused curriculum. Second, the teacher needs to consider carefully how and when interventions in students' learning processes can best be made. We argue that teacher modeling of learning strategies has a central role in such interventions.

References

Lunzer, E. A., & Gardner, K. (Eds.). (1979). *The effective use of reading*. London: Heinemann.

Lunzer, E. (1984). *Learning from the written word.* Edinburgh: Oliver & Boyd.

Mallett, M. (1992). *Making facts matter: Reading non-fiction 5–11.* London: Paul Chapman.

Neate, B. (1992). *Finding out about finding out: A practical guide to children's information books.* Sevenoaks, UK: Hodder & Stoughton.

Wray, D., & Lewis, M. (1994). Extending literacy in the junior school: A curriculum development project. In A. Littlefair (Ed.), *Literacy for life.* Widnes, UK: United Kingdom Reading Association.

Chapter Thirteen

Different Cultural Views of Whole Language

Lee Gunderson
University of British Columbia

Whole language is widely known, discussed, and debated in North America. It represents a view of learning and teaching that has developed from a consensus of multiple viewpoints. Harste and Burke (1977) noted that whole language as a theoretical orientation "views reading as one of four ways in which the abstract concept of language is realized" (p. 37). Yetta Goodman (1989), in a comprehensive review of the history of whole language titled "Roots of the Whole-Language Movement," details the multiple influences on whole language. She suggests that the Harste and Burke reference is the first instance in which the term "whole language" appears in print. She also notes that Goodman and Goodman published an occasional paper in 1979 that discussed whole language comprehension–centered reading curricula. These early contributors to whole language had distinct reading orientations. Indeed, Kenneth Goodman is known for his formulation of a top-down model of reading which posits that meaning is a feature of the reader, not the text, a model that has contributed to whole language theory. He is also known for his comprehensive and varied views associated with whole language (see, for instance, Goodman, 1986a, 1986b, 1989).

Read's (1971) study of spelling development showed that a child's early independent writing was logical and revealed a developing understanding of grapheme-phoneme correspondences. The results of Read's study have been used as evidence to support whole language. His orientation was to studies of the developing phonological awareness in the early spelling attempts of very young individuals. Whole language theorists believe, as a consequence, that children should be allowed to invent spellings and view the activities as meaningful language explorations. Graves's (1983) efforts in the area of writing have also contributed to whole language theory. His view is informed by his studies in writing development, which suggest to whole language theorists that children should be encouraged to explore writing. Studies of emergent literacy have further contributed to whole language theory (Teale & Sulzby, 1986). Rosenblatt's (1978) reader response theory is a prominent feature of most views of whole language. Y. Goodman (1989) notes that from Rosenblatt's theories "whole language incorporated the term *transaction* to represent a rich complex relation between the reader and the text" (p. 117). Atwell's (1987) notions of reading and writing integration represent another major influence on whole language theory.

Efforts have been made recently to investigate the epistemological issues related to whole language and instruction (Harste, 1993, 1994; Gunderson, 1993, 1994, 1995; Leland & Harste, 1994), which propose that teachers and students be involved in questioning knowledge, what is worth knowing, and the worth of knowledge. In recent work (Gunderson, 1995), I propose that it is essential for teachers to judge what students must know and what they should know, and recommend that students be included in such decisions. Harste (1993) suggests, "To the question of what knowledge is most worth teaching, an educator holding an inquiry position would argue 'underlying processes in inquiry'" (p. 15).

Issues related to assessment and evaluation in whole language have been both contentious and pioneering. Goodman, Watson, and Burke (1987) propose that underlying comprehension processes could be inferred from an analysis of oral reading miscues. Generally, the notion of using standardized tests to assess the reading achievement of students is dismissed, and more holistic measures are recommended (Goodman, Goodman, & Hood, 1989).

Y. Goodman (1989) describes the multiple sources of influence on whole language including areas such as language experience approach, early childhood education, integrated education, and assessment and evaluation and concludes that

> the history of whole language shows that many groups and individuals have made continuous attempts to consider issues such as curriculum; individual differences; social interaction; collaboration; language learning, the relation between teaching, learning, and evaluation; and their influences on the lives of teachers and students. (p. 122)

This is a positive view of the contributions different researchers have made to whole language theory, but not one shared by all. Walmsley (1989), for instance, notes that "Donald Graves, Nancie Atwell, Jane Hansen (all of whom have written about "process-approaches" to reading and writing) have been co-opted into the movement, whether they wanted to or not" (p. 1).

The term "whole language" is a fairly geocentric term, one developed in North America, which has been applied to educational trends in other parts of the English-speaking world. It's a term, however, that is not generally used in places such as New Zealand or Australia (Turbill, personal communication, 1993). Swiniarski (1992) proposed that whole language theorists in North America have credited the literacy program in New Zealand as being built on whole language principles, but she notes of New Zealand teachers that "while many were familiar with whole language literature, they regarded the term as a purely American interpretation of their literacy programs" (p. 225). Anderson et al. (1985) refer to the literacy instruction occurring in New Zealand as whole language. Ashton-Warner's (1963) language experience concepts have influenced whole language; indeed, some researchers have considered the two to be synonymous (Stahl & Miller, 1989). Holdaway (1979) introduced the use of shared reading, a development that also influenced literature-based and whole language programs. Clay (1979, 1985, 1991) contributed significantly to the development of programs in New Zealand. In Australia, Cambourne developed a natural learning theory "from naturalistic research that sets out to describe and explain how language learning occurs in the everyday ebb and flow of human activity" (Cambourne & Turbill, 1990, p. 338). Cambourne (1988) sets out seven conditions for literacy acquisition: immersion, demonstration, expectation, responsibility, employment, approximation, and response. Cambourne and Turbill note,

"Teachers who implement this theory create classrooms in which the conditions of learning that accompany natural language learning are simulated for pupils learning to control the written form of language" (Cambourne & Turbill, 1990, p. 338). They suggest that such conditions can be used to teach both young students and those who are older. Cambourne and Turbill (1988, 1989) have also influenced whole language through their studies of "teacher-as-co-researcher." In North America, the concept of teacher as researcher has profoundly affected the way teachers view research and researching. Whole language educators promote the concept of research as collaboration (cf. Harste, 1993): "The teacher as researcher movement embodies not only curriculum and a new view of literacy but a new view of literacy instruction" (Harste, 1989, p. 248).

Whole language has developed over the last twenty years or so. Its origins are complex, its nature multifaceted. Watson (1989) believes that whole language is difficult to define because most whole language advocates reject definitions; those who demand definitions usually disapprove of whole language; and teachers—those who are the experts and have developed their own personalized whole language programs—are not asked; they remain silent. Harste, however, admonishes that "it is our theory and we must take responsibility for it" (1989, p. 247).

Although Harste (1993) proposes that whole language advocates should search for the universals in literacy learning, whole language is not a philosophy in the traditional sense; it does not seek to formulate metanarratives. It does, however, appear to be a complex and changing chronicle representing the communication of multiple voices. It is a text in the postmodern sense of text (Gunderson, 1997). I argue that "whole language is not a philosophy in the traditional sense, rather each construal is a framed composite propositional intertext" (p. 225).

As I have pointed out elsewhere, there are advantages and disadvantages to the view that whole language is an intertext built on the multiple voices of teachers and researchers:

> A propositional intertext may contain philosophical, educational, sociological, perceptual, and literacy propositions generated by

> an individual teacher in response to the multiple sources that inform her. In this respect a propositional intertext is an individual view of teaching and learning, one that varies from teacher to teacher, from school to school, and from region to region. In this sense it does not represent universals, it represents local belief, the interpretive voice of the teacher. This is an advantage in that intertexts evolve over time as new propositions are added or existing ones are altered or eliminated. Individual teachers develop their literacy programs on the basis of a propositional intertext that is complex, one that evolves. (Gunderson, 1997, p. 225)

A propositional intertext represents the voices of those who view literacy as a basic, perhaps natural, human activity framed by the teacher, whose view is often similar; it does not necessarily represent the voices of the students. Whole language teachers appear to propose a view of learning—an extremely complex model of language learning—that is literacy centered, that is, that views reading and writing as integral activities of thinking human beings, and designed to produce independent critical learners. These are fairly well ingrained North American views not necessarily shared by individuals from other cultures (Early & Gunderson, 1993). Reading and writing are not necessarily inherently good. An intertext is a composite of propositions contributed by many individuals, most often well-known educator-researchers, not usually teachers (Watson, 1989), a majority of whom are North American. Delpit (1988, 1991) argues that whole language involves a focus on process, one that benefits students from the middle class, which denies minority students access to the "power code." Anderson (1994a) found "that parents from different cultural groups held different perceptions of literacy learning" (p. 13). Indeed, he also found that "while parents from all three cultural groups supported some aspects of emergent literacy, parents from non-mainstream were less supportive of this perspective than were their mainstream counterparts," and "each of the non-mainstream groups unanimously rejected some aspects of emergent literacy" (p. 13). Whole language would appear to be a pedagogical phenomenon uniquely imbued with mainstream North American cultural features.

Whole Language as North American Text

Cummins (1991) believes that "students from 'dominated' societal groups are 'empowered' or 'disabled' as a direct result of their interactions with educators in the schools" (p. 375). Indeed, teachers consciously or unconsciously reproduce the political system of domination. Eurocentric views and beliefs form the core of the educational thought that guides curriculum development and instructional practice. While the demographic data indicate that "five out of six people in the world are non-White" and that the "vast majority of the world's population is non-Christian" (Banks, 1991, p. 147), North American educators continue to view education from a "mainstream" viewpoint that focuses on European values and beliefs, even though their school populations grow increasingly multicultural. Whole language advocates hold a view of teaching, learning, and the role of text that is imbued with the features of their culture. The new primary program in British Columbia, Canada, for instance, begins its section on children's intellectual development with the following quotation:

> If intelligence develops as a whole by the child's own construction then what makes this construction possible is the child's curiosity, interest, alertness, desire to communicate and exchange points of view, and a desire to make sense of it all. (British Columbia, 1988, p. iv)

Inherent in these words and, indeed, in a whole language approach is the assumption that the development of "questioning" children with a plurality of views and openness to them is meritorious. This is a value by no means universally shared, either by all Western teachers or by all students. As Oster (1989) explains:

> When we ask students who come from such diverse places as the Middle East, the Far East, Africa, or Latin America to argue an opinion, especially an opinion different from that of a teacher or a text, or more threatening yet, to take a stand when there has

> been no direction from the teacher, we are often reversing assumptions deeply ingrained in the value system of their culture, implicitly telling them, for example, that a younger person has something new to say to an older one (Anderson and Powell 1988, 208), that words can have value in argument (Barnlund 1987, 164; Becker 1988, 251), that no one will be offended or feel personally attacked (Becker 1988, 245; Osterloh 1986, 81) if a pupil or fellow student openly disagrees with her or him. (pp. 87–88)

These generalizations are based broadly on the interpretations of findings of research conducted in classroom environments. They are, therefore, not necessarily indicative of students' behaviors in noneducational settings. In many countries, however, books are the embodiment of knowledge, wisdom, and truth. Many of the texts read by students from preindustrial countries are exclusively sacred and not open to question. Recent Kurdish refugees to Vancouver, British Columbia, for instance, report that they and their children first learned to read using the Koran and that the only generally available reading material for them was sacred. Recent works by Maley, 1985; Matalene, 1985; Parker et al., 1987; Valdes, 1987; and Young and Lee, 1985 have increased our awareness of intercultural differences in attitudes to learning in general and to a whole language approach to teaching in particular. They have shown how and why students from education systems such as that of the People's Republic of China rely on memory and quotation and find our insistence on originality and analysis difficult to embrace.

While whole language approaches, often based on notions of risk taking and personal empowerment, appear to be increasing in North America, so does the population of students who come from cultures which espouse different ideologies. In the Vancouver, Canada, school district, for example, 53 percent of the students speak a language other than English at home, representing 118 distinct ethnocultural groups, and their numbers continue to grow (Gunderson & Hu, 1994). The ESL population in the United States increased 56 percent from 1985 to 1992, while the overall school population decreased by 3 percent (Lara, 1994). Those of us who encourage students to be curious, interested, critical, and communicative, and to hold a plurality of points of view and a desire to question and make sense of it all, need to be acutely aware that we are teaching a value system. Moreover, it is a value system potentially in opposition to that held by the families of many of our students. The purpose of this essay is to describe three schools, each with a teaching staff dedicated to whole language instruction, each with a different cultural population, and the consequent cross-cultural misunderstandings that have taken place.

The province of British Columbia initiated a new elementary program on the findings of a Royal Commission on Education published in 1988. The name "Year 2000" was given to the plan that came out of the findings of the commission, including whole language instruction, ungraded primary education, and anecdotal report cards.

Upton Elementary School

Upton is an elementary school of approximately five hundred students in an upper-middle-class neighborhood of a large western metropolitan area. Students were enrolled in grades kindergarten through 8. The first four grades (K–3) were organized into ungraded family units. The staff of the school consisted of individuals totally committed to whole language instruction. The demographics of the school had changed fairly dramatically during the period of 1989 to 1993, with immigrants primarily from Taiwan and Hong Kong making up the bulk of new students. Indeed, in 1989 the school was approximately 10 percent ESL students, and by 1993 it had become 52 percent ESL students, 96 percent of whom were from either Hong Kong or Taiwan (children from Hong Kong constituted the largest group, representing 80 percent of the ESL students). An interesting feature of the backgrounds of both the Taiwanese and Hong Kong students was that all had attended preschool in their home countries, and while only a small number of their families were Christians, 90 percent of the preschools these children had attended were private Christian schools. Interviews with parents have suggested that preschools are viewed as good preparation for school in general and that Christian schools in Hong Kong and Taiwan are viewed positively because instruction is in English (Gunderson & Hu, 1994).

The Upton program had many of the features commonly associated with whole language, many of which had been mandated by the provincial Ministry of Education. Teachers had abandoned basal readers and workbooks and initiated and maintained literature-based literacy programs. Reports cards were anecdotal, without including traditional letter grades. Classroom newsletters were standard in nearly all of the classes. Parent meetings were held often to explain and describe the whole language programs taking place in the school. The school program was viewed as exemplary by many educators, especially those on the faculties of education at the two local universities. The beginning of the 1993 school year was associated with a number of teacher strikes across the province of British Columbia. The local press, in a sharklike frenzy of attacks on teachers, reported general dissatisfaction with Year 2000 and teaching in general. One of the local newspapers reported, for instance, that there was general dissatisfaction with teaching and learning and that a poll had shown that 42 percent of those parents polled disliked the whole language approach to teaching and that 58 percent of parents thought that schools were doing a poor job of providing students with the skills needed for the modern economy (Balcom, 1993).

During the period between 1989 and 1991, Upton School and its program had been fairly well received. But as the number of new ESL students increased dramatically during the 1991–92 and 1992–93 school years, and as their numbers approached 50 percent of the overall school population, problems began to arise. Parental discontent with the whole language program initially focused on report cards. After-school meetings with school staff and parents were held to explain the new reporting system and to describe the new ideas of assessment and evaluation that informed their design. Early in the 1992–93 school year, parental dissatisfaction with the whole language program increased; one or two parents led an anti–whole language crusade with letters to the editors of the local newspapers, to officials in the Ministry of Education, and to the school superintendent. The target of their anger was the lack of rote memorization of facts, homework, and workbooks. The rising tide of discontent at Upton was fueled by a general dissatisfaction with whole language that prompted the premier of the province to reconsider the Year 2000 program and bring back letter grades and a focus on basic skills. The teachers at Upton capitulated and brought back workbooks, basal readers, and rote memorization. The situation at Upton was extremely difficult for teachers, administrators, students, and parents because deep-seated value systems were in conflict. Table 13.1 shows the basic conflicts that existed between teachers' and parents' beliefs and expectations about school. These are generalizations drawn from observations of a particular group of parents and students from Hong Kong and Taiwan who had immigrated to Canada since 1989, all of whom were of upper-middle-class and upper-class socioeconomic status. Their views about teaching and learning were not monolithic; there was variation. My interpretations have also benefited from the advice and counsel of a Chinese Canadian, English-Cantonese-Mandarin trilingual Upton parent. Most families had been granted entrepreneurial status, which allowed them to enter Canada as landed immigrants on the promise that they would invest at least $500,000 in the Canadian economy. It is not unusual to see such immigrants arriving at the school reception center with real estate agents to attempt to locate housing near desirable schools. Table 13.1 contains some observations of differences that were generally apparent at Upton School. Scarcella (1990) is an excellent source to consult concerning apparent systematic differences in cultural beliefs.

It is important to remember that differences within a group are almost always greater than differences between groups. There were individual Asian parents who viewed whole language or parts of it positively, and there were White parents who viewed whole language or parts of it negatively. The teachers at Upton have included more skills-based instruction in their classrooms, and the province has moved to return grade-based report cards. Tension at Upton continues as most Asian parents try to bring the school around to their Hong Kong- and Taiwan-based expectations for students, teachers, and learning. They want a skills-based curriculum, workbooks, carefully corrected written work, lots of homework, teacher-centered instruction, a respect for education and for teachers, and a focus on reading, writing, and

Table 13.1. A Comparison of Teacher and Parental Beliefs about Teaching and Learning

Teachers	Parents
Teaching should be learner centered.	The teacher is the source of knowledge and should not be questioned.
Process is more important than product.	Correctness of form is important.
Meaningful language is intact language.	Learning should focus on skills.
Active learning is essential, so students should contribute to discussions and activities.	Students should be told what to learn. It's the teacher who should talk.
Learning should be meaningful.	Learning should involve memorizing.
Speaking, listening, reading, writing, and watching are integrated, mutually reinforcing language activities.	Learning the elements of language is important; a focus on grammar is especially important.
The aesthetics of language are fundamental. Language is functional.	Language is a series of skills to be learned in a particular order.
The learning of content and the learning of language are inseparable.	Content represents a set of facts that should be memorized.
Learning to read and learning to write involve the learning of process. Error correction does not encourage language acquisition.	Learning to read and write means learning phonics, spelling, and how to write. The student should learn to produce a good product. Errors should be corrected and students should be aware of their mistakes.
Invented spelling should be encouraged since it fosters language acquisition.	Poor spelling represents poor learning.
Independence in learning is critical. Critical reading and writing are basic.	Students should work on material given to them by the teacher.
Students should ask questions.	The teacher is the source of knowledge and should not be questioned.
Students should explore and attempt to solve problems.	The teacher should show students how to solve problems.
Workbooks are mindless make-work activities.	Practice is positive evidence that students are learning. The number of items correct is used to judge students' learning.
Skills are learned through interaction with good literature, not through explicit teaching.	Important skills are learned through explicit teaching and rote memorization.
Assessment and evaluation should be holistic.	Assessment should focus on how many skills a student has learned.
Problem solving should be deductive; learning should be exploratory.	Problem solving should be taught, and students should learn it through induction.

arithmetic. School staff members have met repeatedly with these parents and tried unsuccessfully to convince them that whole language is based on sound learning and teaching principles. Meetings tend to be sessions during which unhappy parents come to complain about the school and its program. One particularly difficult session involved the principal trying to demonstrate the school's holistic assessment procedures. Rather than convincing parents that anecdotal grades were superior, the principal's use of cookies to demonstrate her points convinced them that holistic scoring was silly. Upton presents an interesting situation because the parents have determined that they want the school to change to reflect their beliefs, and they have considerable political power. As successful entrepreneurs, these parents understand how to set goals and find the strategies to achieve them. It is my impression that they view education within a business framework, one that has debits and credits and a clear-cut, success-oriented goal. The features of skills-based instruction become more apparent at Upton as time goes by. A number of families have also enrolled their children in private schools, mostly Catholic institutions, featuring more traditional skills-based instruction.

Oakville School

Oakville is in an affluent suburb of a large West Coast city. Indeed, the median income is one of the highest in Canada. Oakville School enrolls about five hundred students in grades kindergarten to 8. The school is made up primarily of students from upper-middle-class families. At the time of this study, approximately forty-five of the students were Farsi- and Persian-speaking immigrants from Iran. About 50 percent of the immigrant students were English-speaking bilinguals. All but two of the families were Muslim. A cultural liaison worker, one who considered herself a part of the community, reported that parents of this group were devout Muslims but not fundamentalists. She noted that many had left their home country because of fears of religious persecution. Oakville is a relatively conservative community that normally elects conservative, local, non-ESL politicians. The teachers at Oakville School were openly divided in their opinions about and enthusiasm for whole language as mandated by the Year 2000 program. The school's primary teachers were the most enthusiastic, while the intermediate teachers were mostly skeptical and unreceptive. Indeed, the school became two-schools-in-one with a whole language program in the primary grades (kindergarten to 3) and a fairly traditional skills-based program in the intermediate grades (4 to 8). Some intermediate teachers did adopt "literature-based programs" that featured trade books and reading centers, but they also continued to use traditional spelling and basal reading instruction, even though the use of basal readers was no longer prescribed by the Ministry of Education. One primary teacher opined that the intermediate teachers had become involved with literature programs because the province had authorized the expenditure of funds for children's trade books. Workbooks, both reading and spelling, continued to be used, often paid for through teachers' personal funds.

The primary teachers were enthusiastic whole language advocates who encouraged their students—even the kindergartners—to write as soon as they entered school. They involved them in the language-rich, meaning-centered activities that have become associated with whole language teaching and learning (cf. Gunderson & Shapiro, 1988). During the 1991–92 school year, two distinct antipathies developed, one between primary and intermediate teachers and one between the parents of primary students and the school.

As students "graduated" from primary to intermediate school, they crossed a boundary, one that separated two distinctly different views of teaching and learning. In intermediate classrooms, they were asked to do workbook activities and memorize spelling words. Their independent invented spellings were corrected and their work was "set aflame in red." Intermediate teachers complained about their students' writing habits, their apparent dislike for workbooks, and their inability to sit still for long periods filling in workbooks. There was much teacher-room talk about poor work habits, sloppy learning attitudes, and students who had apparently been taught nothing. Primary teachers strongly defended their programs and their students' achievements. As criticism across the province escalated in the popular media, the cleft between primary and intermediate teachers widened, intensifying the conflict developing between the immigrant parents' expectations for their children and the implicit and explicit expectations of the whole language program their children were experiencing.

Meetings at Oakville, informational sessions organized by teachers, were not well attended. In general, most of the immigrant parents did not attend. Formal individual parent-teacher meetings were scheduled during November and May. These sessions were led by students as part of a program designed to include them in discussions. The student-led conferences were extremely successful for all except the immigrants. These students were unable to lead conferences, and their parents were unable to accept what the children said about their own progress. These student-led conferences appeared to generate distrust. Individual parent-teacher contacts were made mostly as students were being picked up after school by their parents, almost always their mothers. Mothers were reluctant to speak with teachers about their children's progress, but when they did they were mostly concerned about their primary student's progress and the apparent lack of traditional school methods and approaches. They appeared to want to be told what to do with and for their children. The set of parent beliefs listed in Table 13.1 is fairly reflective of the beliefs of the immigrant parents at Oakville School.

Parent-teacher contacts were difficult for the primary teachers and were apparently very difficult for the parents, who always seemed uncomfortable. A cultural liaison worker informed the teachers that the parents had a deeply ingrained reticence about dealing with authority, and that they, the teachers, were viewed as authorities. Parker et al. (1986) note that "hostility and suspicion may well be characteristics of the Middle Eastern student when he first arrives in the United States" (p. 96). It should be noted that hostility and suspicion are often displayed by students who experience culture shock in culturally unfamiliar contexts (Furnham & Bochner, 1986; Storti, 1990, 1994). But it is not completely accurate to describe these parents' behavior as hostile or suspicious. They displayed reticence about interacting with teachers, a result, the cultural liaison worker suggested, of their experiences with authorities in their home country. As time passed, the number of primary-age immigrants decreased dramatically as their parents enrolled them in a nearby private school that featured traditional skills-based instruction, until none remained in the primary grades in 1994 except for newly arrived immigrants.

Bottomland School

Bottomland School is located in a suburb of a West Coast metropolitan center. The community is situated on an island formed at the mouth of a major river; its rich earth had been used primarily as farmland until the 1970s, when the expanding population of the nearby metropolitan center began to encroach. The late 1980s and early 1990s saw the immigrant population expand and the number of ESL students increase from about 1 percent of the school population to about 35 percent in 1994 (Gunderson & Carrigan, 1993), mostly Chinese from Hong Kong and Taiwan. Bottomland School is located in an area still used exclusively for farming. It is a small school of about 175 students from kindergarten to eighth grade; some of the grades are combinations, e.g., third-fourth grade. About 80 percent of the students are Punjabi-speaking South Asians from farming families who own or work on the surrounding farms. All parents had been educated in India; none had attended or sat for examinations for university. During the 1991–92 school year, Bottomland's kindergarten class enrolled nineteen boys, sixteen of whom were Punjabi-speaking; all had been born in Canada.

Bottomland's primary teachers had already begun to implement their whole language programs when the Year 2000 program was adopted as official policy by the Ministry of Education. The intermediate teachers adopted many of the features of whole language. Since the school was small (only eight teachers), there was a positive sense of togetherness. The all-male kindergarten class exemplified the inevitable consequences of the interfacing of two sets of cultural beliefs, both about whole language teaching and learning specifically and about behavioral expectations generally.

Punjabi-speaking Indian Muslim farmers have a strong sense of commitment to the land. Their families are patriarchal, sons are highly valued, and it is generally acknowledged that they are overindulged. Indeed, a great deal of antipathy was generated in the wider community by a news report that a U.S. medical doctor travels to British Columbia to provide services allowing South Asian women to tell the sex of their unborn babies so that female fetuses can be aborted ("American Doctor," 1994). Most Indian marriages in the Bottomland area are arranged; potential wives are brought to Canada from India. Bottomland farming families are extended families with grandparents, cousins, aunts, uncles, brothers, and sisters often living together. All family members, except the young boys, are expected to work on the farm, especially during harvest season. It is not uncommon for relatives to visit from India during harvest season to work, often bringing a suitcase full of farming tools.

While it was not the purpose of the study to observe a particular class at Bottomland School, the kindergarten was so extraordinary that I have included a description of it here. The teacher of the all-male kindergarten class was a veteran of fourteen years, a middle-aged White Canadian woman known to be an outstanding teacher by her principal and colleagues. One of the first clues that the kindergarten class would be unique involved students' artwork. When one visits most kindergarten classrooms, they are filled with finger-painted icons, rainbows, sunflowers, and houses with green grass and suns. They represent a veritable dictionary, an epistemological storehouse of salient items. That they can be construed to say, "This is a rainbow," or "This is a house," does not mean that they are in fact representations of syntactic structures or utterances. Indeed, they signify a stage of representing thought, one that finds oral expression in a single spoken word, e.g., "rainbow," "ship," or "house." Kindergarten classrooms around the world abound with such expressions. Indeed, there seem to be universals in the icons produced by five-year-old artists, the most prevalent icon being, of course, "me," followed by icons such as "butterfly," "house and trees," and "rainbow." Such peaceful icons may be an artifact of the school and schooling, however. Indeed, it may be that the female-oriented kindergarten classroom fosters such peaceful, benign images. After an initial period in which boys seem to draw self-images, they begin to represent rockets, bombs, tanks, airplanes, and monsters in their independent drawings, images that are usually abandoned in public art activities in some but not all kindergartens. Bottomland's kindergarten was different. After the initial "me" period seen in their art early in the school year, the iconic stage involved "ghosts," "ghostbusters," "slimers," "tanks," "cars," and "destruction races." Students' play behavior was considerably different. Their make-believe sessions focused on war, rockets, bombs, and destruction. Almost always the block constructions were designed to be blown up.

Bottomland's kindergarten students were behaving in thoroughly North American ways that reflect the influence of mass media. The violent images they painted and acted out were those they saw on television and at the movies. It would appear that the most salient features of North American culture for these young boys, both South Asian and White, were acts of violence portrayed by the media. The kindergarten was unique primarily because it was an all-male class, not because it had sixteen South Asian boys in it. That sixteen out of nineteen students were South Asian, however, made it easy for visitors to the classroom to conclude there was a causal link between cultural background and behavior. That the teacher had an especially difficult time dealing with the boys' behavior was related to their culturally accepted way of relating to women. The portrayal of violence in the media affects both immigrants and natives and is discussed in other chapters in this volume (see Boran, Lensmire, and Vasquez). There was a complex interaction of cultures in this classroom, especially in situations involving the teacher and the students.

The teacher was particularly frustrated by the apparent disregard students had for her. The boys did not listen to her, choosing instead to interact with each other. This was especially apparent when it was time to clean up or go to recess. She found that parent conferences were difficult. It was always the father who came to see her in response to a telephone request. Conversation was difficult because the fathers tended to look away from her as she spoke to them. They did not speak directly to her, especially when their sons were present, choosing to speak through them. The teacher's communicative style was typically American, direct and open, while the South Asian men were behaving in a way that was traditional for them, one which places women in a subordinate position, a behavior already adopted by their sons.

As Bottomland's program became more student centered and individualized as a result of the provincial trend to whole language, parental dissatisfaction grew and was communicated to teachers and the principal through increased personal after-school contacts by fathers. Cumulatively, the whole language program was rapidly becoming viewed as suspect. Students were not given regular homework assignments; they did not have regularly scheduled spelling tests; they were not involved in formal reading groups; their written work was not corrected; they did not "sit" for formal tests; and they did not receive traditional grades. What bothered most fathers was that their children were asked to select their own books depending on what they wanted to read. This was incomprehensible to parents. In addition, as Muslims these parents indicated to both teachers and the cultural liaison worker that they were offended that their children were encouraged to read and guess about what they were reading if they did not know words. It made no sense to these parents that their children were asked to make predictions about their texts. Most of the South Asian boys at Bottomland attended classes at a mosque where they learned to read the Koran. The parental view of reading had been formed by their experiences as Muslims. As Baker (1993) notes:

> Islam is a religion of the Book, and although it is exclusive with respect to other religions of other books, it cannot exclude from among its own adherents the promise of what its own scripture reveals. Submission to a single, complete, and unchanging scripture is the bedrock of Islam's radical monotheism. The ability to affirm a faithful commitment to what has been revealed in this one text by reciting the words precisely as they have been written must extend to all Muslims. Koranic recitation, then, is especially noteworthy as a mode of literacy that cuts across all segments of society; it serves to absolutely distinguish believers from nonbelievers without yet distinguishing the more from the less literate. (p. 102)

Baker's conclusions are based on his observations in an Indonesian village. But South Asian parents at Bottomland did feel that to treat reading as an activity that should be enjoyed, and one that should include an often imperfect "oral interpretation" of what is written, was offensive. Teachers are supposed to teach their students to read aloud the words perfectly, not to guess or predict or interpret. This view was confirmed by the cultural liaison worker, who was a member of the community. It does not, however, necessarily suggest that thinking critically is not a feature of the South Asian culture. It was a view that seemed to result from a complex interaction between parents' religious beliefs and their own expectations for school and schooling that they had learned in India as elementary students.

The intermediate teachers, motivated by a rapidly growing number of requests, began a policy of assigning homework, only to find that it was rarely completed, a major dilemma. Fathers wanted their children to have homework, yet they did not seem concerned that it was almost done. A Punjabi-speaking cultural aide visited homes and reported back to teachers that the extended family was the apparent source of the difficulty students had in attending to their homework. Farm life and extended families resulted in a great number of individuals entering and leaving homes during the afternoons and evenings. It was considered bad manners for a child not to pay attention to visitors, especially those who were relatives. A consequence of the attention students paid to their visiting family members was that they often did not have time to complete their homework.

The whole language program in Bottomland School was designed on a set of beliefs about teaching and learning that focused on the central view that language is inquiry. The parental view of teaching and learning differed. The teacher was viewed as the center of the classroom, the one who had knowledge to be communicated to students. That the primary teachers were female caused considerable difficulty for many Bottomland parents because it violated their own notions of power and authority. The parental view of reading was that books contained knowledge that students could come to know through perfect oral reading. The parental view also included the notion that learning was like any task that consisted of steps learned in order. A learner's task was to acquire the knowledge represented by each step and to be awarded a grade that revealed how well he or she had succeeded.

Communication difficulties continue to be a feature of the program at Bottomland School. Cultural aides, those who are knowledgeable, have attempted to bridge the gap between the cultural notions parents and students have for school and schooling and the explicit and implicit beliefs that informed the school's program. Accommodation on the part of teachers, parents, and students has ameliorated the difficulties somewhat, but Bottomland continues to be a school where whole language beliefs and practices conflict with Eastern beliefs and notions. Presently there is an uneasy peace, two sides trying to get along, each trying not to offend and not to capitulate completely.

Conclusion

I have returned on many occasions to the schools that form the focus of the discussion in this chapter to talk with students, teachers, administrators, cultural aides, and parents to confirm or disconfirm the observations and conclusions made. I have been reminded many times that I bring a particular set of beliefs to my observations, beliefs that establish an interpretive framework, but in many respects whole language itself is an interpretive act.

Whole language is not a unitary and systematic teaching program that is applied the same everywhere. I have concluded elsewhere (Gunderson, 1997) that whole language is a set of beliefs about teaching and learning that "may contain philosophical, educational, sociological, perceptual, and literacy propositions generated by an individual teacher in response to the multiple sources that inform her" (p. 225). In this respect, whole language:

> is an individual view of teaching and learning, one that varies from teacher to teacher, from school to school, and from region to region. In this sense it does not represent universals, it represents local belief, the interpretive voice of the teacher. This is an advantage in that intertexts evolve over time as new propositions are added or existing ones are altered or eliminated. Individual teachers develop their literacy programs on the basis of a

propositional intertext that is complex, one that evolves. (Gunderson, 1997, pp. 238–39)

Whole language is an instructional approach based on a particular teacher's interpretation of a set of beliefs about teaching and learning. As such, it is a uniquely local manifestation that varies from other manifestations.

The research reported in this chapter involves an analysis of three groups identified by culture. The reader should not conclude, however, that the groups are monolithic. Each is unique in that it represents different mosaics of beliefs. The members of each group, in fact, differ from each other in their beliefs. It is critical to remember that the generalizations suggested in this chapter relate specifically to the groups discussed, and they represent only what appear to be general trends. It cannot be said that they are representative in any systematic way of larger populations, only that they do to some degree represent the beliefs of these particular groups at a particular time. Variation should not be surprising. The debate among North American educators about whole language and phonics is eloquent testimony to the variation that exists among teachers.

What the observations in this chapter suggest is that the way individuals view teaching and learning, including the role of literacy, varies across cultural groups, especially those views regarding whole language teaching and learning. This is not a particularly surprising finding considering that the view of whole language, even among middle-class mainstream families, is mixed. Indeed, those who report that they are in favor of whole language instruction also report that skills such as phonics should be explicitly taught (Anderson, 1994b).

Although Harste (1993) proposes that whole language advocates should search for the universals in literacy learning, whole language is not a philosophy in the traditional sense—it does not seek to formulate metanarratives. It does, however, appear to be a complex and changing chronicle representing the communication of multiple voices; it is a text in the postmodern sense of text. Harste (1989) concludes that "whole language is essentially a theory of voice that operates on the premise that all students must be heard" (p. 245) and that students should be asked, "How are you different now that you have finished reading this text than you were when you began?" (Harste, 1989, p. 244). He adds, "Whole language theory is changing. More and more whole-language theorists are talking about reading and writing as tools for learning rather than using such terms as 'learning to mean,' 'reading to mean' and the like." Harste (1993) also suggests that research itself is changing, that the truth about teaching and learning does not exist independently, and that the researcher's task is not simply to discover the truth but also "to uncover the theory of meaning that was operating in the group" (p. 17). Harste predicts that whole language programs "will anchor themselves on such processes as transmediation or, said differently, on universal processes which undergird literacy across sign systems and disciplines" (1993, p. 12). The present study suggests that such an approach, one which seeks to search out literacy universals or universal processes of literacy, may be a thoroughly Western-oriented undertaking. There is an essential conundrum: whole language seeks to empower individual students, to give them voice, yet individual voice is antipathetic to some cultural views. Whole language seeks to teach students that meaning is not in text and that reading is creative prediction, yet in some cultures text represents truth.

The schools described in this chapter represent three different situations and three different outcomes: (1) confrontation, (2) avoidance, and (3) uncomfortable coexistence, three solutions that took place within an overall context of anti–whole language sentiment. The paradox is clear; solutions are not. There do, however, appear to be some bottom-line conclusions.

If we are to help students from other cultures become academically successful in our Western system, one that may feature whole language teaching and learning, we have a responsibility to help them engage in the kind of seeing and thinking that this system demands, to understand "mainstream" literacy attitudes and strategies, and to empower them by learning the discourse of the dominant culture (Delpit, 1988). We must also keep in mind, however, as Harman and Edelsky (1989) note, that "literacy is not necessarily liberating." They further caution that "*merely knowing how to read and write guarantees neither membership in the dominant culture nor the concomitant political, economic, cognitive, or social rewards of that membership*" (pp. 393, emphasis in original). Students are empowered by learning that their voices are heard and valued in the school community. We can come to know about these value systems by involving our students in community ethnographies (Early & Gunderson, 1993) and by changing our strategies to account for them. We must always be aware, however, that we are teaching students views they may consider antithetical or heretical, notions that are viewed with disgust by members of the cultures from which they come. We must also be aware that there may be some cases in which a student's or a parent's view, one that is culturally based, may be abhorrent to North Americans. Some views that are violent, racist, or sexist should be confronted in thoughtful ways. It is not acceptable in North America, for instance, to abort fetuses simply because they are female. What the teacher does to confront and educate students about such an issue is vital.

Schools and teachers are in many respects the instruments by which governments both national and local inculcate in their citizens the set of beliefs deemed correct and appropriate, beliefs that include the dominant social values that may reproduce an oppressive stratified society (cf. Giroux, 1983). Dominated individuals may "buy in" to the system and recreate their own domination (see Canagarajah, 1993, for example). Whole language, like other teaching approaches, is imbued with values and beliefs about teaching, learning, and voice. Whole language teachers believe in the value of process and critical, independent thinking and inquiry.

What seems true across cultures and political affiliations is that parents, teachers, and other interested adults seek "the best" for students. The upper-middle-class Asian parents in this study viewed the best as a product, the accumulation of knowledge that would enable their children to pass a test that would allow them to enter a university and subsequently graduate and become a member of a profession. Some individuals would interpret this as a politically conservative approach to the values of schooling, one which aims to maintain an oppressive, stratified society. But it is an approach that has worked for the parents themselves. The Asian parents in this study believed passionately that a whole language approach violated their children's right to acquire the knowledge they needed to succeed, a cultural view of teaching and learning shared by parents in immigrant and non-immigrant groups across North America.

Traditional schooling has empowered the dominant classes in North America and in other countries. Whole language teachers value the notion that the empowerment of all students is a central pedagogical objective, that it is liberating, and that everyone's voice should be heard. It is not enough simply to dismiss divergent views as wrong. Traditional schooling clearly works for some individuals within the established system—that is, it empowers some students to acquire the knowledge they need to be successful in school and subsequently in a class-stratified society. Whole language must work for all students. To achieve this goal is no easy task. One view might be that traditional schooling should be changed or "fixed" so that it empowers all students. Another view might be that schooling should be "fixed" so that its focus on the elements of language, tests, measures, grades, and product is changed. But these are epistemological issues related to knowledge and to knowing. An essential question is, "Who is right?" This is a question that cannot be answered by considering epistemological issues, because it involves values. The whole language answer is clear: the voices of all people should be heard, and their answers may differ. The more important general philosophical consideration for whole language may be axiological. For the whole language teacher in particular, the understanding that whole language represents a view of learning and teaching that differs from the view held by many parents and students is an important step. Traditional teaching does not empower teachers to consider issues related to voice, power, and values. Whole language does. Such consideration is difficult, filled with potential disagreement and discord, yet it is essential. The norm in many districts across North America is no longer middle-class White. Whole language has evolved over time and it will continue to do so as it empowers both students and teachers from diverse cultures. The recognition and accommodation of difference will drive—empower, if you will—change in whole language. Further research in multicultural and international contexts is essential.

References

American doctor criticized for providing gender revealing services in British Columbia. (1994, March 12). *Vancouver Sun,* A1, Vancouver, BC.

Anderson, J. (1994a). Parents' perceptions of emergent literacy: An exploratory study. *Reading Psychology, 15*(3), 165–87.

Anderson, J. (1994b, November). *Parents' perspectives of literacy acquisition: A cross-cultural perspective.* Paper presented at the Conference of the College Reading Association, New Orleans, Louisiana.

Anderson, J. F., & Powell, R. (1988). Cultural influences on educational processes. In L. Samovar & R. Porter (Eds.), *Intercultural communication: A reader* (5th ed., pp. 201–29). Belmont, CA: Wadsworth.

Anderson, R. C., and the United States Commission on Reading. (1985). *Becoming a nation of readers: The report of the Commission on Reading.* Washington, DC: National Institute of Education.

Ashton-Warner, S. (1963). *Teacher.* New York: Bantam Books.

Atwell, N. (1987). *In the middle: Writing, reading, and learning with adolescents.* Upper Montclair, NJ: Boynton/Cook.

Baker, J. N. (1993). The presence of the name: Reading scripture in an Indonesian village. In J. Boyarin (Ed.), *The ethnography of reading* (pp. 98–138). Berkeley: University of California Press.

Balcom, S. (1993, March 5). Parents are unhappy about schools. *Vancouver Sun,* A1, Vancouver, BC.

Banks, J. A. (1991). *Teaching strategies for ethnic studies* (4th ed.). Boston: Allyn & Bacon.

Barnlund, D. C. (1987). Verbal self-disclosure: Topics, targets, depth. In L. F. Luce & E. C. Smith (Eds.), *Toward internationalism: Readings in cross-cultural communication* (2nd ed., 147–65). Cambridge, MA: Newbury House.

Becker, C. B. (1988). Reasons for the lack of argumentation and debate in Far East. In L. A. Samovar & R. Porter (Eds.), *Intercultural communication: A reader* (5th ed., pp. 87–101). Belmont, CA: Wadsworth.

British Columbia Ministry of Education. (1988). *The British Columbia primary program*. Victoria, Canada: The Queens Printers.

Cambourne, B. (1988). *The whole story: Natural learning and the acquisition of literacy in the classroom*. Auckland, New Zealand: Ashton Scholastic.

Cambourne, B., & Turbill, J. B. (1988). *From guinea pigs to coresearchers*. Brisbane, Australia: Pre-Conference Institute, World Reading Conference.

Cambourne, B., & Turbill, J. B. (1989). *Whole language all day, every day*. New Orleans, LA: Pre-Conference Institute, International Reading Association National Conference.

Cambourne, B., & Turbill, J. B. (1990). Assessment in whole-language classrooms: Theory into practice. *Elementary School Journal, 90*(3), 337–49.

Canagarajah, A. S. (1993). A critical ethnography of a Sri Lankan classroom: Ambiguities in student opposition to reproduction through ESOL. *TESOL Quarterly, 27*(4), 601–26.

Clay, M. (1979). *Reading: The patterning of complex behavior* (2nd ed.). Portsmouth, NH: Heinemann.

Clay, M. (1985). *The early detection of reading difficulties* (3rd ed.). Portsmouth, NH: Heinemann.

Clay, M. (1991). *Becoming literate: The construction of inner control*. Portsmouth, NH: Heinemann.

Cummins, J. (1991). Empowering minority students: A framework for intervention. In M. Minami & B. P. Kennedy (Eds.), *Language issues in literacy and bilingual/multicultural education* (pp. 372–90). Cambridge, MA: Harvard Educational Review. (Original work published 1985 in *Harvard Educational Review, 56*[1], 18–36).

Delpit, L. (1988). The silenced dialogue: Power and pedagogy in educating other people's children. *Harvard Educational Review, 58*(3), 280–98.

Delpit, L. (1991). A conversation with Lisa Delpit. *Language Arts, 68*, 541–47.

Early, M., & Gunderson, L. (1993). Linking home, school and community literacy events. *TESL Canada Journal, 11*(1), 99–111.

Furnham, A., & Bochner, S. (1986). *Culture shock: Psychological reactions to unfamiliar environments.* London: Methuen.

Giroux, H. (1983). *Theory and resistance in education: A pedagogy for the opposition.* South Hadley, MA: Bergin & Garvey.

Goodman, K. S. (1986a). Basal readers: A call for action. *Language Arts, 63*(4), 358–63.

Goodman, K. S. (1986b). *What's whole in whole language?* Portsmouth, NH: Heinemann.

Goodman, K. S. (1989). Whole-language research: Foundations and development. *Elementary School Journal, 90*(2), 207–21.

Goodman, K. S., & Goodman, Y. M. (1979). Learning to read is natural. In L. B. Resnick & P. A. Weaver (Eds.), *Theory and practice of early reading* (Vol. 1, pp. 137–54). Hillsdale, NJ: Erlbaum.

Goodman, K., Goodman, Y., & Hood, W. (1989). *The whole language evaluation book.* Portsmouth, NH: Heinemann.

Goodman, Y. M. (1989). Roots of the whole-language movement. *Elementary School Journal, 90*(2), 113–27.

Goodman, Y., Watson, D. & Burke, C. (1987). *Reading miscue inventory: Alternative procedures.* New York: R. C. Owen.

Graves, D. (1983). *Writing teachers and children at work.* Exeter, NH: Heinemann Educational Books.

Gunderson, L. (1993, August). *Whole language: Whose voice?* Paper presented at the Whole Language Umbrella Conference, Winnipeg, Manitoba, Canada.

Gunderson, L. (1994). Reading and language development. In V. Froese (Ed.), *Whole-language: Practice and theory* (pp. 199–240). Scarborough, Ontario: Allyn & Bacon Canada.

Gunderson, L. (1995). *The Monday morning guide to comprehension.* Markham, Ontario: Pippin.

Gunderson, L. (1997). Whole language approaches to reading and writing. In S. Stahl & D. Hayes (Eds.), *Instructional models in reading* (pp. 221–47). Norwood, NJ: Erlbaum.

Gunderson, L., & Carrigan, T. (1993, December). *A three-year study of the achievement of immigrant students.* Paper presented at the National Reading Conference, Charleston, South Carolina.

Gunderson, L., & Hu, J. (1994). *A study of the personal, familial, cultural, and literacy backgrounds of school-age immigrant students.* Paper presented at the National Reading Conference, San Diego, California.

Gunderson, L. & Shapiro, J. (1988). Whole language instruction: Writing in 1st grade. *Reading Teacher, 41*(4), 430–37.

Harman, S., & Edelsky, C. (1989). The risks of whole language literacy: Alienation and connection. *Language Arts, 66*(4), 392–406.

Harste, J. (1989). The future of whole language. *Elementary School Journal, 90*(2), 243–49.

Harste, J. (1993). Curriculum for the millennium: Putting an edge on learning through inquiry. *Australian Journal of Language and Literacy, 16*(1), 6–22.

Harste, J. (1994). Literacy as curricular conversations about knowledge, inquiry, and morality. In R. B. Ruddell, M. R. Ruddell, & H. Singer (Eds.), *Theoretical models and processes of reading* (4th ed., pp. 48–69). Newark, DE: International Reading Association.

Harste, J. C., & Burke, C. L. (1977). A new hypothesis for reading research: Both teaching and learning of reading are theoretically based. In P. D. Pearson (Ed.), *Reading: Theory, research and practice: Twenty-sixth yearbook of the National Reading Conference* (pp. 32–42). Clemson, SC: National Reading Conference.

Holdaway, D. (1979). *The foundations of literacy.* Sydney, Australia: Ashton Scholastic.

Lara, J. (1994). Demographic overview: Changes in students enrollment in American schools. In K. Spangenberg-Urbschat & R. Pritchard (Eds.), *Kids come in all languages: Reading instruction for ESL students* (pp. 9–21). Newark, DE: International Reading Association.

Leland, C. H., & Harste, J. (1994). Multiple ways of knowing: Curriculum in a new key. *Language Arts, 71*, 337–45.

Maley, A. (1987). XANADU—A miracle of rare device: The teaching of English in China. In J. M. Valdes (Eds.), *Culture bound: Bridging the culture gap in language teaching* (pp. 102–11). Cambridge: Cambridge University Press.

Matalene, C. (1985). Contrastive rhetoric: An American writing teacher in China. *College English, 47*, 789–808.

Oster, J. (1989). Seeing with different eyes: Another view of literature in the ESL class. *TESOL Quarterly, 23*(1), 85–103.

Osterloh, K. (1986). Intercultural differences and communicative approaches to foreign-language teaching in the Third World. In J. M. Valdes (Ed.), *Culture bound: Bridging the cultural gap in language teaching* (pp. 77–84). Cambridge: Cambridge University Press.

Parker, O. D., & Educational Staff of AFME. (1986). Cultural clues to the Middle Eastern student. In J. M. Valdes (Ed.), *Culture bound: Bridging the culture gap in language teaching* (pp. 94–101). Cambridge: Cambridge University Press.

Read, C. (1971). Preschool children's knowledge of English phonology. *Harvard Educational Review, 41,* 1–34.

Rosenblatt, L. (1978). *The reader, the text, the poem: The transactional theory of literary work.* Carbondale: Southern Illinois University Press.

Scarcella, R. (1990). *Teaching language minority students in the multicultural classroom.* Englewood Cliffs, NJ: Prentice-Hall Regents.

Stahl, S. A., & Miller, P. D. (1989). Whole language and language experiences approaches for beginning reading: A quantitative research synthesis. *Review of Educational Research, 59*(1), 87–116.

Storti, C. (1990). *The art of crossing cultures.* Yarmouth, ME: Intercultural Press.

Storti, C. (1994). *Cross-cultural dialogues: 74 brief encounters with cultural difference.* Yarmouth, ME: Intercultural Press.

Swiniarski, L. B. (1992). Voices from down under: Impressions of New Zealand's schooling. *Childhood Education, 68*(4), 225–28.

Teale, W. H., & Sulzby, E. (1986). *Emergent literacy: Reading and writing.* Norwood, NJ: Ablex.

Valdes, J. M. (Ed.). (1987). *Culture bound: Bridging the culture gap in language teaching.* Cambridge: Cambridge University Press.

Walmsley, S. (1989, December). *Whole language: Definition, issues and concerns.* Paper presented at the National Reading Conference, Austin, TX.

Watson, D. J. (1989). Defining and describing whole language. *Elementary School Journal, 90*(2), 129–41.

Young, R., & Lee, S. (1985). EFL curriculum innovation and teachers' attitudes. In P. Larson, E. L. Judd, & D. S. Messerschmitt (Eds.), *On TESOL '84, a brave new world for TESOL: Selected papers from the eighteenth annual convention of Teachers of English to Speakers of Other Languages, Houston, TX, March 6–11, 1984* (pp. 183–94). Washington, DC: TESOL.

CHAPTER FOURTEEN

Inviting Reflective Global Inquiries: Politicizing Multicultural Literature, Mediated Student Voices, and English Literacies

SIBEL BORAN
University of Wisconsin Oshkosh

As the lives of our children and youth are touched by or distanced from global issues, the challenge for teachers lies in establishing literacy partnerships with their students to help them create a more peaceful and democratic world as empowered global citizens.

> I just came to the United States, in the beginning of this semester, and most of my friends are international students because we take the same ESL class. We kind of stick together. Like this Russian girl is my best friend because we can understand each other better.
>
> MARYAM, an Iraqi high school student

> Talking to my American friends who have been to other countries, like Russia, helped me understand how nice the Russian people were compared to all the "stern and aggressive" stereotypes we see on television. . . . And there are always the new international students at our school and I really wanna get to know them too but . . . like when I go to the cafeteria they all sit together and I wanna go talk to them but I feel like I'd be an intruder if I break in.
>
> PETER, a U.S. high school student

These two accounts illustrate both the potential and the missed opportunities for international communication that occur in multiethnic high schools. These illustrations are drawn from a broader qualitative research study on global understanding that I conducted during the 1990–91 school year at Worldville High School, a midwestern school in the United States.[1] As examples of cultural communication barriers in a mini-community—i.e., the school—they call for inquiries about the politics of our English literacy agendas and of our students' voices. The question is: Are our literacy practices really overloaded with diversity and social justice issues, as was suggested at the 1994 International Whole Language Umbrella Conference in San Diego? Or do we have a long way to go before the politics of the kinds of literacies we envision for our future citizens reflect experiences for critically and responsibly participating in our global community?

Earlier studies on international understanding reported a serious lack of world knowledge, lack of knowledge about world problems, and often stereotyped perceptions of non-European cultures by most U.S. students. Global educators, who criticized the U.S. curriculum for lacking international perspectives, called for intensified efforts to prepare future citizens to live in an increasingly interdependent world society. With heightened world conflicts, increased international connectedness, and increased dependency for solving common world problems shared by members of our single planet, global educators stressed the inadequacy of both Eurocentric and nationally centered multicultural education for the development of global citizenship. They emphasized the urgency of merging multicultural and international education to help students realize the interdependence of human survival and welfare, not only in their culturally pluralistic national communities but also in the multicultural world community (Cakmak [Boran], 1993).

Significant theoretical strides have been made in the area of global education, especially since the 1980s, despite opposition from advocates of European-centered cultural literacy such as Bloom (1987) and Hirsch (1987). In implementation, while social studies courses have been the most successful in joining the global education movement (see Becker, 1982; Hanvey, 1982; Reardon, 1988), some ESL educators (see Ashworth, 1991; Brown, 1991; Cakmak [Boran], 1989; Fine, 1990; Fox, 1990) also showed concern for global understanding and world peace.

On a national scale, literature texts read in most U.S. high school English courses remain those considered part of the European canon (Applebee, 1989; Oliver, 1994). With the increasing impact of multicultural education on English curricula, today we encounter some ethnic American literature in some literacy classrooms committed to education about historically neglected cultures. Unfortunately, in practice we have yet to witness full-scale globalization of our literacy curricula, although the international status of the English language (Kachru, 1988) allows us to access the human experience not only through ethnic American literature but also through international literature.

Interested in the implications of global education for literacy, in my 1990–91 study I explored:

- the meaning of global understanding based on students' perceptions of diverse cultures and universal human issues, and
- what social (academic or nonacademic) experiences shaped students' perceptions.

My purpose was to find out what possibilities and challenges existed for reforming our literacy agendas to include global perspectives, i.e., diverse ethnic perspectives within a nation and international perspectives from abroad.

Besides highlighting communication barriers between U.S. and international students, my findings suggested challenging possibilities for partnerships between English and ESL courses for enhancing global understanding, including:

- the positive impact on students' global understandings of in-depth international experiences provided by interpersonal communications and courses
- stereotypical perceptions or attitudes and behaviors, usually toward mostly neglected new international students, especially those from non-European cultures often categorized as "Middle Eastern" or "Asian," due to differences in dress or physical features
- initial self-alienation of new ESL students from U.S. students while adjusting to their new school culture

- the negative impact of cultural stereotypes on some students' perceptions of international political issues, or vice versa
- the inability of some U.S. students to challenge injustices committed against some unfamiliar non-Western cultures, as opposed to their ability to challenge such injustices against national ethnic or familiar international cultures
- in contrast to globally oriented social studies courses, a lack of global perspective in English courses that included ethnic American and European literature but excluded non-European international literature in exploring "universal" human experiences.

Elaborating on this last item, the English courses fostered inquiries about and understandings of European or major ethnic U.S. cultures to the exclusion of international non-European cultures and conflicts. This situation challenges us to determine how ESL-English partnerships can serve to help students inquire about the perceptually distant cultures and issues.

My purpose was to introduce partnerships between secondary ESL and English classes as "a continuum for global experiences" provided in social studies courses (Cakmak [Boran], 1990, 1993)—an idea often overlooked at the high school level. The need to challenge cross-disciplinary boundaries in seeking knowledge "for purposes of producing a more equitable, a more just, a more thoughtful world" is strongly advocated by Jerome Harste in Chapter 1 of this volume.

Here, I seek to show from a global literacy perspective that within each discipline—in this case, English—we also need to provide "diverse ethnic and international perspectives" on global human issues. Further, I take the position that, prejudiced or not, while all student voices must be heard, the political consequences of each voice and the social sources that shape them must also be problematized and challenged. Likewise, since different disciplinary perspectives are only reflections of certain voices serving certain political and cultural interests, they also must be challenged. It should be stressed that perspectives conveyed by different disciplines are only some among many social sources that shape student voices and perceptions of global cultures and issues. Whole language, which values the power of not just texts but also diverse sign systems (such as music, art, drama) on literacy, can set the context for pursuing globalized inquiries, rather than perpetuating inquiries that politically sanitize the controversial realities of communities and the world.

The Impact of International Experiences

International experiences that enhance global understanding may not be experienced only through firsthand sources such as travel to overseas contexts that can directly challenge one's prior cultural assumptions; they also can be experienced through local social contexts. I discovered that in local social contexts students' global understandings of diverse world cultures and conflicts were shaped by the following environments:

- academic environments such as courses with an international focus or socialization with international or U.S. peers with international experiences, particularly those related to non-Western countries
- social environments outside the school such as U.S. or international family members or friends with diverse international experiences and diverse political perspectives on global cultures and conflicts
- experiences at home with literature, newspapers, and mass media reflecting diverse international perspectives or global issues
- religious institutions, etc.

But what helped students the most in inquiring about their own and others' perceptions of global cultures and conflicts was not only the source but also the nature of that source and the depth of their engagement with it. For instance, exposure to a global conflict on television, or sharing lessons with an international student whose country was involved in that conflict, did not affect students' perceptions of the issue. However, students' initially stereotyped perceptions of that country and the social, economic, environmental, psychological, and political consequences of their views on that conflict became objects of self-inquiry when challenged by various sources that allowed discussion and reflection from diverse and contradictory perspectives.

I found that in-depth international experiences with classmates or other people from different countries helped students to (a) discover similarities and differences, (b) view their culture from different cultural perspectives, (c) question cultural supremacy, cultural biases, and cultural stereotypes, and (d) enhance their transcultural respect for human dignity and welfare, even if they disagreed with some non-West European traditions, especially concerning women's rights. Unless coupled with other in-depth experiences that provided substantive knowledge and discussion of human issues from multiple cultural perspectives, however, local or overseas international contact alone did not enhance critical thinking on such political issues but instead perpetuated unquestioned, biased views. Research studies on critical thinking (Paul, 1992) and on political socialization that focus on perceptions of international conflicts (Knowles, 1993; Buergenthal & Torney, 1976) also confirm this finding.

The positive impact of interpersonal international experiences on global understanding has been noted by other researchers from a range of contexts. Bachner and Zeutschel (1990), who studied German and U.S. high school students, found that overseas exchange experiences taught students not to stereotype people by nationality but to individualize them. Case (1991) reports that international experience contributes to open-mindedness, resistance to stereotyping, the tendency to empathize with other people, and a lack of chauvinism. Furthermore, research that focused on local international experiences between U.S. and visiting foreign students also yielded encouraging findings, especially for those students who lacked direct overseas experiences. Sharma and Jung (1986) found a significant relationship between U.S. students' cross-cultural interactions with international students and their world-mindedness, cosmopolitan worldview, support for internationalism, and acceptance of cultural pluralism. Wilson (1993) found that conversation partnerships between U.S. and international ESL students benefited both parties by contributing to their substantive cross-cultural knowledge and global open-mindedness. This in turn fostered empathy, the ability to view their own cultures from multiple cultural perspectives, and a reduction in prejudice. The partnerships also helped improve ESL students' English-language abilities.

Wilson (1993) explored the impact of a specific academic program—the Conversation Partner Program at the University of Kentucky—designed to provide ESL international students with conversation partners by pairing them with social studies majors who had plans to teach overseas. The question is, Why not design similar partnership programs at the high school level? If ESL partnerships are established with students in a required English class, a larger number of students could be reached.

The empowering impact of challenging prejudiced thinking and behavior through collaborative learning is supported by studies at secondary and college levels (see Pate, 1989). Student-centered collaborative inquiry and conversations through multiple sign systems across the curriculum have been witnessed as powerful means for effective literacy development and learning at presecondary levels (Harste, 1994).

This chapter strongly recommends continuing the reflective dialogue and inquiry across secondary language classes based on this study and other studies cited in this chapter. In this chapter, I propose to address the perceptions of Middle Eastern cultures that emerged during this study as a result of the reporting of the Persian Gulf War. In the following sections, such cultural perceptions will be related to efforts to broaden both national and other international perceptions based on four major themes that emerged from this study: breaking the communication barriers; sensitivity to stereotypes brought on by international conflicts and war; international women's images; and adolescent life.

The following activities are based on a multicultural global curricular approach to English-ESL curricula (see Figure 14.1), which is theoretically grounded in my 1993 study at Worldville High School. The globally empowering cycle in Figure 14.1 is a reflection of the actual cognitive-affective processes students engaged in in their attempts to understand world cultures and universal human issues from multiple perspectives. By using guiding questions as well as definitions of universal interculturalism and universal ethical-humanism (see Figure 14.2) to generate inquiry themes in order to enhance multicultural global understanding, students in global partnership communities should then be en-

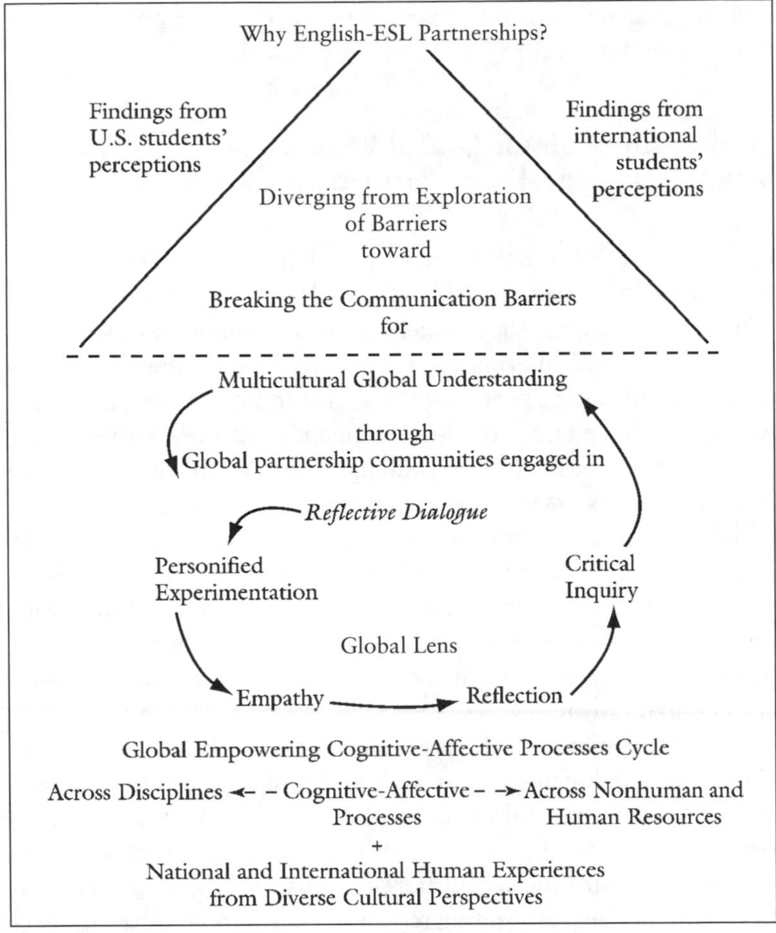

FIGURE 14.1. *A multicultural global approach to English-ESL curricula.*

gaged in "reflective dialogue," i.e., conversations with multiple human and nonhuman resources (see Appendix 14.1 at the end of this chapter) reflecting diverse perspectives within and across world cultures. Such conversations allowed students in this study to reflect on the nature, sources, and consequences of their previous perceptions. Reflective dialogue can be triggered through collaborative learning, which involves cognitive-affective processes including "personified experimentation" (with unfamiliar human experiences) for creating "empathy," "reflection," and "critical inquiry" (questioning and reasoning about human issues from diverse perspectives rather than accepting the dominant perspective at face value).

Looking through the Global Lens Using Whole Language–Based Partnerships

In this chapter, although I focus on explaining partnership activities suited for separate ESL and English classes, modifications can be made to apply similar partnerships in English courses taken by both U.S. and international students (ESL or fluent English-speaking). Initiating partnerships using videos can be a powerful means for challenging students to engage in inquiries about their perceptions of local, national, and international diversity. Because so many youngsters today are mass media–oriented,[2] teachers, as collaborative classroom inquirers, can use multicultural videos to explore their own students' perceptions of the world. Such teacher-initiated inquiry is a means of contextualizing global inquiries[3] according to the needs and background experiences of inquirers in different cultural contexts (classroom, school, local community, nation).

Let's consider an ESL class and a required English class that needs a global dimension. On the first day, students in both classes are invited to write in their dated (and anonymous) journals their perceptions of aspects of U.S. culture and those of international cultures that they view as different. This may be done through freewriting or by responding to a set of questions. Certain questions may help the classes explore whether students have positive or negative attitudes toward different cultures and what experiences shaped those perceptions. Identifying sources of student perceptions will form the potential basis for challenging students' stereotypes by opening avenues for self-reflection and further inquiries from other sources. Having students write responses to journal questions such as the following are helpful:[4]

Identifying cultures perceived as different

- Which ethnic U.S. and international cultures do you view as different from mainstream U.S. culture? How are they different?

Guiding Questions

Invitation to construct a multicultural global exploration activity based on the multicultural global curricular approach represented in Figure 14.1.

1. Selected theme.

2. Purpose.

3. Selected materials to support themes.

4. Activities for ESL-English partnership communities.

(a) Using the above theme and materials, how would you activate reflective dialogue among students and engage them in critical inquiry?

(b) What other materials (human or nonhuman) and activities would you tie in to "personify" culturally distant human experiences?

(c) How will you generate other connected themes?

- -

Core Components of Multicultural Global Understanding Based on Cognitive-Affective Processes of Sixteen U.S. High School Seniors Engaged in Understanding Global Cultural Diversity:

1. Universal Interculturalism: Inquiry for understanding, although not necessarily adopting, national and international cultural differences and for establishing similarities among humankind.

2. Universal Ethical-Humanism: Consistent application of ethically fair criteria across national and international cultures in evaluating human issues, without regard for cultural differences. Ethically fair criteria include respect for the welfare and human dignity of any one culture without favoritist judgments about the welfare or unfair supremacy of one culture over others. Such criteria also include critical inquiry into human issues from multiple perspectives versus passive acceptance of a particular reasoning or action favoring a particular viewpoint.

These two components can be used as major goals for guiding students to approximate "globalism" and as two major criteria for keeping track of students' perceptions of diverse cultures and universal human issues.

FIGURE **14.2.** *Guiding questions for inquiry to enhance multicultural global understanding.*

Identifying initial cultural attitudes

- What do you think and how do you feel about these different cultures? Why?

Identifying sources of students' initial cultural perceptions

- What kinds of firsthand or indirect experiences have you had with these different cultures?
- What were the sources (for example, courses, books, movies, news, parents, peers, etc.) of your indirect experiences?

Encouraging potential self-reflection and action to challenge stereotypes about others and to personify (humanize) the culturally different

- Have you ever experienced a situation in which you felt different or were alienated by others? How did you feel? What did you think? Why? What action have you taken? Why?

Encouraging potential inquiries

- What kinds of questions do you have about these different cultures?

After the journal writing activity, students in both classes watch a video such as *Oprah Winfrey: After School Special.* This program reflects cultural diversity, racism, discrimination, cultural conflicts, and harmony in high schools across the United States, drawing on ethnically, racially, and internationally diverse teenagers' points of view and experiences. Using historical and contemporary snapshots of real events, with political songs playing in the background, the video also captures issues of diversity and conflict from political, historical, economic, and social perspectives. Snapshots of racism and its consequences such as poverty and violence in the inner-city slums, clips showing changes brought about by the civil rights movement, the Rodney King beatings that sparked the California riots, and the impact of international conflicts are included. This video, which also paints a picture of controversies at national and international levels, has the potential to help students link diversity and justice issues to their personal and social lives.

Comparing the journals and students' written responses to the video can then be used to generate various themes for discussion, writing, drawing, and dramatizing, and for potential readings of multicultural literature. Inquiry themes might include views and stereotypes of U.S. culture, similar personal experiences students have had regarding cross-cultural friendships or conflicts, how such conflicts were resolved, the meaning of friendship in diverse world cultures, world peace, and world conflicts. The theme of U.S. diversity is extended to world diversity to explore in particular stereotypical perceptions and student-generated inquiries about U.S. and world cultures.

There are several ways of breaking the communication barriers between English-class and ESL students to help them engage in global inquiries and to challenge each others' assumptions. English and ESL classes may be joined to watch the video together. Students might freewrite their reactions to the video and discuss them in mixed groups of ESL and English-class students in order to generate diverse perspectives.

Pre-freewriting inquiry questions may include

- What is my reaction to issues in the video?
- To which issues can I personally and socially relate or not relate? Why?

Helping students develop empathy—to think and feel from the perspectives of different cultures—is another way to foster global inquiries and understandings. While watching the video, different groups of students may be assigned a teenager from a different ethnic, racial, or international background shown in the video in order to engage in the following inquiries and activities:

Pre-video inquiry questions for writing

- If I were the Asian American (or the White American, African American, Mexican American, Native American, the international student from Taiwan), how would I feel, think, and react if I were discriminated against?
- Have I ever personally experienced or witnessed a similar situation?

Each group can then share its written responses with the entire class through dramatizations in order to share their views, which may be initiated with introductions such as:

- I am an African American teenager from the inner city.

and may continue to be linked to personal and social levels such as:

- I have never personally experienced racism or poverty but have witnessed it in my own (ethnic/international) community.

or

- I can relate to the African American teenager in the video because I feel alienated at school since I'm not as rich as the other kids who dress up differently (or because I am stereotyped as a Middle Eastern person)

After writing and whole-class sharing, students should be encouraged to examine the similar patterns across culturally diverse groups in order to show commonalities in human experience. Most important of all, unless students engage in postreflections, inquiries will not make much progress in revealing potential changes or types of critical consciousness raised about global cultures, issues, and individual lives. Therefore, after partnership activities, both English-class and ESL students should write postinquiry reflections in their journals after rereading their initial journals entries.

Postinquiry reflection questions might include

- Now how do I feel and think about diverse cultures? Why?
- In what ways can I relate to human issues experienced by different cultures?
- What personal or social action will I take about diversity issues that influenced me the most?
- What further conversations do I want to engage in with the ESL (or ethnically diverse U.S.) students? What are my major questions?

English and ESL classes can then be guided to read either the same multicultural global literature selections or different selections on a common issue, meeting once a week for literature discussion circles. In schools where resources are available, ongoing English-ESL partnerships may also be established through more sophisticated uses of technology, the simplest being communications through electronic mail. Global educators such as Tucker (1990) and Anderson (1990) also suggest high school-university cooperation and exploration of the community's international links. Issues of interest generated from interpersonal or community-level partnerships within or across national and international communities may guide selection of other appropriate resources.

The powerful impact of diverse resources (such as graphic images in videos or in-depth experiences in literature) on students' more in-depth global understandings was reflected in this study. For instance, reading African literature, some of which describes in detail what a life of imposed poverty meant for children and mothers economically, socially, and emotionally after their fathers and husbands were imprisoned in the struggle against apartheid, touched Obi's (an African American student) life more powerfully than factual information in social studies courses or in the mass media. After being exposed to graphic images of the Holocaust in his European history course, Ray (a White American student) became highly psychologically sensitized to "how cruel human beings can be." In her American literature class, reading biographical accounts of injustices experienced by Native Americans and their struggles with conflicting cultures, Michelle (a White American student), claimed she was able to question the stereotypical perceptions of Native Americans she had acquired from TV movies and was able to empathize with the Native Americans who had suffered such injustices.

The potential risks of imposing on students White or European guilt, or of mystifying certain cultures and ethnocentric perceptions of human rights struggles, can be addressed in at least two ways without neglecting the experiences of oppressed cultures: (1) by engaging all U.S. and international students, no matter what their ethnic or social class background, in critical inquiries about injustices in their own lives, communities, and cultures, and (2) by reading about people of diverse ethnic and international backgrounds who have fought for human rights. The inadequacy of implementing multicultural theories that focus on oppressed ethnic cultures only within a nation is illustrated with Bob's (a White American student) comments in our interview:

SIBEL: Bob, why did you choose to explore Nelson Mandela for your anthropology group project on discrimination but not Martin Luther King?

BOB: Well, first I was gonna do Martin Luther King, but then my friend [from Africa] said, "Let's do Nelson Mandela." And I thought we always learn about Martin Luther King anyway and we never get to study other cultures, so I agreed.

SIBEL: What did you learn from this project?

Bob: Before, I used to think that people fought for human rights only in our country but not in other places of the world.

My study found that establishing partnerships around texts such as ethnic American and international adolescent literature is important for at least the following major reasons:

- Reading adolescent literature, biographies in particular, facilitates establishing personal connections with culturally distant others. Sharing something in common such as being from the same age group helps humanize experiences of culturally different people while providing new perspectives on life.
- Literature can provide deeper insights and understandings and lead to further inquiries into global understanding compared to reliance on only one major source or on superficial experiences (such as television news, movies, commercials; simply being in diverse social contexts; cultural images received as a result of international governmental conflicts; or factual knowledge in history textbooks).

Engaging in literacy through literature in order to understand the world and to create democratic communities is essential for the empowerment of tomorrow's citizens since we live in highly literate societies. Literature may provide opportunities for language enrichment and the development needed for effective political, social, and economic participation in our communities.

One way to invite exploration into world cultures and human issues is through reading a variety of short pieces of global literature, which includes ethnic American and international literature. According to my study, such published literature can be used as the medium for generating cross-cultural experiences that international and U.S. students can then write about. Both professional and student writings can then be used as a means for inviting global understanding when shared between ESL and English classes. Such sharing should incorporate other whole language activities including communication through discussions, exchange of journals, dramatizations (based on readings of students' journals or published literature), acting out plays (based on scriptwriting using students' journals or published literature), and inviting to the classroom culturally diverse American and international people from the community and from the student associations of local universities.

Literature, as the transaction between reader and text, allows exploration of the human experience (Rosenblatt, 1976, 1991; Bennett, 1990; O'Connor, 1980; Reardon, 1988). Using ethnic American or immigrant literature in connection with reading response theory and creative writing in English classes has created empathy and understanding of U.S. ethnic cultures (Walker-Dalhouse, 1992; Reissman, 1994; Roseboro, 1994). Mullen and Olsen (1990) report how a creative writing class, of mixed age and ability ESL and native-English-speaking students, helped build a sense of global community across racial and cultural borderlines. Judith Oster (1989), using American literature with her ESL students, found that having students read, write, and discuss an experience from diverse cultural viewpoints fostered critical thinking. Oster's ESL students, who read and discussed American literature, became aware that our experiences and cultures act as lenses through which we read. Freeman and Freeman (1989) showed that culturally relevant readings activated ESL students' schema to write personal experiences and to improve their language skills. I suggest using culturally familiar and unfamiliar international literature with ESL (Robson, 1989) and U.S. students (1) to foster critical thinking from multiple cultural perspectives on human issues, (2) to explore variations in viewpoints within specific cultures, and (3) to provide both

ESL and fluent English-speaking students enriching language experiences through the different writing styles of culturally diverse authors.

Two major collections of short literary pieces that can be used as core collections in both ESL and English classes are:

1. *At the Door: Selected Literature for ESL Students* by McKay and Pettit (1984)
2. *New Kids on the Block: Oral Histories of Immigrant Kids* by Bode (1989)

Because the first collection, *At the Door*, contains original excerpts from literature written by well-known ethnic American authors, it can be used not only in ESL but also in literature classes. The major reason for using *New Kids on the Block* along with the first collection is to build a bridge from understanding the multicultural U.S. society to understanding other world cultures using the experiences of adolescents. Other short or longer international literary pieces can be used in conjunction with these two core collections.

Breaking the Communication Barriers

An appropriate short literary piece for exploring cultural communication barriers is "A Song for the Barbarian Reed Ripe," an excerpt from Maxine Hong Kingston's *Woman Warrior* reprinted in McKay and Pettit (1984, pp. 84–87). Here, Kingston focuses on her own childhood experiences as a Chinese American adjusting to a school in a foreign culture. Kingston describes how painful it was for her to speak out in school and how she could relate only to one ethnic group of students, the Black Americans, who treated her as if she "was a daring talker, too" (McKay & Pettit, 1984, pp. 85).

New students from Malaysia, Russia, Taiwan, and Iraq who reported similar adjustment problems at Worldville High School, as well as students in similar national and international school contexts, should relate well to Kingston's narrative. Sadia from Malaysia explains her culture-bound silence:

> One thing I admire about the American students is they just feel very free in the classrooms, to speak out and say their opinions. I wish I could do that too but I still couldn't get used to speaking out in classes. See, in our culture, in our schools the teacher talks most of the time and the students, especially the girls, are supposed to be quiet. I think it will take me some time to get used to that [the freedom to speak].

Such culture-bound barriers to expressing opinions in class can be challenged by ESL teachers through real-life stories shared by ethnic authors and students. International students also reported alienation and perpetuation of their silence by some content area teachers who assumed that the students' silence derived only from language barriers rather than from culture-bound shyness.[5] According to those content area teachers, not calling on a student who lacks English-language skills helps these students avoid embarrassment. Therefore, it is important for ESL and English teachers to create partnership opportunities through literature in order to prepare silent students to share their voices across content areas.

Another communication barrier at Worldville was the lack of communication between some U.S. and international students. Kingston's writing can be used to generate and explore the interactions between U.S. and international students in this school. While such sharing would alleviate international students' alienation, it would also help both groups of students learn more about each other's diverse experiences and views. Alev, a student from the former Yugoslav republic of Bosnia and Herzegovina, reports her strong reaction when rejected by some U.S. students:

> Most American students accepted me but some of them do not accept you because they think you are from outer space. It takes some time for them to see that you're just a normal person as if they didn't come from other countries. Their grandmothers came from all different countries. They are foreigners themselves too.

Some Malaysian students mentioned how difficult it was to break through communication barriers with some U.S. students. Ali reports his feelings:

> Some of the American students just ignore us. I dunno why they do that but I feel like a subject, hurt, I feel very angry. Because we are trying to make friends with them but they don't want. We say hi, they just pass by.

Those U.S. and international students who were able to break through the communication barriers discussed how their initial stereotypes about each others' cultures were challenged. Amy, another Malaysian student, reports:

> Before I came to the United States I watched American movies of the 1960s and I just thought that all the Americans were wild and liked to party, drink, and had no ethics and did not believe in religion. But one day I met this American girl in the cafeteria and one day in my church. She was so nice. And then this guy told me he never liked to drink and party. So there goes my general bias about Americans!

Stella, a U.S. student with extensive overseas experiences in western and some eastern European countries, reports: "Before meeting my Lebanese friend, I just assumed that all the Middle Easterners were loud and aggressive. But he is very different and polite."

Breaking the cross-cultural barriers and initiating conversations with international students did help both U.S. and international students in this study to question their stereotypes about each other. Sharing experiences such as the ones these students describe in both ESL and literature classes can generate interest in global communication.

Sometimes a cultural mediator might be necessary to help students realize the international diversity within their reach, as illustrated by Sue, a U.S. student:

> Until our sociology teacher asked her a question about the foods in their country, I didn't know that this girl was not American but South American. After class I went to her and said, "I didn't know you were from South America. I'd like to borrow your recipe." She was so excited she said I'll bring you the recipe but my mom can cook it for you one day. She seemed so Americanized I've never before realized that she appreciated her own culture that much. But then I try to talk to this Russian girl. I say hi,

how are you to her in Russian and she just says hi in English. That's all. She seems so shy. I dunno why. She doesn't talk in class either.

Other Literary Works and Suggested Activities

Other literary works that deal with adjusting to a new culture, living in between two cultures, cultural change, communication barriers, and relationships include the following:

Literary Work	Source
From "Medicine Man's Daughter," an American Indian experience	In McKay & Pettit (1984), *At the Door: Selected Literature for ESL Students*
To Live in Two Worlds: American Indian Youth Today	Ashabranner (1984)
The Unbelonging, a Jamaican British experience	Riley (1985)
No Tigers in Africa, a White South African experience in England	Silver (1992)
Shades of Gray, an African American experience	Reeder (1989)
Between Worlds: Contemporary Asian-American Plays	Berson (1990)
Emilio (Filipino), "Tito" (Mexican), and "Abdul" (Afghan)	In Bode (1989), *New Kids on the Block: Oral Histories of Immigrant Teens,* U.S. immigrant experiences of international teenagers

When sharing student-written experiences and published literature between ESL and English classes, students can be asked to dramatize these incidents as if the events had happened to them, so that they can understand what it means to be in another culture. As another assignment, a U.S. student can be assigned an ESL partner, and vice versa, and one shadow the other for one day in an effort to understand what it feels like to be in the other's shoes.

Sensitivity to Stereotypes Created by International Conflicts and Understanding the Experience of War

International conflicts can create opportunities to explore both cultural stereotypes shaped by political propaganda in the media and the experience of war and other human conflicts from various perspectives. At Worldville High School, the Persian Gulf War exacerbated mutual stereotyping and prejudice by some U.S. and international students, as illustrated by Maryam, an Iraqi student:

> Some American students don't understand that it's just ten people in the government, and the innocent people can't do anything about it. During the Persian Gulf War, some would approach me and ask, "Where are you from?" I say, "Iraq." And they'd go, "From Iraq? Why are you killing our people?" I'd just say, "I'm not Saddam Hussein, you know, and I'm not the one killing your people, it's the governments." I wouldn't feel upset because I didn't expect the Americans to like the Arabs. The whole world knows that!

Other international students, U.S. students, and a teacher reported similar attitudes and incidents. According to Obi, an African American student, "Some American students just called the Malaysian students all kinds of names like 'the Malaysian invasion' or the 'Middle Eastern invasion' as if they were responsible for the war, and they are not even from the Middle East." In contrast, Steve, a White American student, admits, "Before talking to Leila, from Saudi Arabia, I guess at first in my ignorance I just felt mad at the Iraqi people too, seeing governments and all Iraqi people the same." Stella, White American student who has international friends, reports her transcultural concerns for people involved in wars:

> I have Jewish friends, a Lebanese friend, and other friends from the Middle East. . . . Especially during the Persian War conflict they'd talk about how worried they were because they have relatives there. Talking to them makes me feel worried about those people. Whereas, for some of my friends war is just a national victory.

Insiders perspectives on conflicts include international students' experiences and fears. David, a Jewish student from Israel, reports: "I really felt scared and insecure when I was living in Israel. I was always worried that I might get killed when I went out, but here I feel safer." Some worries that did not circulate openly among the students included the fear shared with me by Alev, a Bosnian girl, about a possible war between the former republics of Yugoslavia:

> In Yugoslavia a civil war is about to start, but CNN is not showing anything about our country for days. We are so worried about our family. My grandmother called us and told us that war might come. My parents will go back to Yugoslavia soon and they will leave me here. They will take me to stay with their friends in Michigan so I can go to the university because they think if I go back and there is war I might not have a future.

From these comments, we see that international conflicts did not necessarily have to directly affect all our students in order to create conflicts in the hallways and classrooms of Worldville High School. Stella, Obi, and Steve had no relatives fighting in another country to worry about, whereas Maryam, David, and Alev did. Yet, while Obi critically viewed the war from an international perspective and condemned war-related discrimination against Malaysian and Middle Eastern students in their school, Steve needed an encounter with another's perspective, which differed from his own, in order to question his formerly biased perspective. Case studies of Obi (a middle-class African American student) and Stella (a middle-class White American student), reveal how, from childhood years until teenage years, they watched and later engaged in political conversations within their families about international conflicts from different international perspectives.

Michelle (a middle-class White American student) never questioned global conflicts such as the Vietnam or the Persian Gulf Wars from anything but the U.S. perspective. During our interview, however, tears filled Michelle's eyes while talking about the letters her mother received from an American soldier to whom she wrote as an adopted son during the war "because she thought last time we [the Americans] didn't treat fairly the soldiers returning from the Vietnam War." And students such as Obi criticized other students who thought about conflicts only from one national perspective: "Some students cheered for our soldiers during the Persian Gulf War as if it was a football game. . . . They go by whatever our government says on television, but they never talk about the lives of Iraqi babies and children who were killed."

Suggested Activities and Literature

How can we discuss conflict-related experiences and challenge the associated ethnic stereotypes? Such experiences can be generated by using contemporary and past newspaper photos and articles or paintings of war experiences alongside Von's experience of the Vietnam War, Francia's experience of the conflict in El Salvador, and Abdul's experiences in Afghanistan in *New Kids on the Block*. In other words, students' experiences, mass media, literature, and insights from international events can be considered together in order to foster understanding and disrupt assumptions about other world cultures. Following is a list of more literature sources that can be explored from a range of perspectives:

Literary Work	Source
"Baghdad Diary" "Notes from Abroad: What Used to Be Yugoslavia"	In Bufford (1992)
Anton the Dove Fancier: And Other Tales of the Holocaust	Gotfryd (1990)
Farewell Manzanar	Houston (1973)
Don't Cry, Chiisai, Don't Cry	Uyesugi (1977)
Voices from the Civil War	Meltzer (1989)
Echoes of the White Giraffe	Choi (1993)

The Holocaust, the Yugoslav war, and the "Baghdad Diary," which reports experiences and reactions to the Persian Gulf War, can all be part of a discussion of internal national conflicts. *Farewell Manzanar* and *Don't Cry Chiisai, Don't Cry* narrate the

Japanese American internment during World War II, and *Echoes of the White Giraffe* focuses on the brutal treatment by the Japanese of Koreans during World War II. Including excerpts from *Voices from the Civil War*, which also contains real war letters, would bring the war experience to a personal level for the U.S. students. By introducing universal human issues such as war or racism in a global context, we can avoid victimizing or romanticizing specific cultures, as suggested by Stotsky (1994), but also avoid overgeneralizing human rights violators within specific cultures.

Through whole language activities, students' life experiences should also be shared between classes. People from the community such as war veterans, parents, and ethnic and international students from local university student associations can also be invited into classes. Then a play can be staged for the school by ESL and English students on war experiences from multiple perspectives. In such a play, to foster critical thinking and feeling from diverse perspectives, U.S. students simulate the role of international characters while the international students play U.S. characters. The purpose is to experience, reflect on, and inquire about the reasons and consequences of such a major human event. Such inquiries can then be carried over to courses in other disciplines for further reflective dialogue.

From International Women's Images and Roles to Adolescent Life in the United States and around the World

In exploring global diversity, it is crucial to invite the students in the ESL class to discuss and write brief personal essays or incidents on international women's images. Maryam, an Iraqi student who had recently arrived at Worldville High School, produced the following:

> When my American classmates saw my mom one day when she came to pick me up at school, and they saw that she was free and she didn't cover her hair, they were like, "Does she do that? Is that your mom!?" I was like, "Of course, she's my mom. Why?"

> They were so shocked. They said, "Well, how come she doesn't cover herself up?" "Well," I said, "being a Muslim doesn't mean you have to cover yourself up." Although my parents don't, at least I personally pray and fast, but I just don't believe in covering up.

Alev, a Bosnian student, reacting to U.S. students' lack of knowledge about diversity among Muslims, who were often stereotyped as all alike, reported an experience similar to Maryam's:

> When I say I'm a Muslim, my American friends are like "Hah?" They just think that to be a Muslim you have to be covered up and be an Arab or a Malaysian, or from the Middle East. And a few of my Muslim friends, the ones who are strongly religious or who cover up, are that way too. They go, "If you don't at least fast, pray, or if you eat pork, how can you be a Muslim?" But I personally don't practice religion; my grandmother didn't, my mother didn't, and I don't.

Although some of the stereotypes that Maryam's friends held about Muslim or Middle Eastern women may have been challenged by meeting her mother, almost all U.S. students in this study were not aware of the diversity among Muslim women. My conversations with both male and female U.S. students often provoked similar surprised reactions, as illustrated during my second interview with Jane:

SIBEL: Last time you said that Muslims gotta change and become Westernized because they were backward, uneducated, and women wear long garments. And you also said you can tell Muslims by the way they dress. Is that right?

JANE: Yes. . . .

SIBEL: What about your Afghan friend who is a Muslim and who has been your best friend since elementary school?

JANE: Well, she must have changed, Americanized.

SIBEL: Then what about all those Muslim students at school—Malaysian, Yugoslav, Iraqi—who don't wear long garments or cover their heads or who don't believe in religion at all?

JANE: Oh! Are they Muslims?!

In contrast to such cultural generalizations rooted in religion-based gender stereotyping, students such as Tom and Anne, who were more knowledgeable about diversity within European cultures than Middle Eastern cultures, avoided gender stereotyping of European cultures. Anne commented, "I know it was just *this* German girl whom I hosted here and not other Germans I know. I told this girl that I might be interested in becoming a forest ranger, and this girl was like, 'Women don't do such jobs.' That really offended me." Similarly, Tom reported: "Not *all* the Russians were that way, but this Russian man and his son my friends hosted didn't respect the things women did like going shopping or driving when there was a man in the car."

Anne and Tom not only individualized the diversity within European cultures, but they also provided lengthy explanations such as, "This German girl is different because she grew up on a farm where women are not even supposed to feed the chickens but only wash the dishes," or "I know why these Russian men were different from the others . . . 'cause the father worked for the government and he thought he controlled everything." In contrast, students' perceptions of non-European cultures did not often provide hints of any natural curiosity about the possibility of diversity within those cultures.

In order to broaden students' perceptions of international women, especially non-European women, written and anonymous personal narratives such as the ones provided here can be distributed in an English literature class. In pre- or postreading discussion activities, the literature students should be guided to compare and contrast their initial perceptions of international women with their perceptions after reading the narratives. Exploration of U.S. women's diversity, including intergenerational differences, would provide opportunities for discovering similarities and diversity among the world's women. Reading Nadine Gordimer's "A Chip of Glass Ruby" in *Six Feet of the Country* (1982) provides a snapshot of a poor and traditionally perceived Muslim Indian woman's secret participation in the Black movement for social justice in South Africa. Her sacrifices and the sufferings experienced by her husband and children after her imprisonment provides a counterexample for those U.S. students who believe Muslims, in particular Muslim women, do not fight for their rights. Such literature in the classroom, including *Women in the Third World* (Fisher, 1989), or a current newspaper article such as one by the Associated Press in a local newspaper reporting on a visit by two women prime ministers (Benazir Bhutto of Pakistan and Tansu Çiller of Turkey) to Bosnia to protest the war there, may challenge students' stereotyped generalization that non-West European women do not struggle to make changes in their societies. Black American women in *Walking the Road to Freedom* (Ferris, 1988), Mexican American women in *Woman Hollering Creek* by Mexican American Sandra Cisneros (1991), and the Japanese woman Kuniko in *The Paper Door and Other Stories* (Naoya, 1987), are good examples of non-White women who fight for justice.

This theme of international women's images and roles can then be tied into another theme of great interest to adolescents (at least those in this study): male and female teenagers' cultural roles, values, and professional goals. Inviting a group of U.S. and ESL students to make oral presentations in each other's classes is one approach. Follow-up discussion and writing activities focusing on cross-cultural similarities, differences, and cross-cultural adjustment issues will culturally enrich not only ESL students' understanding of the diversity in U.S. society, but also all students' understanding of the world's diversity. Foreign exchange students in language classes can also be included in ESL and English classes. One result in the Worldville High School French class was that students discovered similarities, as illustrated by Michelle: "Talking to French exchange students in our French class, I learned that we are basically similar as teenagers. They talked about the kinds of things they do at school, after school, and for fun." And Ray, having studied adolescence in New Guinea culture in his anthropology class, learned that he

> can't generalize the adolescence turbulence we experience in the American culture to other cultures. Before studying the New Guinea culture, I had just assumed that experiencing adolescent upset was just a biological and not a cultural thing and that it was the same in all the cultures.

Introduction to adolescent life in diverse cultures of the world and in the United States can also be integrated into ESL and literature classes through reading brief oral histories told by immigrant teens in the United States in *New Kids on the Block*. The oral histories by Debbie (Chinese), Emilio (Filipino), Abdul (Afghan), Anna (Greek), and Martha (Dominican) include adolescent issues such as the expected cultural values and behaviors for males and females, dating, marriage, value of school, work, future professional dreams, and parent-teenager conflicts.

Teachers, however, should be careful not to perpetuate stereotypes; therefore, they need to emphasize that each oral history represents only a specific experience and a specific perspective from that specific world culture. For instance, by comparing Abdul's traditional views about Muslim women in *New Kids on the Block* with Maryam's views expressed in her interview, students can learn to be skeptical about stereotyping, to question generalizations, and to keep an open mind to the possibility of diversity within cultures. For instance, Anna's views on the Greek culture may not be generalized to her entire country since she describes traditional women's and men's roles as experienced in her village, not in cities.

Why We Can't Rely on Natural Curiosity Alone in Global Inquiry

An important lesson we can learn from the experiences related here is that these teenagers do not have a natural curiosity for inquiries about diversity within stereotyped cultures unless confronted by a contradicting experience that challenges their stereotypes, as in Holly's case:

> Just like many other people, I thought all the Middle Easterners, except of course the people from Israel, were backward, but then when I chose to study Egypt as my anthropology project—to understand the backgrounds of the cultures involved in the Persian Gulf War—I found out that women in Egypt are different and can be similar to us. . . . There are women lawyers, doctors.

But not every student had an opportunity like Holly's to inquire about their stereotyped perceptions of other cultures. The following were some of the reasons:

- A globally oriented social studies course such as anthropology was an elective course not taken by all students.
- Required courses such as U.S. history and English lacked a global perspective.
- The elective world literature course, in which some students enrolled out of curiosity about world cultures, emphasized European literature.
- Some students lacked firsthand or indirect experiences with non-European cultures.

The findings show that students do not naturally become aware of their stereotypical beliefs unless challenged, and this is one reason we cannot rely on natural curiosity in global inquiry.

To illustrate the point that students' natural curiosities or ethnicities cannot always be taken for granted in global inquiry, I share a glimpse of David's case study, which is an interesting contrast to Holly's. David, like Holly, has ethnically different parents. While both their fathers are White southerners of west European background, David's mother is Hawaian of Asian origin and Holly's mother is of European Jewish origin. Due to his father's military service, David spent part of his childhood in Hawaii, where he says his "school curriculum was just the same [U.S. and European-centered] as on the mainland." Holly has never traveled overseas but heard lots of European travel experiences from her mother, who reminded Holly that "people are similar everywhere." Neither Holly nor David looks White American, but both are good-looking kids. Holly is a confident girl, but David cynically claims, "They just think I am a little Asian" as the reason for the international students' "feeling safe" in sharing with him a political perspective contradicting that of the U.S. or British governments. David is a friend of Holly's but does not blame her for any political differences as he does his non-European peers.

David, very proud of his White heritage, views U.S. and European cultures as "the most elegant cultures" in the world and others as backward except for the ones he is connected to by blood ties. These include Native American through his father's side and East Asian through his mother's Asian Hawaiian heritage. Holly talked critically about some White southerners' stereotypes and racism against non-White cultures, which she also had "seen among some of [her] father's older relatives." While Holly condemned racism and discrimination, David showed signs of selective discrimination, especially against people he categorized as "Muslims," explaining: "All Pakis, Indians, Afghanis in California, they smell bad. Like, I have this friend who is from Pakistan, ughhh he smells bad. . . . I think it's because of their religious rituals; they don't bathe but wash only parts of their bodies."

During our second conversation, David felt challenged to question his stereotyped reasoning about the Persian Gulf War—not naturally, but when given the opportunity for self-reflection. Another important point is that David's cultural stereotypes of ethnic Muslims in the United States tend to influence his political viewpoint of global conflicts and justice issues related to Muslims in international contexts, demonstrating how cultural stereotypes may influence judgments of political conflicts. Both points are illustrated in the following exchange:

DAVID: This Pakistani guy, he is just against the war because I think he supports Saddam because he is a Muslim and I think he hates all the White people

SIBEL: Why do you think he hates the White people?

DAVID: . . . Like, he talks about how the British invaded his country and he doesn't like that and that he would have fought against them. . . .

SIBEL: What is your viewpoint about the war?

DAVID: I am for the war because I am a Christian and that's why I support Israel not the Arabs.

After some opportunity for reflection, David diverges:

SIBEL: David, you told me that you support the war because you are a Christian and that's why you support Israel; can you share with me what you know about the conflict between Israelis and Arabs?

DAVID: . . . I don't really know anything. . . . We never studied that conflict. . . .

SIBEL: How would you have felt if they said they didn't support you because you were a Christian?

DAVID: *Mad!* Real mad. . . . Sorry, guess it's all . . . just my ignorance. . . . Did I really say that?!

What David's interviews show, as do case studies of other students, is that given the opportunity for reflection, students are often challenged to inquire about their perceptions and assumptions. Therefore, this should not be taken as a negative illustration but as a potential opportunity for global inquiry.

Given opportunities to pursue his personal choices and natural curiosities about people for projects in anthropology or art history projects, David had chosen to indulge his appreciation for the cultures he already admired, i.e., European and Native American cultures. Those were the cultures he did not stereotype at all. Like all students not exposed to global issues and diversity in required courses, David was not given the opportunity to challenge his international cultural stereotypes. Yet, guaranteed the anonymity and safe environment of this research, David voiced his prejudices. David's case is highlighted to show that we can neither completely count on students' natural inquiries nor assume that all students can rely on their families, peers, or other sources to compensate for the missing global components in the school curriculum. Such missing global components will not challenge cross-cultural communication barriers, as in the case of David, who distanced himself from people and peers he stereotyped, unless we create risk-taking, reflective environments.

International students were concerned about some of the communication barriers that result from not exploring cultural backgrounds. Sheila, a Taiwanese student, noted: "The American students, they just ask, 'Where're you from?' I say my country's name and they don't know where it is and then I explain. But they stop there; they just don't ask many questions about our cultures." Among the reasons reported by those U.S. students who had difficulties approaching international students were fear of offending, language barriers, lack of time at school to make new friends, and prejudice toward those students who did not look Americanized. Anne, a U.S. student, explained: "If I ask too many questions about their culture because I don't know how they'll react, I feel like I might offend them."

Conclusion

Multicultural education has taken up the responsibility for helping students explore ethnic diversity and justice issues at the national level. It is my position that, as literacy educators, we have a responsibility to prepare our future citizens to be inquirers about the political roots and consequences of their positions on diversity issues at the international level as well. Without national and international inquiries about the human experience, it would be hard for students to imagine the power they have to influence global issues as today's and tomorrow's literate citizens.

Today's world includes not only increased international communications but also increasingly heightened ethnic conflicts. It is hardly possible to paint a sanitized picture of cultural harmony and social justice in our local communities and nations. Similar problems are reflected in our classrooms and schools, which continue to be enriched through the increased influx of immigrants, mostly from non-European countries. Immigrant or not, all our students learn to communicate through English as their first or second language. They all become literate in English, the dominant international language, and literature can make global issues which, as reflected in the mass media, seem depressing, dehumanizing, and overwhelming more understandable and relevant to our students.

Global English literature can help students gain personal and psychological insights about social, political, and economic questions from other cultural perspectives, not only within our own nation but also across many others that seem culturally distant or irrelevant. How our students position themselves politically on world issues tends also to be influenced by how far they distance themselves from other world cultures based on superficial knowledge. As literacy educators, using literature and other resources, we can act as mediators to personify, problematize, and politicize our students' perceptions of global cultures and issues to help them engage in responsible inquiries and actions about their lives and about local, national, and global communities.

In multiethnic classrooms, schools, and communities, we have the opportunity to establish cross-cultural partnerships in order to break through communication barriers. Does that mean we cannot or should not engage our future citizens in global inquiries in culturally homogeneous contexts? If global literacy is viewed as social empowerment for human survival and welfare in our global village and multicultural nations, the answer is, "Yes, we should!"

I would like to end this chapter with an excerpt from a journal entry I kept about my former midwestern global neighborhood, where some of the high school students in this study also grew up, a place they called "the mini-United Nations":

> And while I sat on my porch writing this chapter, every day I watched three-, four-, and five-year-old boys of highly educated parents play with genuine-looking guns and rifles, while innocent children all over the world die from war, hunger, or violence. When I asked the little boys why they like to play with guns, they responded, "It's only pre-t-e-e-nd." And I had to ask myself, who makes the pretend real and who allows the real to be treated as if it's pretend? While these middle-class boys of American and international backgrounds say they "pretend" to kill, I wonder who is the "pretend" victim? If their parents keep buying them Power Ranger toys; if their parents let them watch violence on television; if the day after the Oklahoma bombing, while we all watched babies die, these boys dramatize a war scene in front of my porch as a birthday party game organized by a parent, who is the victim? Is violence culture free? Is violence gendered? Mothers of two of the boys I watched play with "pretend" guns are teachers, and most of the boys' fathers are future university professors. Just like the female teachers I worked with in our neighborhood's international preschool, I listened to these mothers complain of violence and conflicts among children. And again I had to ask if violence is gendered. Can we claim that violence is gendered if mothers and teachers, most of whom are women in many communities, tolerate "pretend" violence? What can we do as mothers, fathers, and teachers with the rich ethnic and international human resources of our communities and schools to encourage global citizenship? I no longer unquestionably embrace the following gendered declaration from the Preamble to the Constitution of UNESCO, which I had intentionally quoted in my dissertation to mean "men," not "man" in the generic sense of the word "human": "Since wars are created in the minds of man, it is in the minds of man that the defences of peace must be constructed" (O'Connor, 1980, p. 10).

Appendix 14.1

Annotated Resources

Literary Resources

Mohr, Nicholasa. (1993). "The Wrong Lunch Line." In Mazer, Anne (Ed.), *America Street: A Multicultural Anthology of Stories.* New York: Persea Books.

A Spanish American girl is humiliated and prevented by a teacher from eating a special Jewish American lunch together at school with her closest Jewish American friend. The incident is incomprehensible to both.

Namioka, Lensey. (1993). "The All-American Slurp." In Mazer, Anne (Ed.), *America Street: A Multicultural Anthology of Stories.* New York: Persea Books.

A Chinese American girl discovers that the way to eat celery in China is as mysterious to her friend Meg as the American way of drinking a milkshake is to her.

Silver, Norman. (1992). *No Tigers in Africa.* New York: Faber.

Selwyn, a White boy of South African heritage, is adjusting to a new life in England but losing his identity. Pursued by thoughts of having killed a Black boy back home, he can find no reassurance. His classmates taunt him for being a bigot, although he has always considered himself anti-apartheid. This novel offers insights into the debilitating effects of a young man's South African upbringing on his perceptions of human relationships. He looks not just to society but also within himself for a moral solution to prejudice.

Meltzer, Milton. (1989). *Voices from the Civil War: A Documentary History of the Great American Conflict.* New York: HarperTrophy.

A documentary history of the Great American Conflict from the views of ordinary people, Northerners and Southerners, through their letters, diaries, interviews, ballads, and public speeches. Includes drawings and a few graphic photographs. Issues such as death, life, racism, and the Ku Klux Klan are vividly reported.

Reeder, Carolyn. (1989). *Shades of Gray.* New York: Macmillan.

The Civil War is over but the Yankees are still enemies of a boy who lost his immediate family during the war. This story is about his reignited anger toward a traveling Yankee who comes to his uncle's house and about how he comes to grips with it. The boy's humanity finally prevails, helping him realize that good people may hold opposite views and that all people needlessly suffer during war.

Schami, Rafik. (1990). *A Hand Full of Stars.* New York: Dutton Children's Books.

A Syrian boy's discovered hidden diary recounts his daily adventures but also his frustrations with the government injustices he witnesses. He finds his political voice in a message of rebellion that echoes throughout Syria and as far away as western Europe. This is a symbolic novel of the difficult and committed actions taken by young people around the world.

Videos/Audiotapes

The purpose of showing these audiovisuals in the classroom is to help U.S. and international students critically examine and discuss conflict and solutions for peaceful communication. Audiovisual texts give voice and face to the people affected by global conflicts, allowing them to present the issues from a different perspective. Audiovisuals provide animated graphics that can enhance reflective thinking about the consequences of cross-cultural conflict by stirring multiple senses, intelligences, and learning styles, especially when coupled with multicultural literature and other language arts activities.

Witness to Apartheid.

A look at how racism and police violence affect children. 50 min.

Beyond War: A New Way of Thinking.

Explores why war has become obsolete and ways for relating to other nations, cultures, and people through interviews. 22 min.

Guernica: Pablo Picasso.

The horror and ugliness of war and inhumanity are passionately depicted in Picasso's paintings. 15 min.

Israel, The Other Reality: Jew & Arab

Israel's Arabs and Jews explain why hatred has prevailed between their peoples for thousands of years and why and how some find ways to get along. 58 min.

Vietnamese and American Veterans.

Two American veterans and two Vietnamese veterans discuss the Vietnam War from their perspectives. 30 min.

Planting Seeds for Peace.

Focuses on the relationships among four teenagers (Israeli, Arab, Jewish, and Palestinian) who come together in the United States to share their cultures, share their personal lives, break down stereotypes, and present their views to U.S. teens. 23 min.

Caring.

Focuses on the urban Chinese family. 50 min.

Dim-Sum: A Little Bit of Heart.

Intergenerational differences in a Chinese American family. 80 min.

Miles from the Border.

Twenty years after immigrating from rural Mexico to southern California, Manuela and Ben, who arrived in their teens and now work as counselors with other young newcomers, share their experiences of dislocation and pressures to succeed in an ethnically divided society. 15 min.

Latin America, An Overview. 25 min.

A Veiled Revolution.

Explores the views of secular Egyptian feminist women who oppose their fundamentalist granddaughters rejecting Western dress and adopting the veil, which was cast off by revolutionary Egyptian women in 1932. 27 min.

Angelou, Maya: Our Sheroes and Heroes.

Discusses her first friendship with a White woman, her sense of religion, and the differences between Black and White women. Audiocassette. 34 min.

Bridging the Culture Gap.

Some of the cultural differences Americans must be attuned to overseas. 30 min.

Notes

1. This broader study, conducted during 1990–91 for my doctoral dissertation, coincided with the Persian Gulf War and the initial tensions of the ethnic conflict in former Yugoslavia. The impact of such global conflicts on students' political positions and cross-cultural behaviors are also highlighted in this chapter. Data for this study were collected through classroom observations and intensive interviews with U.S. and international high school students, their teachers (English, social studies, and foreign language), the principal, and some parents. The name "Worldville High School" is a pseudonym, as are all names of students quoted in this chapter. For further details about the major study, see Cakmak (Boran), 1993, in the references.

2. As reported by the students in my study, most of their cultural stereotypes and perceptions of international conflicts were shaped by the mass media, particularly by movies and news on television, when they lacked challenging counterknowledge and perspectives from other sources such as the school, parents, peers, or firsthand or indirect cross-cultural contact.

3. My study and other studies (see Buergenthal & Torney, 1976) show that students' perception of diverse cultures and international conflicts varies depending on the depth and politically challenging nature of their experiences, rather than on their race or ethnicity.

4. In my 1995–99 research in Rio Grande Valley schools in south Texas, responses to these types of initial inquiry questions proved useful in generating reflective inquiries about global diversity and justice issues

both in students' own lives and in other global communities with elementary and secondary students.

5. For other related perspectives on culture-bound silence and teachers' attitudes toward ethnic students, see Chapter 10 by Vivian Vasquez in this volume.

References

Anderson, C. (1990). Global education and the community. In K. Tye (Ed.), *Global education: From thought to action* (pp. 125–41). Alexandria, VA: Association for Supervision and Curriculum Development.

Applebee, A. N. (1989). *A study of book-length works taught in high school English courses*. Albany, NY: Center for the Study of Teaching and Learning of Literature, SUNY, School of Education.

Ashworth, M. (1991). Internationalism and our "strenuous family." *TESOL Quarterly, 25*(2), 231–43.

Bachner, D., & Zeutschel, U. (1990). *Students of four decades: A research study of the influences of an international exchange experience on the lives of German and U.S. high school students*. Washington, DC: Youth for Understanding.

Becker, J. (1982). Goals for global education. *Theory into Practice, 21*(3), 228–33.

Bennett, C. (1990). *Comprehensive multicultural education: Theory and practice* (2nd ed.). Boston: Allyn & Bacon.

Bloom, A. (1987). *The closing of the American mind: How higher education has failed democracy and impoverished the souls of today's students*. New York: Simon & Schuster.

Brown, H. D. (1991). TESOL at twenty-five: What are the issues? *TESOL Quarterly, 25*(2), 245–60.

Buergenthal, T., & Torney, J. (1976). *International human rights and international education*. Washington, DC: U.S. National Commission for UNESCO.

Cakmak (Boran), S. (1989). English literacy redefined: Promoting intercultural literacy through English as a search for better cross-cultural understanding and communications. ERIC Clearinghouse #CS 506-604, 1–28.

Cakmak (Boran), S. (1990). Multidisciplinary perspectives on cross-cultural education. Pilot study research report. ERIC Clearinghouse #CS 212-523, 1–20.

Cakmak (Boran), S. (1993). *Educational and sociocultural roots of prejudices and approximations to globalism: American high school students' perceptions of cultural diversity and concerns for humanity.* Unpublished doctoral dissertation, Indiana University, Bloomington.

Case, R. (1991). Key elements of a global perspective. Occasional Paper No.25, *Exploration in development/global education* (published with support of the Canadian International Development Agency). Vancouver: University of British Columbia.

Fine, L. (1990). Resolving conflict creatively: Peace education concepts in the ESL classroom. *TESOL Newsletter, 24*(1), 19.

Fox, L. (1990). Planethood: An ESL writing course on the global community. *TESOL Newsletter, 24*(2), 19.

Freeman, Y., & Freeman, D. (1989). Whole language approaches to writing with secondary students of English as a second language. In D. Johnson & D. Roen (Eds.), *Richness in writing: Empowering ESL students* (pp. 177–92). New York: Longman.

Hanvey, R. (1982). An attainable global perspective. *Theory into Practice, 21*(3), 162–67.

Harste, J. (1994). Literacy as curricular conversations about knowledge, inquiry, and morality. In M. R. Ruddell, R. B. Ruddell, & H. Singer (Eds.), *Theoretical models and processes of reading* (4th ed., pp. 1220–42). Newark, DE: International Reading Association.

Hirsch, E. (1987). *Cultural literacy: What every American needs to know.* New York: Vintage Books.

Kachru, B. (1988). Teaching world Englishes. *ERIC/CLL News Bulletin, 12*(1), 1–8.

Knowles, T. (1993). A missing piece of heart: Children's perceptions of the Persian Gulf War of 1991. *Social Education, 57*(1), 19–22.

Mullen, N. A., & Olsen, L. (1990, Spring). You and I are the same. *California Tomorrow, 26*(34).

O'Connor, E. (1980). *World studies in the European classroom.* Strasbourg, France: Council for Cultural Co-operation, Council of Europe.

Oliver, E. I. (1994). *Crossing the mainstream: Multicultural perspectives in teaching literature.* Urbana, IL: National Council of Teachers of English.

Oster, J. (1989). Seeing with different eyes: Another view of literature in the ESL class. *TESOL Quarterly, 23*(1), 85–103.

Pate, G. S. (1989). Reducing prejudice in the schools. *Multicultural Leader, 2*(2), 1–3.

Paul, R. (1992). *Critical thinking: What every person needs to survive in a rapidly changing world* (2nd ed.). Rohnert Park, CA: Foundation for Critical Thinking.

Reardon, B. (Ed.). (1988). *Comprehensive peace education: Educating for global responsibility.* New York: Teachers College Press.

Reissman, R. C. (1994). Leaving out to pull in: Using reader response to teach multicultural literature. *English Journal, 83*(2), 20–23.

Robson, A. (1989). The use of literature in ESL and culture learning courses in U.S. colleges. *TESOL Newsletter, 23*(4), 25–27.

Roseboro, A. J. S. (1994). Student choice/teacher control: "Braided lives" in the classroom. *English Journal, 83*(2), 14–19.

Rosenblatt, L. (1976). *Literature as exploration* (3rd ed.). New York: Noble and Noble.

Rosenblatt, L. (1991). Literature—S.O.S.! *Language Arts, 68,* 444–48.

Sharma, M., & Jung, L. (1986). How cross-cultural participation affects the international attitudes of U.S. students. *International Journal of Intercultural Relations, 10,* 377–87.

Stotsky, S. (1994). Academic guidelines for selecting multiethnic and multicultural literature. *English Journal, 83*(2), 27–34.

Tucker, J. (1990). Global education partnerships between schools and universities. In K. Tye (Ed.), *Global education: From thought to action.* Alexandria, VA: Association for Supervision and Curriculum Development.

Walker-Dalhouse, D. (1992). Using African-American literature to increase ethnic understanding. *Reading Teacher, 45*(6), 416–22.

Wilson, A. H. (1993). Conversation partners: Helping students gain a global perspective through cross-cultural experiences. *Theory into Practice, 32,* 21–26.

Suggested Multicultural International Literature Core Collections of Short Literary Pieces

Bode, J. (1989). *New kids on the block: Oral histories of immigrant teens*. New York: Franklin Watts. (Ethnic American)

McKay, S., & Pettit, D. (1984). *At the door: Selected literature for ESL students*. Englewood Cliffs, NJ: Prentice-Hall. (Ethnic American)

Other Collections

Adler, D. (1989). *We remember the holocaust*. New York: Henry Holt. (Jewish American)

Ashabranner, B. (1984). *To live in two worlds: American Indian youth today*. New York: Dodd, Mead. (American Indian)

Berson, M. (1990). *Between worlds: Contemporary Asian-American plays*. New York: Theatre Communications Group. (Asian American)

Bufford, B. (Ed.). (1992, Winter). *Krauts! Granta, 42*. (International)

Choi, S. N. (1993). *Echoes of the white giraffe*. Boston: Houghton Mifflin. (Asian American)

Cisneros, S. (1991). *Women hollering creek*. New York: Random House. (Hispanic American)

Cisneros, S. (1989). *The house on Mango Street*. New York: Vintage Books. (Hispanic American)

Ferris, J. (1988). *Walking the road to freedom: A story about Sojourner Truth*. Minneapolis, MN: Carolrhoda Books. (African American)

Fisher, M. (1989). *Women in the third world*. New York: Franklin Watts. (International)

Gordimer, N. (1982). A chip of glass ruby. In N. Gordimer, *Six feet of the country*. Harmondsworth, UK: Penguin. (Ethnic South African)

Gotfryd, B. (1990). *Anton the dove fancier: And other tales from the Holocaust*. New York: Washington Square Press. (Jewish American)

Houston, J. W. (1973). *Farewell Manzanar: A true story of Japanese American experiences during and after the World War II internment.* New York: Bantam Books. (Japanese American)

Johnston, R. (1973). *Iyabo of Nigeria.* Claremont, CA: Alpha Iota Chapter of Pi Lambda Theta, Claremont Graduate School. (Nigerian African)

Meltzer, M. (1989). *Voices from the Civil War: A documentary history of the great American conflict.* New York: Crowell. (American)

Miller, J. (1989). *Newfound: A novel.* New York: Orchard Books. (Appalachian American)

Naoya, S. (1987). Kuniko. In S. Naoya, L. Dunlop (Trans.), *The paper door and other stories.* San Francisco: North Point Press. (Japanese)

Riley, J. (1985). *The unbelonging.* London: Women's Press. (Ethnic British)

Uyesugi, R. (1977). *Don't cry, Chiisai, don't cry.* Paoli, IN: Stout's Print Shop. (Japanese American)

Index

Editors

Sibel Boran is assistant professor of language arts at the University of Wisconsin Oshkosh, where she emphasizes the integration of critical inquiry, multiple literacies/intelligences, multicultural international literature, and technology into language arts curricula. Originally a Turkish Cypriot from North Cyprus, Boran received a bachelor's degree in linguistics from Hacettepe University in Ankara, Turkey, before moving to the United States, where she earned master's and doctoral degrees from Indiana University in applied linguistics/TESOL and language education, respectively. As assistant professor of reading at the University of Texas-Pan American, she taught technology-linked undergraduate courses in reading/literacy with a field-based component in low-performing, low-income schools, as well as multicultural child and adolescent literature and research courses. In the Mexican American Rio Grande Valley public schools in South Texas, she educated, trained, and guided inservice and preservice teachers as collaborative researchers on inquiry-based literacy curricula and explored social justice issues. A recently completed manuscript, *The Politics of Literacy, Culture, and Social Justice Issues: Critical Inquiry in K–Middle Classroom Practice*, is based on her research findings at these schools. As part of her work in the Rio Grande Valley schools, Boran launched "Parental Involvement Literacy/Drama Fiestas," showcasing critical inquiry-literacy projects with K–5 students in order to enhance family involvement in school literacy issues. Boran has presented at various local, national, and international conferences, including the National Council of Teachers of English, the Whole Language Umbrella, the International Reading Association, and Teachers of English to Speakers of Other Languages.

Barbara Comber is associate professor at the Centre for Studies in Literacy, Policy and Learning Cultures at the University of South Australia, where she teaches in master's of education and Ph.D. programs. From 1996 to 1999, she directed a teacher-researcher network, exploring responsive and critical literacies in diverse communities. She is committed to extending and publishing teacher research. Her research interests include literacy development, teachers' work, social justice, critical literacies, public education, and school-based collaborative research. Comber's doctoral thesis, *The Discursive Construction of Literacy in a Disadvantaged School*, employed ethnographic and poststructuralist discourse analytic methods and won the Australian Association for Research in Education Thesis Award in 1997. With Bill Green and a team of school and university-based researchers, she recently completed a study, funded by the Department of Education, Training and Employment, South Australia, concerned with information technology, literacy, and educational disadvantage. She is engaged in several research projects that explore the literacy learning over time of primary school children who are disadvantaged by poverty. Comber has published in *Language Arts, Elementary School Journal, Australian Journal of Language and Literacy, Discourse,* and *Australian Educational Researcher.* She is currently editing a book titled *Negotiating Critical Literacies in Classrooms,* due out in 2001.

CONTRIBUTORS

Carolyn L. Burke is professor emeritus of language education at Indiana University Bloomington. She has done extensive research in miscue analysis, early language development, and inquiry-based curriculum. Her previous books include *Reading Miscue Inventory* (with Yetta Goodman and Dorothy Watson), *Language Stories and Literacy Lessons* (with Jerome Harste and Virginia Woodward), and *Whole Language: Inquiring Voices* (with Dorothy Watson and Jerome Harste). She was a contributing author to *Creating Classrooms for Authors and Inquirers* (with Jerome Harste and Kathy Short).

Susan M. Church is currently assistant superintendent of schools with the Halifax Regional School Board in Nova Scotia, Canada. She has fulfilled a variety of teaching and administrative roles within the public education system and has provided leadership in teacher education through university courses and a wide range of professional development activities. Church has published widely in educational journals and is the author of *The Future of Whole Language: Reconstruction or Self-Destruction?* She is completing doctoral research through the University of South Australia with a focus on educational leadership.

Carolyn Cox is the deputy head teacher of a primary school in Kent, England, and has been a school language coordinator for many years. She has two young children of her own and has a particular interest in the language and literacy development of children in the early years.

Lee Gunderson is professor and head of the Language and Literacy Education Department at the University of British Columbia, where he teaches undergraduate and graduate courses in first- and second-language reading acquisition. He has been a classroom teacher, a special education teacher, a Title I teacher, and an elementary vice-principal and principal. He has conducted a longitudinal study of the language and academic achievement of approximately 25,000 immigrant students.

Jerome C. Harste is professor of language education at Indiana University, where he holds an endowed chair in teacher education. He is the co-author of several professional videotape series and texts, the latest of which is *Beyond Reading and Writing: Inquiry, Curriculum, and Multiple Ways of Knowing* (with Beth Berghoff, Kathryn A. Egawa, and Barry T. Hoonan, 2000). Together with a group of teachers from Indianapolis, Harste is exploring what it means to put a critical edge to inquiry-based instruction.

Robyn Jenkin, who has a master's in literacy and language education from the University of South Australia, has been teaching in elementary schools for over twenty-five years. She has been a classroom teacher at all year levels, and has been a teacher-librarian as well as a Reading Recovery teacher. For the last seven years, Jenkin has worked as a literacy consultant in a nongovernment schooling sector. Her current work involves the provision of professional development in literacy teaching and learning. She also works with teachers, particularly those whose students are in the early years of schooling, to provide balanced literacy teaching and learning programs designed to meet the needs of all students. Jenkin has a particular interest in early intervention teaching strategies. In recent years, much of her work has been in the area of explicit teaching, especially in aspects of reading and writing.

Timothy J. Lensmire's teaching, research, and writing focus on the promise and problems of critical literacy education. His recent book, *Powerful Writing/Responsible Teaching* (2000), draws on Bakhtin and Dewey to affirm, criticize, and reconstruct workshop approaches to the teaching and learning of writing in public schools.

Maureen Lewis is currently on leave of absence from her position as senior lecturer at the University of Plymouth, England, in order to spend time as a regional director for the UK government's National Literacy Strategy. She has a particular interest in how children interact with nonfiction texts and has researched and published widely in this area, including six books and numerous articles in both research and practitioner journals. She was a primary teacher for many years before becoming a research fellow at the University of Exeter and the co-director of several literacy research projects.

Jennifer O'Brien and her young students explore all kinds of texts from a critical perspective. She has written about some of these experiences for educational policy documents, literacy journals, and books about critical literacy and social justice. Her current research interests include investigating how Australian policy documents provide opportunities for teachers and students to work critically across the English/literacy curriculum and the stories recently retired literacy teachers have to tell. Since retiring from classroom teaching, O'Brien has worked as a researcher at the Centre for Studies in Literacy, Policy and Learning Cultures at the University of South Australia and continues to write for teachers and children.

Patrick Shannon is a former preschool and primary grade teacher. He is currently professor of education at Penn State University. His most recent book, *iSHOP, You Shop: Raising Questions about Reading Commodities*, is concerned with the commodification of literacy and literacy education.

Timothy Shannon is a former middle and high school teacher and principal. He is currently a superintendent of schools in Janesville, California. His research interests include environmental education, cross-disciplinary teaching, and student voice.

Kathy G. Short is currently professor of education in the Department of Language, Reading and Culture at the University of Arizona, where she teaches courses on children's literature, curriculum, and inquiry. She has worked extensively with elementary teachers to develop curricula that actively involve students as authors and inquirers. She is the author of *Literature as a Way of Knowing* (1997), co-author with Carolyn L. Burke of *Creating Curriculum* (1990), co-author with Jerome Harste, with Carolyn L. Burke, of *Creating Classrooms for Authors and Inquirers* (1996), and co-author with Birchak et al. of *Teacher Study Groups* (1998), as well as author of numerous other articles, chapters, and books. She is co-editor of *Language Arts*.

Vivian Vasquez is currently assistant professor in the School of Education at American University in Washington, D.C. Previous to this she was an elementary school teacher in Canada as well as professional growth consultant for Evergreen Child Care Centre. She has also worked with Andy Manning from Mt. Saint Vincent University in supporting M.Ed./M.A. students through an external graduate program. Her research interests include explorations of critical literacy and inquiry curriculum in practice with young children. She is also interested in exploring the social construction of English as a second language learners, looking specifically at visible minority groups. Vasquez has presented at international, national, and local conferences and has had her work published in *UKRA Reading*, *Reading Teacher*, *Reading Today*, and *Language Arts*.

Connie L. White has been an elementary classroom teacher for twenty years and is currently a resource teacher at an elementary school in rural Nova Scotia, Canada. She is involved in distance education, both as an instructor and as a student. She works as part-time faculty for Mount St. Vincent University, Halifax, Nova Scotia, teaching literacy courses for their Web site master's of education programs. She is currently a Ph.D. student with the University of South Australia. Connie has been actively involved in teacher research for the past decade. Her book, *Jevon Doesn't Sit at the Back Anymore,* was the first in Scholastic Canada's Teacher's Forum series. She has also published in several professional reading journals and presented at a number of national and international conferences. Her most passionate research interests are in the areas of gender, poverty, and schooling.

David Wray taught in primary schools in the United Kingdom and is currently professor of literacy education at the University of Warwick, England. He has published over thirty books on aspects of literacy teaching and is best known for his work with Maureen Lewis on the Nuffield Extending Literacy (EXEL) project, which has been concerned with helping learners of all ages access the curriculum more effectively through literacy. The work of this project was made an integral part of the National Literacy Strategy in the United Kingdom, and Wray was a founding member of the Advisory Group to the National Literacy Project.

This book was typeset in Sabon by Electronic Imaging.
The typeface used on the cover is Frutiger.
The book was printed on 50-lb. Williamsburg Offset paper by Versa Press.